INTRODUCTION TO GRAPHICS

Microcomputer Power

INTRODUCTION TO GRAPHICS

John P. Grillo/J. D. Robertson
Bentley College
Waltham, Massachusetts

wcb
Personal Computer Series
Wm. C. Brown Company Publishers
Dubuque, Iowa 52001

Library of Congress Catalog Card Number: 81-65444

ISBN 0—697—09953—9

Third Printing, 1982

Printed in the United States of America

Contents

Introduction

The purpose of this book is to explore the computer's special abilities to produce graphic displays. The book is geared toward one microcomputer, the Radio Shack TRS-80, and one computer language, BASIC. However, due to the generalized nature of the discussion, we feel that the techniques employed in the many sample programs can be adapted to other hardware and other languages.

Three general methods for producing computer graphics are examined in depth. The most traditional method of creating pictures with a computer, *line printer graphics*, is treated first. With line printer graphics, the picture is considered to be a set of horizontal lines whose components are the letters, digits, and special symbols that make up BASIC's character set. This method of producing outlines, silhouettes, graphs, and other visually appealing pictures takes up the largest part of the book, as it should. Line printer graphics can be produced using any language and with any computer, with or without printer.

Character graphics is the second method for creating graphics and relies on the TRS-80's 64-character set of graphic symbols. Many microcomputer makers besides Radio Shack have adopted special graphic characters, and for good reason. These characters allow the video screen to display a wide variety of special effects, such as game boards and pieces, lunar landers and space ships, faces and entire bodies, even schematics and blueprints. The popularity of this technique has increased significantly since the appearance of the many microcomputer chess games on the market in the late 1970's.

The third technique for producing graphics is *pixel graphics*. The pixel is to visual information what the binary digit or bit is to stored information. The bit is the smallest amount of storable information, a 1 or a 0, whereas the pixel is the smallest amount of pictorial information, an addressable area of the screen that can be turned on or off, bright or dark. The microcomputer programmer who can deal with pixel graphics on the TRS-80 can produce computer displays at moderate resolution. While the normal display density of a TRS-80 screen is 64 characters across and 16 lines down, the display density increases by a factor of 6, to 128 pixels across and 48 down.

As you proceed through the discussion of the three graphics methods, you will discover a diversity of techniques exemplified by many complete programs, both short and long. We hope you will try them out and modify them as you see fit. We have purposely left some programs in skeletal form so that you can adapt them more easily to your particular taste.

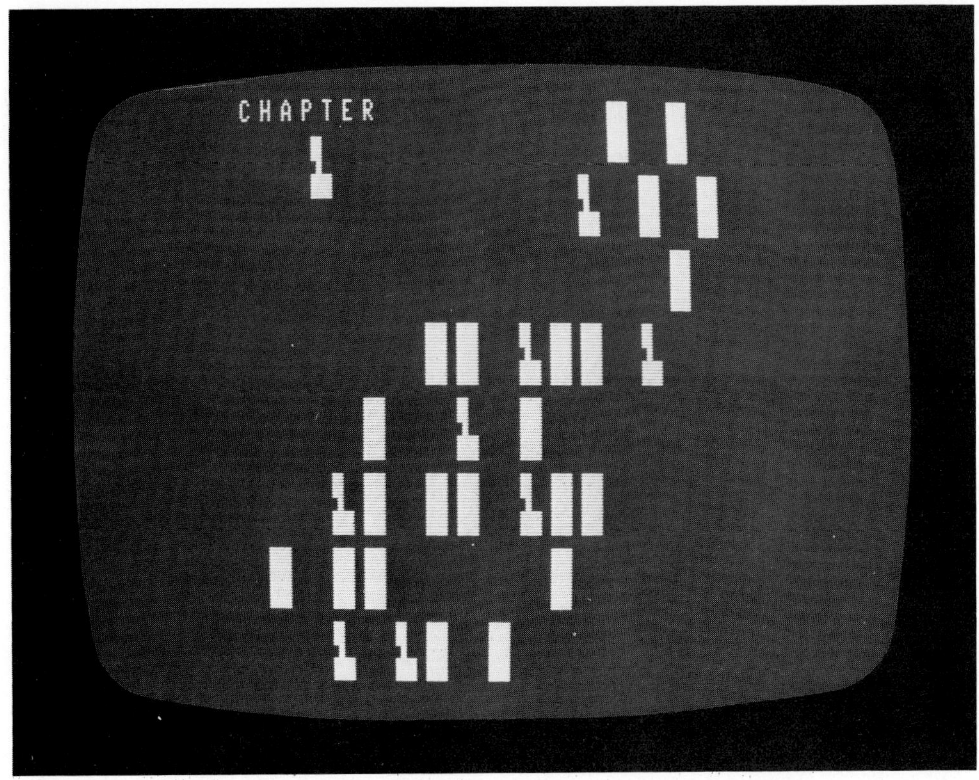

The Program Is the Picture

The simplest form of line printer graphics is when the program is the picture. Each program statement is a PRINT statement which outputs a line of the picture. An overwhelming advantage of this technique is that the programmer can detect and correct errors in the picture easily by inspecting a listing of the program.

Problem 1.1

Draw a picture of the Virgo zodiac sign.

Solution

```
10 'filename:"sip1"
20 '  purpose:  draw a picture of the Virgo zodiac sign
30 '   author: jdr 8/80
40 '
50 PRINT "    0000      0000      0000      0000"
60 PRINT "  000000    000000    000000    000000"
70 PRINT "00000000000000000000000000000000      00"
80 PRINT "    00000000  00000000  00000000      00"
90 PRINT "    0000      0000      0000        0000"
100 PRINT "    0000      0000      0000      0000"
110 PRINT "    0000      0000      0000    0000"
120 PRINT "    0000      0000      0000  0000"
130 PRINT "    0000      0000      00000000"
140 PRINT "    0000      0000      000000"
150 PRINT "    0000      0000      0000"
160 PRINT "    0000      0000    000000"
170 END
```

```
    0000      0000      0000      0000
  000000    000000    000000    000000
00000000000000000000000000000000      00
    00000000  00000000  00000000      00
    0000      0000      0000        0000
    0000      0000      0000      0000
    0000      0000      0000    0000
    0000      0000      0000  0000
    0000      0000      00000000
    0000      0000      000000
    0000      0000      0000
    0000      0000    000000
```

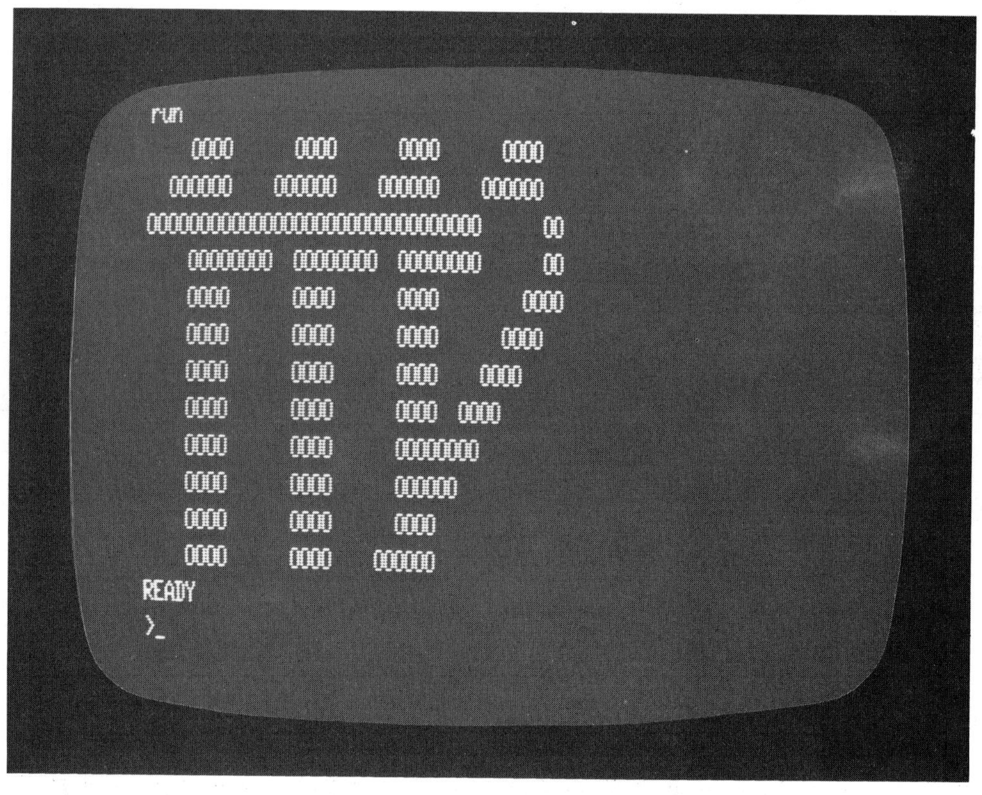

Problem 1.2 Draw a picture of the state of Massachusetts.

Solution

```
10 'filename:"s1p2"
20 '  purpose: Massachusetts
30 '    author: jdr 8/80
40 '
50 PRINT "                                        ****"
60 PRINT "     *******************************************"
70 PRINT "    *******************************************"
80 PRINT "    ****************************************"
90 PRINT "   *******************************************"
100 PRINT "  **********************************************        ***"
110 PRINT " *************************************************        ****"
120 PRINT " *************************************************************"
130 PRINT "                                          ******   ******"
140 PRINT "                                            ***     *"
150 END
```

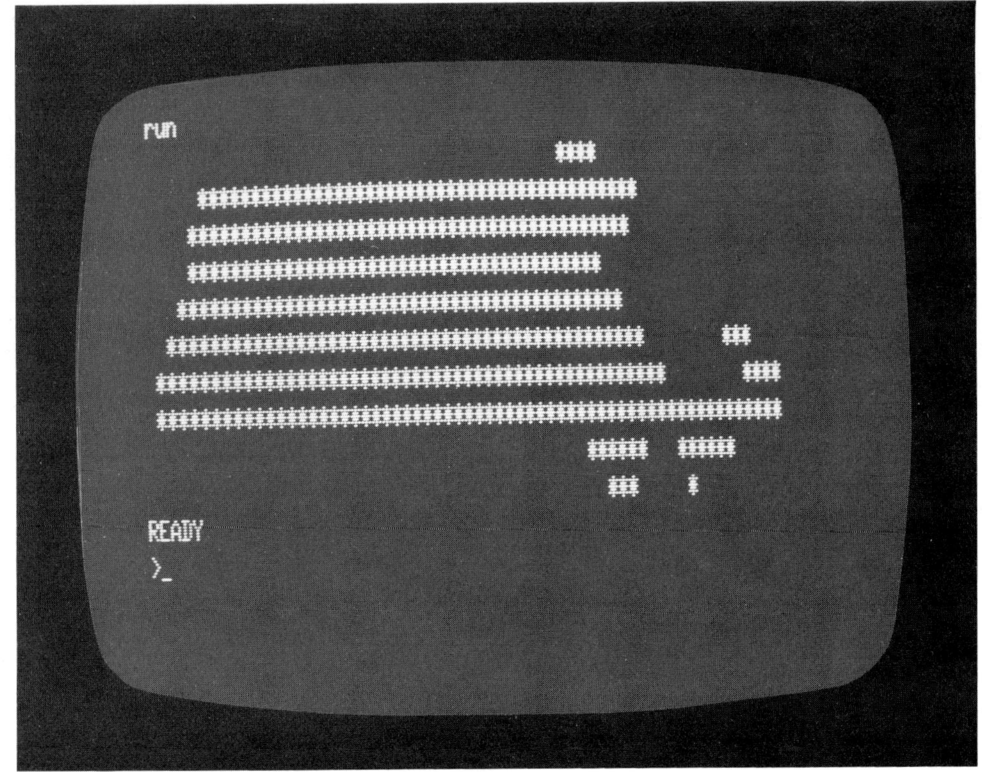

Problem 1.3 Draw the logo for Bentley College.

Solution

```
10 'filename:"s1p3"
20 '  purpose: produce logo of Bentley College
30 '   author: jdr 8/80
40 '
50 PRINT "::::::::::::::::::::::::::::::::::::::::::::::::"
60 PRINT "::                                            ::"
70 PRINT "::                            ::::::::        ::"
80 PRINT "::                          ::::::::::::      ::"
90 PRINT "::                        ::::        ::::    ::"
100 PRINT "::        ::::::::        ::::        ::::    ::"
110 PRINT "::      ::::::::::::      ::::        ::::    ::"
120 PRINT "::    ::::        ::::    ::::        ::::    ::"
130 PRINT "::    ::::        ::::    ::::        ::::    ::"
140 PRINT "::    ::::        ::::    ::::        ::::    ::"
150 PRINT "::    ::::        ::::    ::::        ::::    ::"
160 PRINT "::    ::::        ::::    ::::        ::::    ::"
170 PRINT "::    ::::        ::::    ::::        ::::    ::"
180 PRINT "::    ::::::::::::::::    ::::::::::::::::    ::"
190 PRINT "::                                            ::"
200 PRINT "::::::::::::::::::::::::::::::::::::::::::::::::";
210 IF INKEY$="" THEN 210
220 END
```

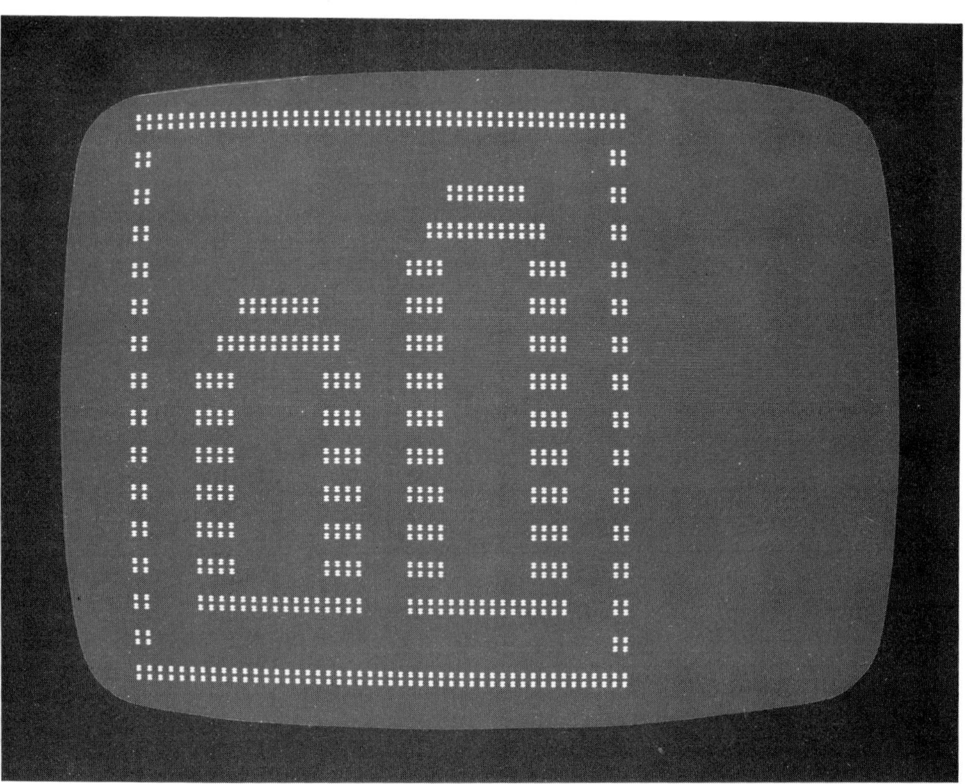

Problem 1.4 Sketch a picture of Woodstock.

Solution

```
10 'filename:"g1p4"
20 '  purpose: draw Woodstock
30 '    author: jdr 8/80
40 '
50 LPRINT "            ,   -"
60 LPRINT "            ,  (   -"
70 LPRINT "            , (  -=  -"
80 LPRINT "            -  -=  -="
90 LPRINT "          -(     -== ---"
100 LPRINT " ,======== *     -=="
110 LPRINT "(                -------"
120 LPRINT ",                 --"
130 LPRINT " --------           ===="
140 LPRINT "         -        ==--"
150 LPRINT "          -  -=----   ="
160 LPRINT "          -        =-"
170 LPRINT "         (  ,"
180 LPRINT "        ( ,  ,"
190 LPRINT "       ,  ,   ,"
200 LPRINT "       ,  ,  , ,"
210 LPRINT "       ,  ,  , ,"
220 LPRINT "       ,   , , ,"
230 LPRINT "        ,   ,  ,"
240 LPRINT "         =--,-==========-"
250 LPRINT "            I   =========="
260 LPRINT "      (((((((((-"
270 LPRINT "          ,("
280 END
```

```
            ,   -
            ,  (   -
            , (  -=  -
            -  -=  -=
          -(     -== ---
 ,======== *     -==
(                -------
,                 --
 --------           ====
         -        ==--
          -  -=----   =
          -        =-
         (  ,
        ( ,  ,
       ,  ,   ,
       ,  ,  , ,
       ,  ,  , ,
       ,   , , ,
        ,   ,  ,
         =--,-==========-
            I   ==========
      (((((((((-
          ,(
```

Discussion

- Producing pictures in this way is simple, if you trace either an existing sketch or an original drawing onto a coding form.
- If you use a variety of characters to produce the output, you can more closely approximate the subtle shadings, pleats, highlights, and other details in the picture.

Don't let the simplicity of this graphics technique dissuade you from using it. The very fact that it is so simple makes it immensely popular. Using someone else's artistic ability or your own as a pattern, persistence in the face of tedium coupled with this technique can provide some pleasant computer graphics.

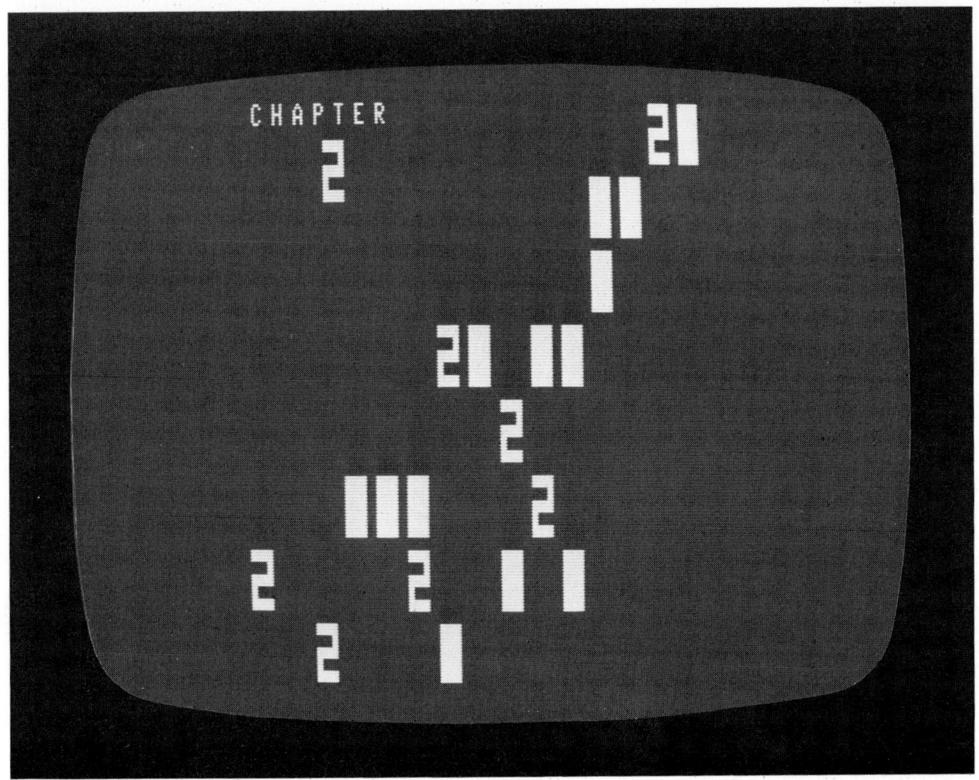

TABbed Pictures

All versions of BASIC have a TAB function that allows positioning of the carriage or print head or cursor anywhere across the output line. Also, the execution of a PRINT statement that doesn't end with a comma or semicolon results in a carriage return-linefeed. With these controls in two dimensions, a wide variety of pictures can be produced. As in the previous chapter, we will illustrate the techniques using both output on a line printer and pictures of actual screen output.

Problem 2.1

List a table of strings in a variety of ways using the TAB function for positioning the string on the output line.

Solution

```
10 'filename:"s2p1"
20 '  purpose: output table in sundry ways using TAB function
30 '   author: jdr 8/80
40 '
50 DIM P$(15)
60 FOR I=1 TO 15 : READ P$(I) : NEXT I
90 CLS : RANDOM
100 FOR I=1 TO 15
110     PRINT TAB(25);P$(I)
120 NEXT I : GOSUB 1000 'pause and clear screen
```

```
140 FOR I=1 TO 15
150     PRINT TAB(I);P$(I)
160 NEXT I : GOSUB 1000 'pause & clear
180 FOR I=1 TO 15
190     PRINT TAB(2*I);P$(I)
200 NEXT I : GOSUB 1000 'pause & clear
220 FOR I=1 TO 15
230     PRINT TAB(3*ABS(8-I));P$(I)
240 NEXT I : GOSUB 1000 'pause & clear
260 FOR I=1 TO 15
270     PRINT TAB(RND(40));P$(I)
280 NEXT I : GOSUB 1000 'pause & clear
300 FOR I=1 TO 15
310     PRINT TAB(40-LEN(P$(I)));P$(I)
320 NEXT I : GOSUB 1000 'pause & clear
340 STOP
350 DATA "parrot","pheasant","ptarmigan","pelican","penguin"
360 DATA "pochard","pipit","purple martin","pardalote","pewee"
370 DATA "pintail","puffin","phoenix","phoebe","plover"
1000 'pause and clear screen subroutine
1010 FOR J=1 TO 200 : NEXT J : CLS : RETURN
9999 END
```

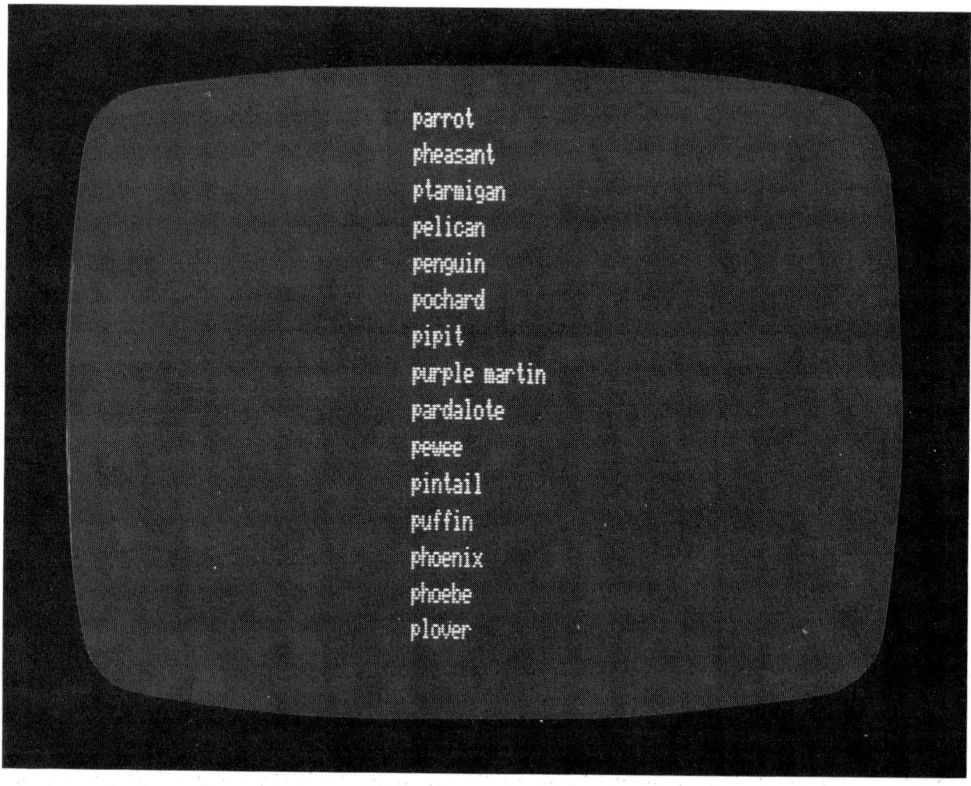

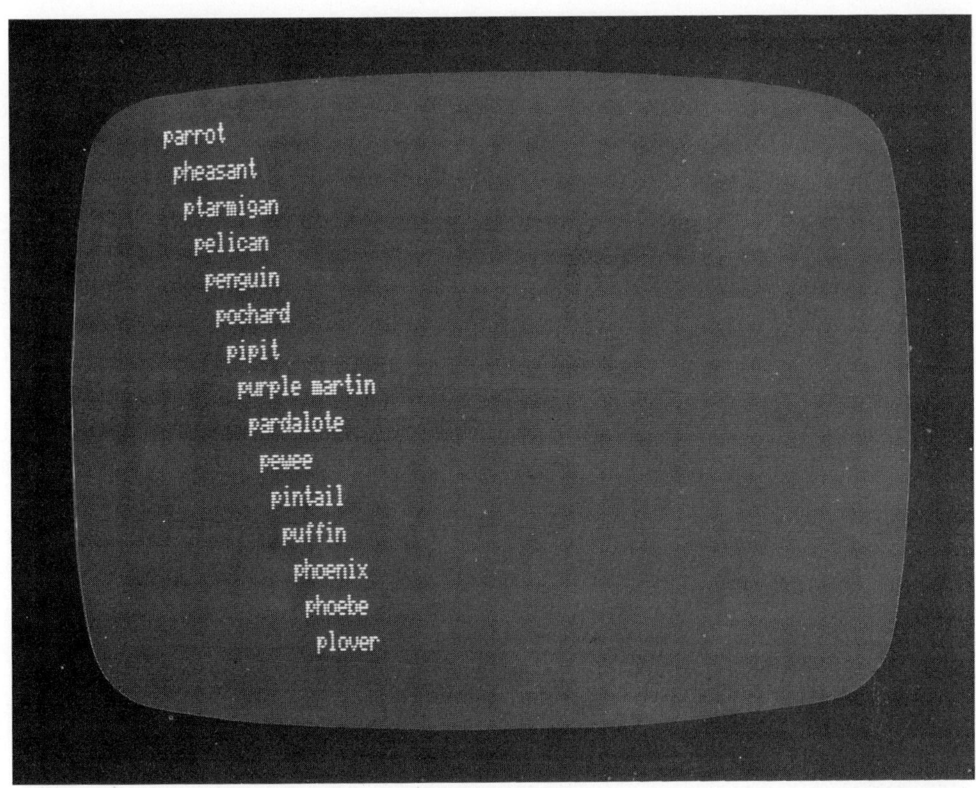
parrot
pheasant
ptarmigan
pelican
penguin
pochard
pipit
purple martin
pardalote
pewee
pintail
puffin
phoenix
phoebe
plover

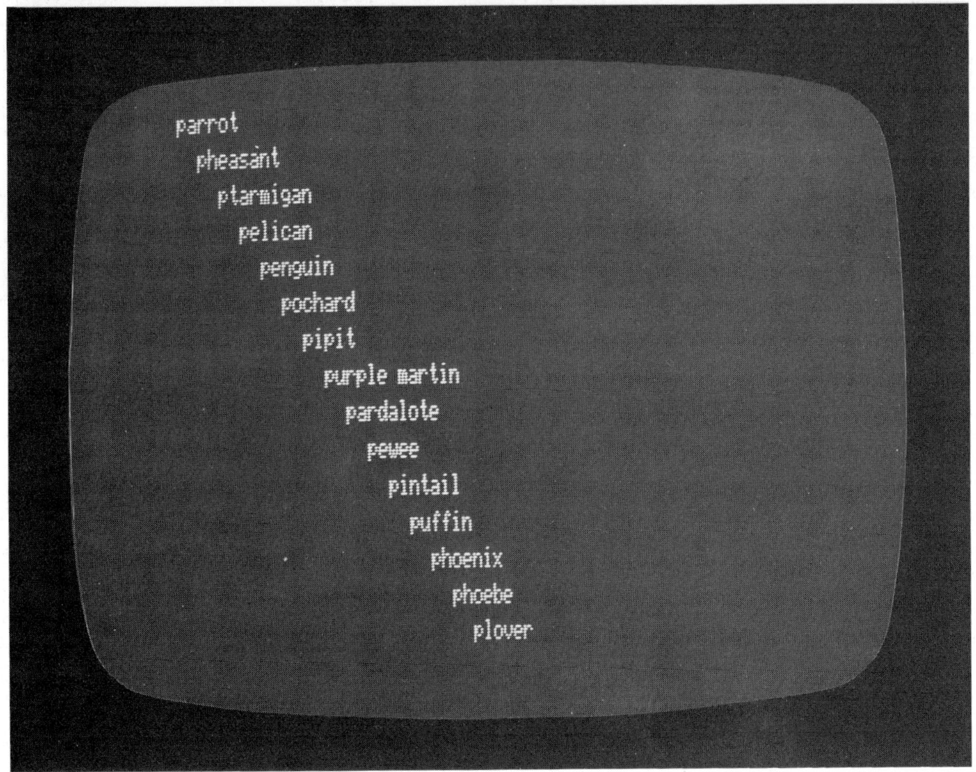
parrot
pheasant
ptarmigan
pelican
penguin
pochard
pipit
purple martin
pardalote
pewee
pintail
puffin
phoenix
phoebe
plover

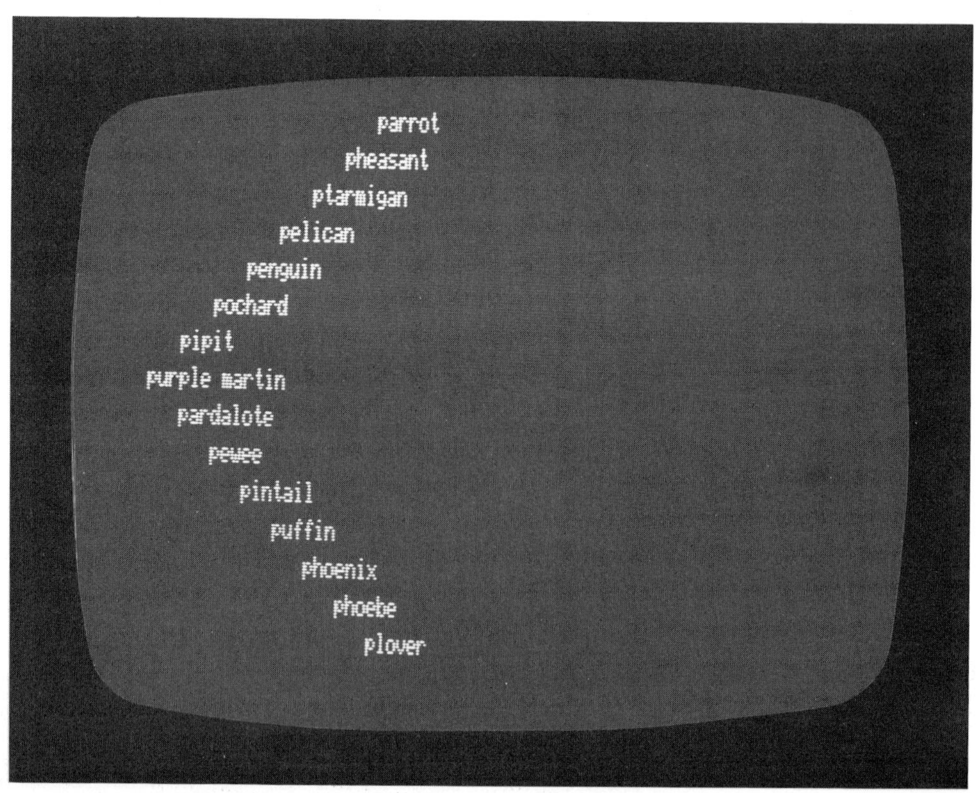
parrot
pheasant
ptarmigan
pelican
penguin
pochard
pipit
purple martin
pardalote
pewee
pintail
puffin
phoenix
phoebe
plover

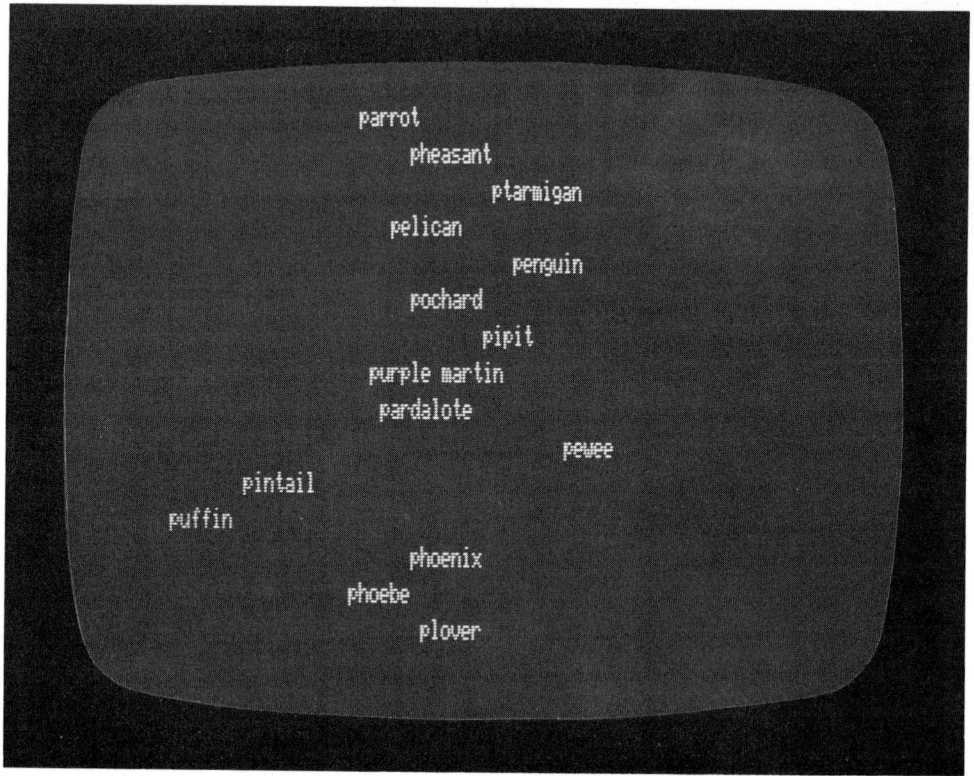
parrot
pheasant
ptarmigan
pelican
penguin
pochard
pipit
purple martin
pardalote
pewee
pintail
puffin
phoenix
phoebe
plover

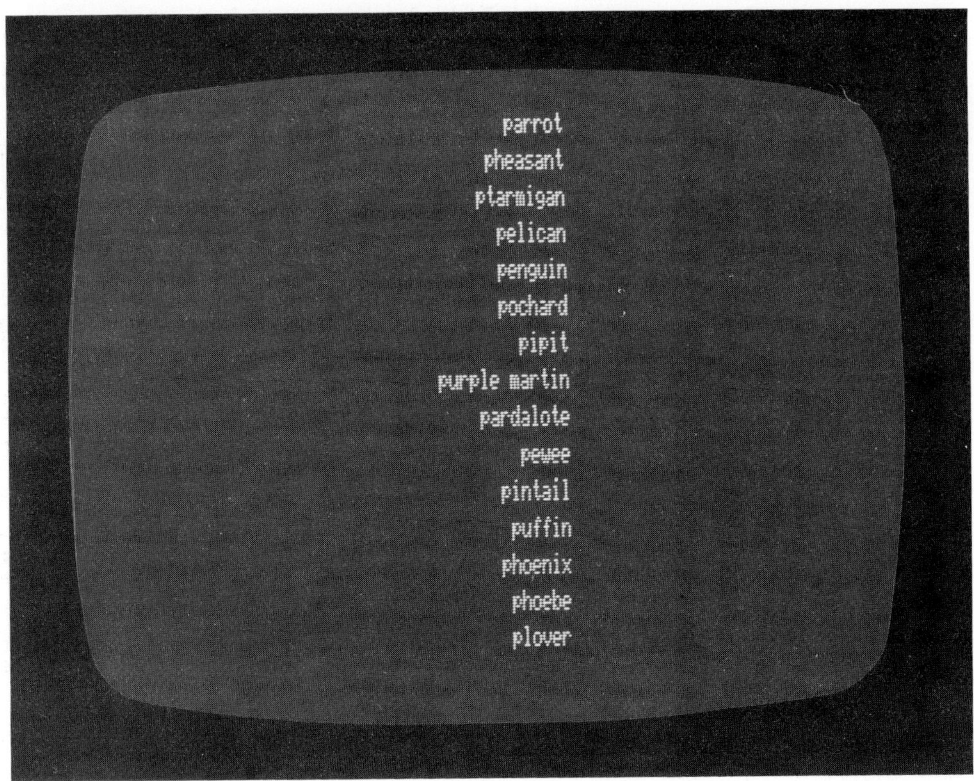

Discussion

- When the argument of the TAB function is a more complex expression than a constant, some otherwise prosaic output can be transformed into a graphic presentation of information.

Suggestions

- Modify the argument of the TAB function to produce other interesting visual patterns.

Problem 2.2

Produce a visual representation of the sine curve, y=sin x.

Solution

```
10 'filename:"s2p2"
20 ' purpose: graph the sine function
30 '   author: jps 1/80
40 '
50 '          let the X axis vary from 0 to 2 pi radians.
60 FOR X=0 TO 6.28 STEP .25
70     '          calculate displacement from 0 on Y axis,
80     '                                  then expand by 30.
90     Y=SIN(X)*30
100    LPRINT TAB(Y+30); "*"
110 NEXT X
9999 END
```

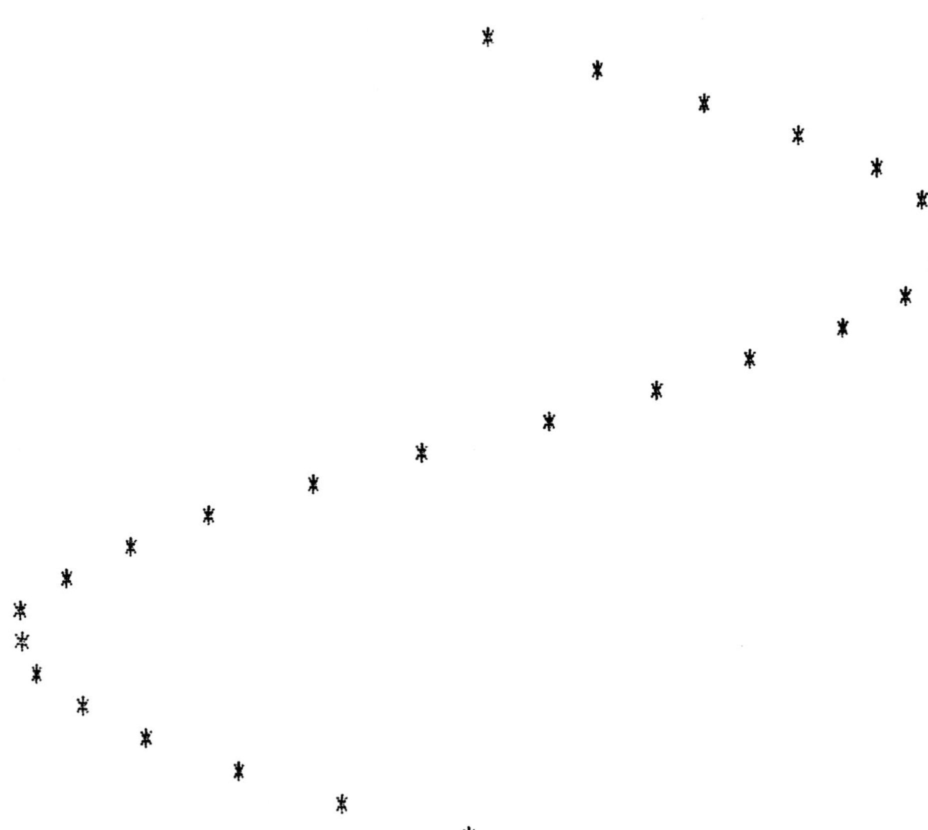

Discussion

- The Y-axis is across the print line and the X-axis is down the page. Thus, the tabbed position of Y, as represented by the asterisk ("*"), varies according to the sine of the line count X.

- The increment between calculated points is .25 radians. To squeeze the sine wave (increase its frequency), increase the increment. To expand the sine wave (decrease its frequency), reduce the increment.

- The sine wave is shown between 0 and 6.28 radians, or 0 to 360 degrees. To see more waves, increment from 0 to 10 (or more) radians. To see the sine function before 0 degrees, increment from -6.28 to 6.28 radians. Note that 6.28 is approximately two times pi, or almost a full circle of 360 degrees.

Suggestions

- Make the following changes in the statements indicated.

```
60 FOR X=0 TO 6.28 STEP .5
60 FOR X=0 TO 6.28 STEP .1
60 FOR X=-6.28 TO 6.28 STEP .35
60 FOR X=-20 TO 20 STEP .7
90 Y=ABS(30*SIN(X))+32
```

Problem 2.3

Produce a visual representation of three functions simultaneously; a=sin x, b=sin 2x, and c=a+b

Solution

```
10 'filename:"g2p3"
20 '  purpose: graph of multiple functions
30 '   author: jps 1/80
40 '
50 '  vary X from .1 to 6.28 radians
60 FOR X=.1 TO 6.28 STEP .1
70      '      set original values of desired functions
80      S=SIN(X): S2=SIN(3*X): SS=S+S2
90      '      adjust values of functions for printer
100     A=20*S+32: B=20*S2+32: C=20*SS+32
110     IF A<=B AND A<=C THEN LPRINT TAB(A)".";:
            IF B<=C THEN LPRINT TAB(B)"+" TAB(C)"*"
                    ELSE LPRINT TAB(C)"*" TAB(B)"+"
120     IF B<=A AND B<=C THEN LPRINT TAB(B)"+";:
            IF A<=C THEN LPRINT TAB(A)"." TAB(C)"*"
                    ELSE LPRINT TAB(C)"*" TAB(A)"."
130     IF C<=A AND C<=B THEN LPRINT TAB(C)"*";:
            IF A<=B THEN LPRINT TAB(A)"." TAB(B)"+"
                    ELSE LPRINT TAB(B)"+" TAB(A)"."
140 NEXT X
9999 END
```

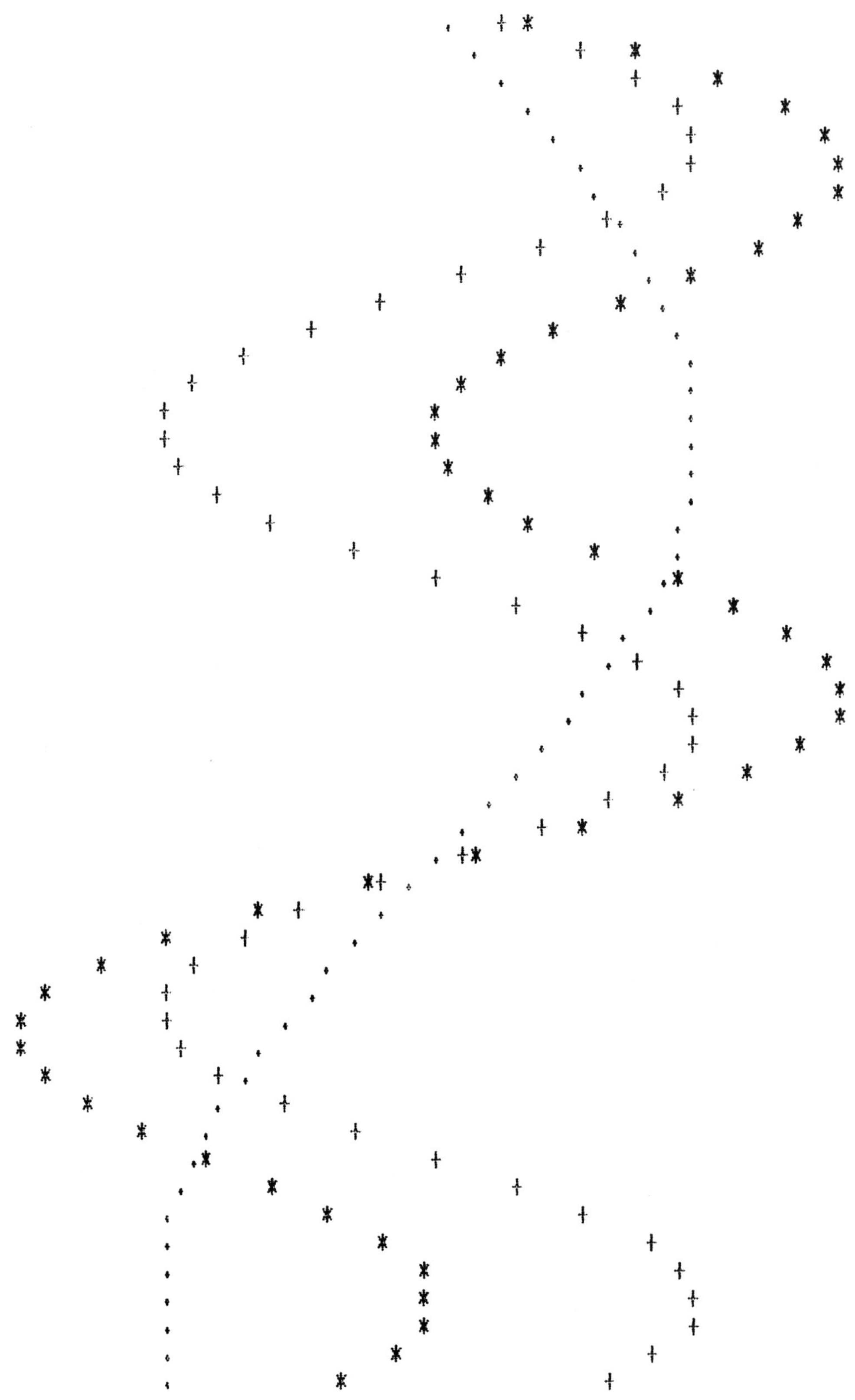

Discussion

- Once you find out which one of the points is lowest in value, print it. Then print the lesser of the remaining two. Then print the one that's left.

- If you graph this kind of multiple function, it is usually necessary to use different characters to plot the different functions.

Suggestions

- Add the first five harmonics of x:
  y=sin x + sin 2x + sin 3x + sin 4x + sin 5x
  Then, graph y versus x. The result will be a sawtooth wave form.

- Add the first five odd harmonics of x:
  y=sin x + sin 3x + sin 5x + sin 7x + sin 9x
  Then graph y versus x. The result will be a square wave form.

- Graph sin x and cos x together.

Problem 2.4

Graph a damped cosine curve. More specifically (and complicated sounding), graph two full cycles of a rectified sinusoidal curve that decays exponentially.

Solution

```
10 'filename:"s2p4"
20 '  purpose: absolute cosine function decaying exponentially
30 '   author: jps 1/80
40 '
50 INPUT "Enter the decay factor (.01 to .3)";DF
60 INPUT "Enter the step size in degrees (5 to 30)";S
80 LPRINT ,"Decay factor: ";DF, "Step size:";S
90 LPRINT: LPRINT
100 'print vertical grid header
110 LPRINT TAB(10)".0" TAB(20)".2" TAB(30) ".4" TAB(40)".6"
          TAB(50)".8" TAB(60)"1.0"
120 '   print vertical grid itself
130 LPRINT TAB(10);
140 FOR I=10 TO 60
150    IF I/10=INT(I/10) THEN LPRINT "+"; ELSE LPRINT "-";
160 NEXT I: LPRINT
170 ' step from 0 to 720 degrees by steps of S degrees
180 FOR D=0 TO 720 STEP S
200    R=D*.017  ' convert degrees to radians
210    Y=49*ABS(EXP(-DF*R)*COS(R))
220    IF D/90=INT(D/90) THEN LPRINT USING "### deg.";D;
230    LPRINT TAB(10)"." TAB(Y+11)"*"
240 NEXT D
9999 END
```

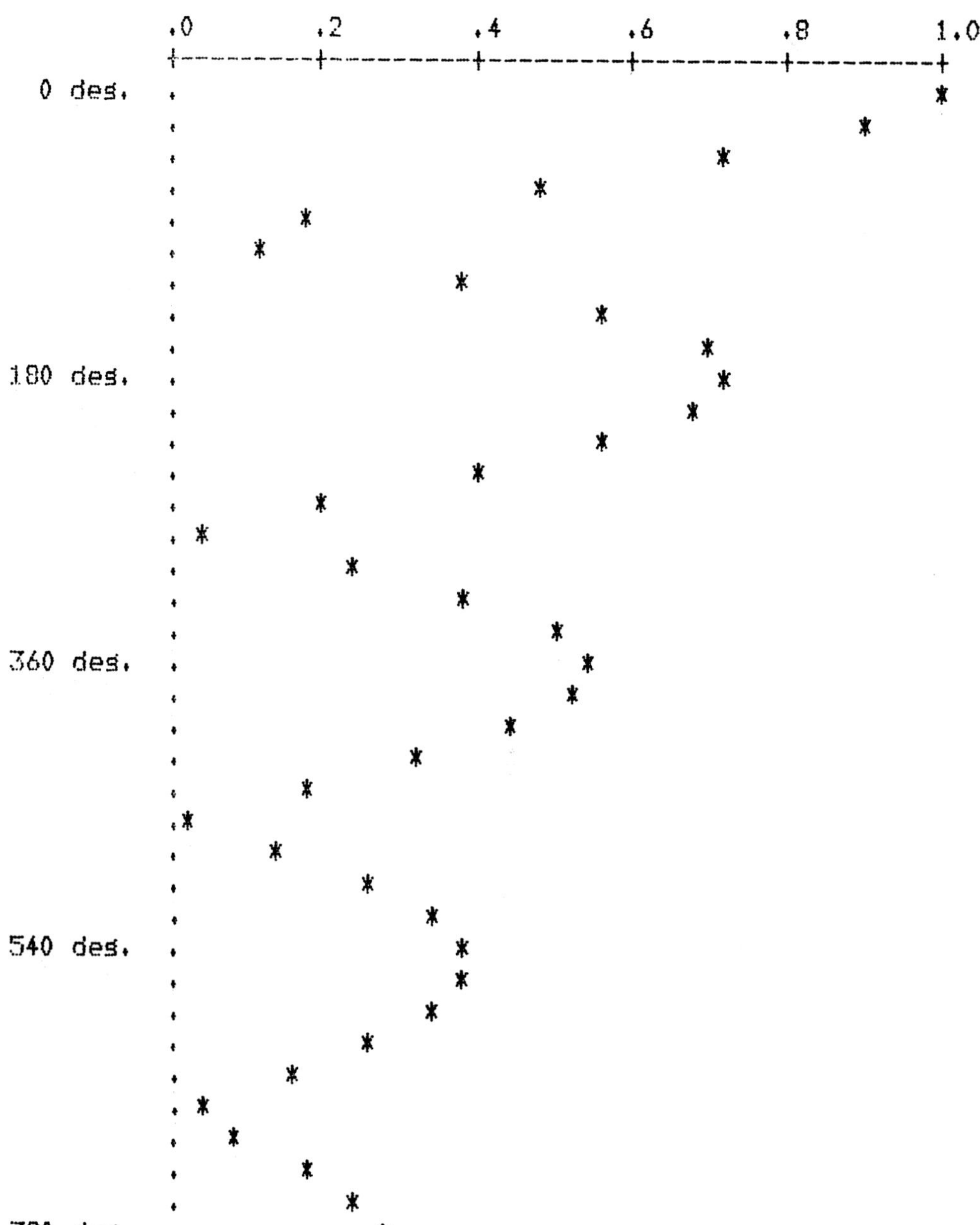
Decay factor: .1
Step size: 20
.0
.2
.4
.6
.8
1.0
0 deg.
180 deg.
360 deg.
540 deg.
720 deg.

Decay factor: .2   Step size: 20

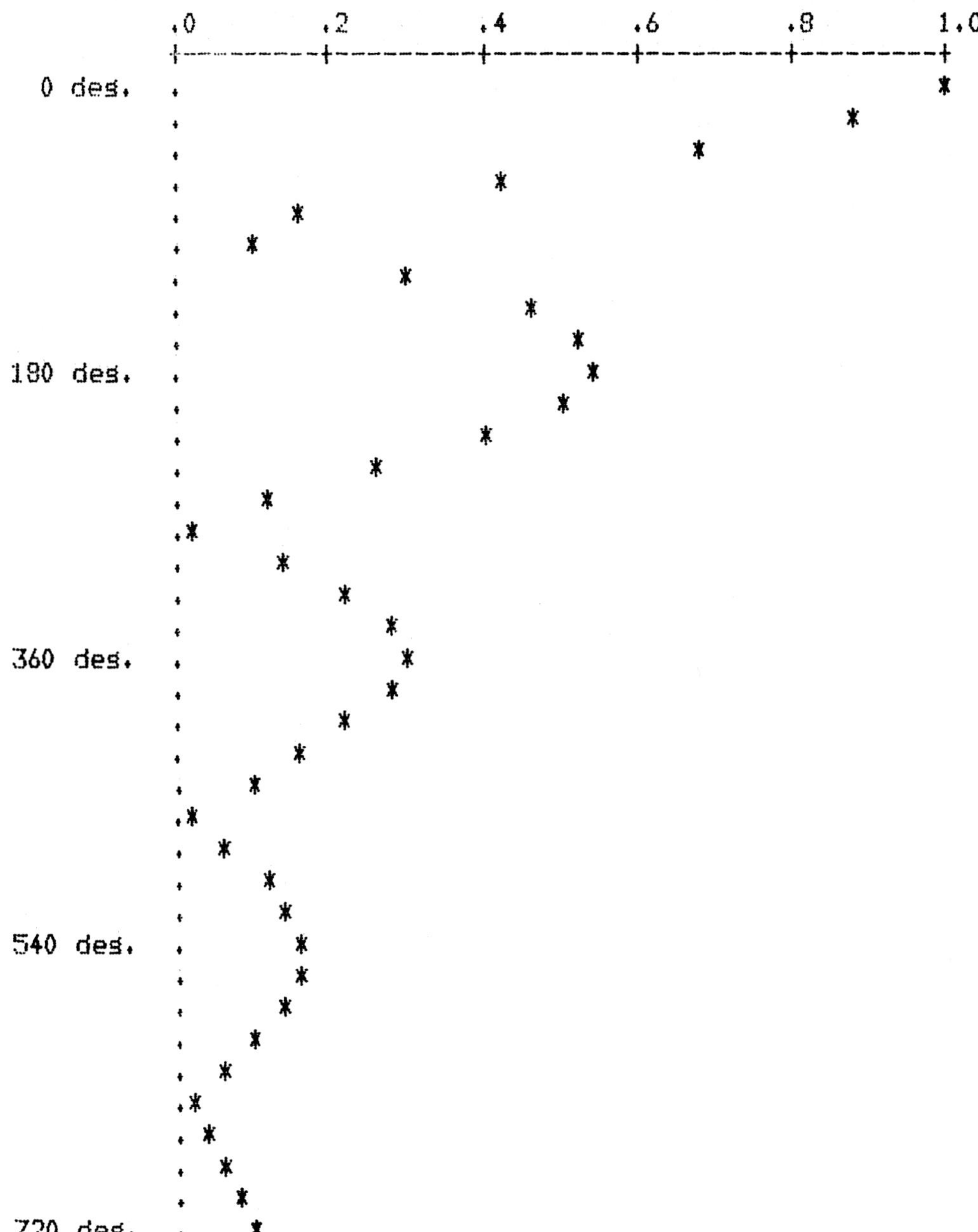

Discussion

- The absolute value function ABS in line 210 does the rectifying by converting all negative values of the cosine function into their positive counterparts.

- The exponential function EXP in line 210 produces the damping effect on the curve.

Suggestions

- Remove the ABS function and shift the graph to the center of the screen: The output is the trace of a moving pendulum as it loses its momentum.

- Modify the program to show two traces at different frequencies.

- Change the EXP function's argument from negative to positive. The effect will be to display an increasing amplitude. This is what happens when an object begins to vibrate at its resonant frequency.

The TAB function can be very useful in the plotting of curves. The examples shown above should provide sufficient patterns for you to explore its use in graphing more exotic or more useful functions.

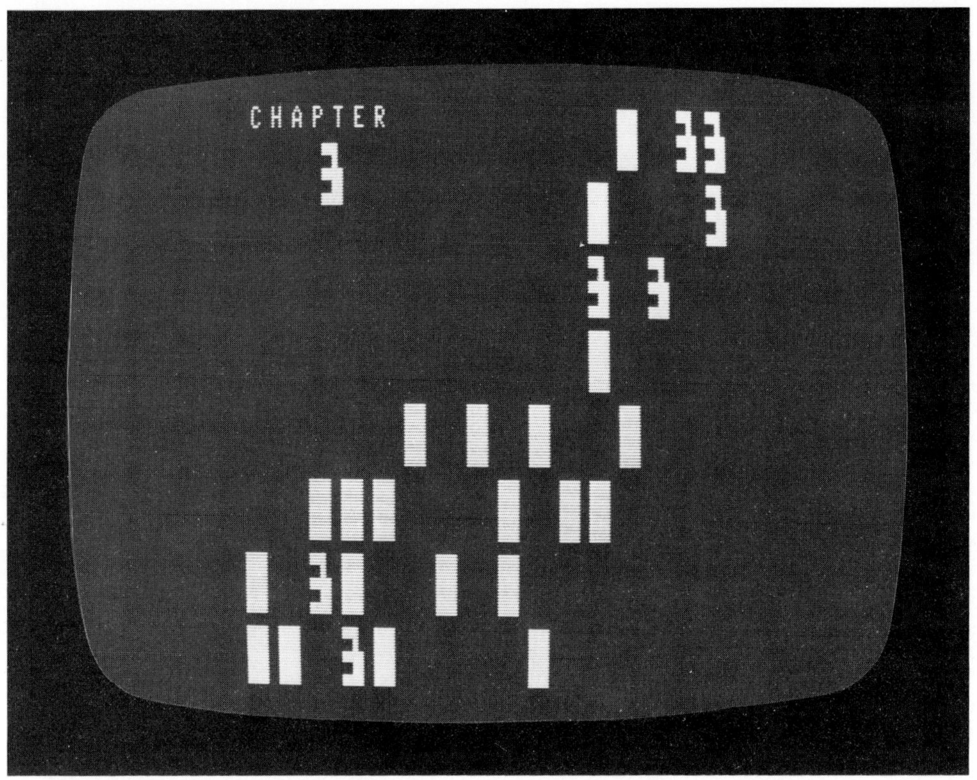

Bar Graph Pictures

The pictorial representations that are variously called bar graphs or histograms are easy to understand but can be difficult to get the computer to produce them. If the bars are arranged horizontally, the bar graph's generation is relatively simple to program but the descriptive text is arranged contrary to custom.

Problem 3.1

Depict the rate of reported crimes in five large metropolitan areas in 1976 using a bar graph.

Metropolitan area	Population, thousands	Crime index, thousands of reported crimes
New York	9,635	658
Chicago	6,982	214
Los Angeles—Long Beach	6,945	247
Philadelphia	4,797	77
Detroit	4,444	154

Solution

```
10 'filename:"s3p1"
20 ' purpose: horizontal bar chart
30 '  author: jps 1/80
40 '
50 DIM C$(5), P(5), C(5)
60 FOR I=1 TO 5: READ C$(I), P(I), C(I): NEXT I
70 DATA "NEW YORK", 9635, 658, CHICAGO, 6982, 214
80 DATA "L.A.-LONG BEACH", 6945, 247
90 DATA PHILADELPHIA, 4797, 77, DETROIT, 4444, 154
95 CLS
100 PRINT TAB(15)"REPORTED CRIMES PER THOUSAND POPULATION"
110 PRINT
115 FOR I=15 TO 60 STEP 10: PRINT TAB(I);(I-15)*2;: NEXT I: PRINT
120 FOR I=1 TO 5: L=500*C(I)/P(I)
130 PRINT
140 PRINT C$(I);: GOSUB 500
160 NEXT I
170 GOTO 170
500 FOR J=1 TO L: PRINT TAB(15+J)"*";: NEXT J: PRINT: RETURN
9999 END
```

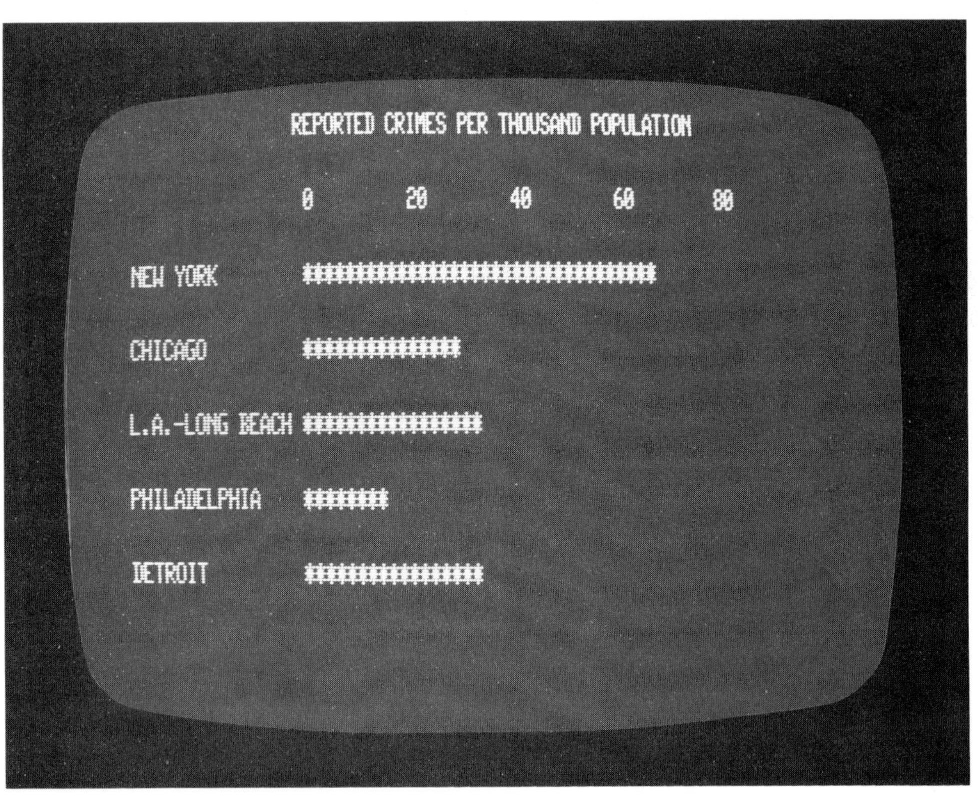

Discussion

- The program graphs the number of reported crimes per ten thousand population.
- Each one of the rightmost 50 columns of the screen represent one reported crime per 500 population.
- This program could be improved by generalizing it to allow flexibility in defining the tabular data.

Suggestions

- Provide a dialog before the DIM statement that allows a variable number of cities to be analyzed. This would require the input of the data interactively, rather than through DATA statements.

Problem 3.2

Rotate the bar graph produced in problem 3.1 so that the bars are vertical.

Solution

```
10 'filename:"s3p2"
20 ' purpose: vertical bar chart
30 '   author: jps 1/80
40 '
50 DIM C$(5), P(5), C(5)
55 DIM L(5)
60 FOR I=1 TO 5: READ C$(I), P(I), C(I): L(I)=500*C(I)/P(I): NEXT I
70 DATA "NEW YORK", 9635, 658, CHICAGO, 6982, 214
80 DATA "L.A.-LONG BEACH", 6945, 247
90 DATA PHILADELPHIA, 4797, 77, DETROIT, 4444, 154
95 CLS
100 PRINT TAB(15)"REPORTED CRIMES PER THOUSAND POPULATION"
130 FOR Y=0 TO 15
132 M=(15-Y)*5
135 IF M/20=INT(M/20) THEN PRINT @ Y*32+160, M;
138 FOR I=1 TO 5
140 IF L(I)>(Y+1)*4 THEN PRINT @ 64*(10-Y)+I*13-8, "******";
150 NEXT I
160 NEXT Y
162 FOR I=0 TO 4: PRINT @ 708+I*13, C$(I+1);: NEXT I
170 GOTO 170
9999 END
```

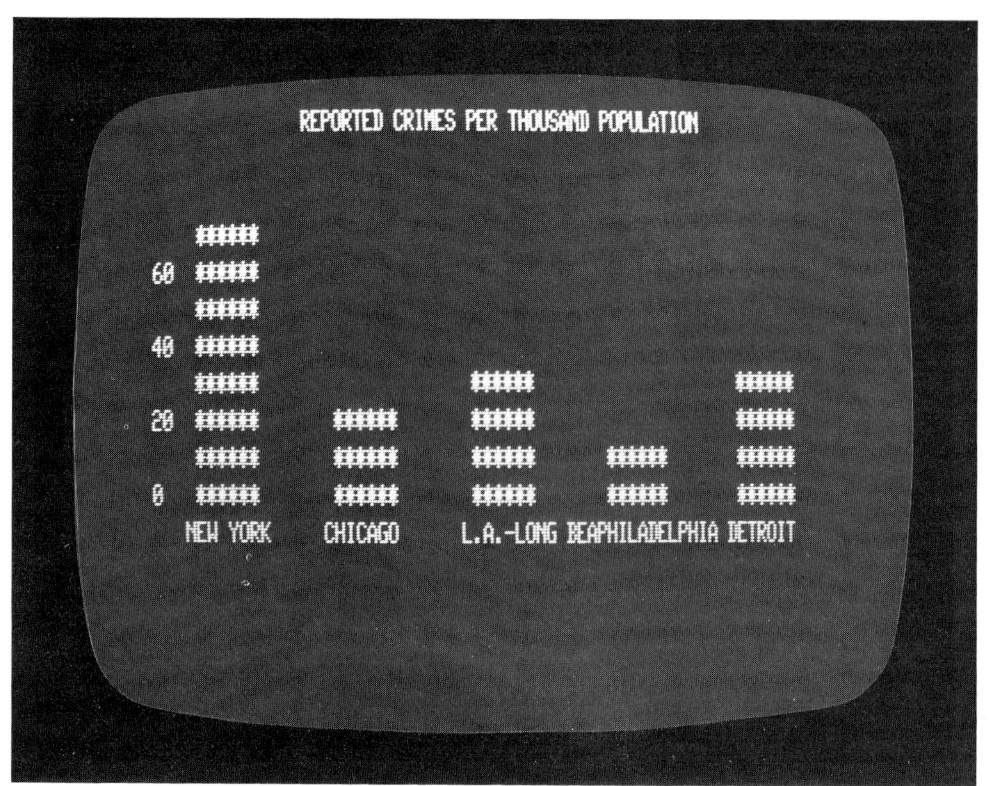

Discussion

- Note the clumsy subtitling when the city names are very long.

- Also note the lack of resolution in the heights of the bars. One might assume from looking at this bar graph that Philadelphia's crime rate is two thirds that of Chicago's when in fact it is about half. The flaw lies in the restriction on the height of the bars to just 15 units in order for the bar graph to fit on the screen. This low resolution was not apparent in the previous program because each bar could be as long as 45 characters, yielding a threefold increase in detail.

Suggestions

- Rewrite the program to accept the data interactively. Suggest to the user that city names be abbreviations, such as "CHI", "LA-LB", or "DET", each limited to five characters. With such a restriction, you should be able to graph about twice as many cities, and the titles won't run into each other.

- Alter the program to provide more resolution, say bar heights to 30 or 40. Notice that this restricts the program's output to the printer.

Problem 3.3 Write a generalized bar graph generator program.

Solution

```
10 'filename: "s3p3"
20 '  purpose: generalized histogram
30 '   author: jps 1/80
40 '
60 INPUT "HOW MANY DATA POINTS";N: DIM D(N)
70 INPUT "WHAT IS LOW VALUE";L: MIN=L
80 INPUT "WHAT IS HIGH VALUE";H: MAX=H
90 LPRINT "Num=";N,"Low=";L,"High=";H
100 '    Generate N random data points between MAX and MIN
110 FOR I=1 TO N
120 D(I)=RND(MAX-MIN+1)+MIN-1
130 LPRINT D(I);
140 IF I=INT(I/10)*10 THEN LPRINT
150 NEXT I
160 LPRINT
170 '    Get height interval size.
180 H=INT(MAX-MIN+1)/10
190 DIM B(10)
200 FOR I=1 TO N
210 ' P is proper bar pointer
220 P=(D(I)-MIN+1)/H + .5
230 B(P)=B(P)+1
240 NEXT I
250 LPRINT
260 FOR I=1 TO 10: LPRINT B(I);: NEXT I
270 LPRINT : LPRINT : LPRINT
280 HT=B(1)
290 FOR J=1 TO 10
300    IF HT<B(J) THEN HT=B(J)
310 NEXT J
320 '   II is vertical interval size (integer)
330 II=INT(HT/10+1)
340 FOR I=10 TO 1 STEP -1
350 LPRINT II*I; TAB(5); " ";
360 FOR J=1 TO 10
370    IF B(J)>=I*II THEN LPRINT " *** ";
                    ELSE LPRINT "-----";
380 NEXT J: LPRINT
390 NEXT I
400 LPRINT "Size>";
410 T=7
420 FOR I=MIN TO MAX STEP H
430 K=INT(I+H/2)
440 LPRINT TAB(T); K;: T=T+5
450 NEXT I
9999 END
```

```
Num= 200        Low= 0          High= 99
 31  49  25  48  70  22  37  52  4  39
 61  74  77  20  62  43  18  3  83  26
 15  1  53  71  67  31  76  23  3  19
 89  15  84  80  98  38  72  71  94  80
 85  25  31  48  14  48  93  53  25  8
 28  85  31  81  58  49  42  88  67  86
 87  94  61  64  12  92  1  44  56  53
 20  23  97  62  4  53  75  17  55  31
 93  10  25  65  89  86  30  21  84  64
 35  36  6  52  12  10  88  19  80  75
 44  51  13  39  12  86  28  99  82  10
 44  34  95  45  21  76  11  98  67  47
 65  94  26  81  82  77  40  11  84  95
 81  42  56  50  69  89  1  30  49  95
 58  13  59  23  2  47  65  26  20  4
 66  86  56  11  88  30  37  54  41  28
 70  55  53  54  16  34  85  32  37  29
 14  50  23  9  96  58  86  50  1  26
 36  87  24  97  30  51  68  94  93  66
 12  20  20  34  41  20  45  87  58  26


 18  22  24  18  25  16  17  16  24  13


 30    --------------------------------------------------
 27    --------------------------------------------------
 24    ---------- ***  -----  ***  --------------- ***  -----
 21    -----  *** ***  -----  ***  --------------- ***  -----
 18     ***   *** ***   ***   ***  --------------- ***  -----
 15     ***   *** ***   ***   ***   ***  ***  ***  ***  -----
 12     ***   *** ***   ***   ***   ***  ***  ***  ***   ***
 9      ***   *** ***   ***   ***   ***  ***  ***  ***   ***
 6      ***   *** ***   ***   ***   ***  ***  ***  ***   ***
 3      ***   *** ***   ***   ***   ***  ***  ***  ***   ***
Size>    5    15   25    35    45    55   65   75   85    95
```

Discussion

- This is a generalized bar graph generator which can apply to most kinds of data. It provides for 10 bars oriented vertically.
- Note that the program's calculations are almost entirely for purposes of scaling the vertical and horizontal dimensions of the graph.
- The data values that are graphed are produced by the program itself in lines 110-150. Of course this section of the program should be rewritten to allow the user to either enter the data conversationally or provide DATA statements which the program would READ.

Suggestions

- Rewrite the program to have the user provide the data.
- Modify the program to give the user the choice of symbol used for printing the bars.
- Rewrite the program to give the user the choice of screen or printer output.

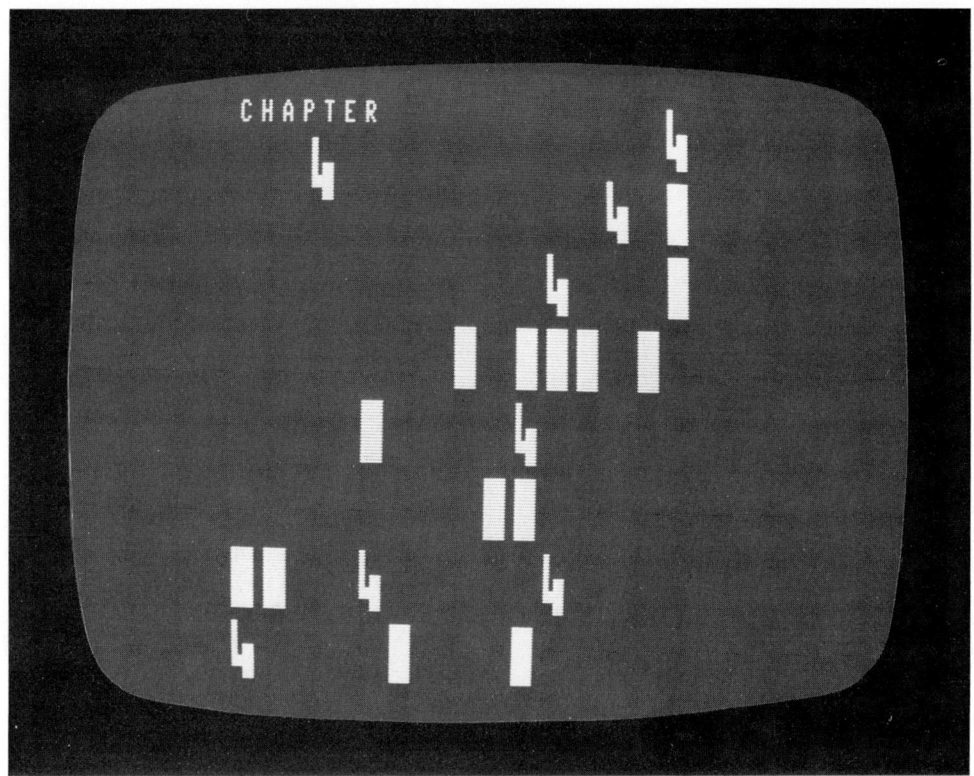

Computed Pictures

This chapter illustrates a technique that uses a two-dimensional table to hold numeric values that have been computed according to the solution of some problem. This table is then outputted with conversion of the numeric table elements to a symbol that provides a meaningful "picture" of the computation.

Problem 4.1

Rotate the graph of the sine curve of problem 2.2 so that the X-axis is horizontal and progresses across the screen.

Solution

```
10 'filename:"s4p1"
20 ' purpose: sine wave across screen
30 '   author: jps 1/80
40 '
45 CLEAR 200: DEFINT P: DIM P(64,16): CLS
70 FOR A=0 TO 8 STEP .25
80   X=A*7: Y=SIN(A-1)*7+8: P(X,Y)=1
100 NEXT A
140 FOR Y=14 TO 0 STEP -1: X$=""
150   FOR X=1 TO 62
160     IF P(X,Y)=1 THEN X$=X$+"*" ELSE X$=X$+" "
190   NEXT X: PRINT X$
200 NEXT Y
210 GOTO 210
9999 END
```

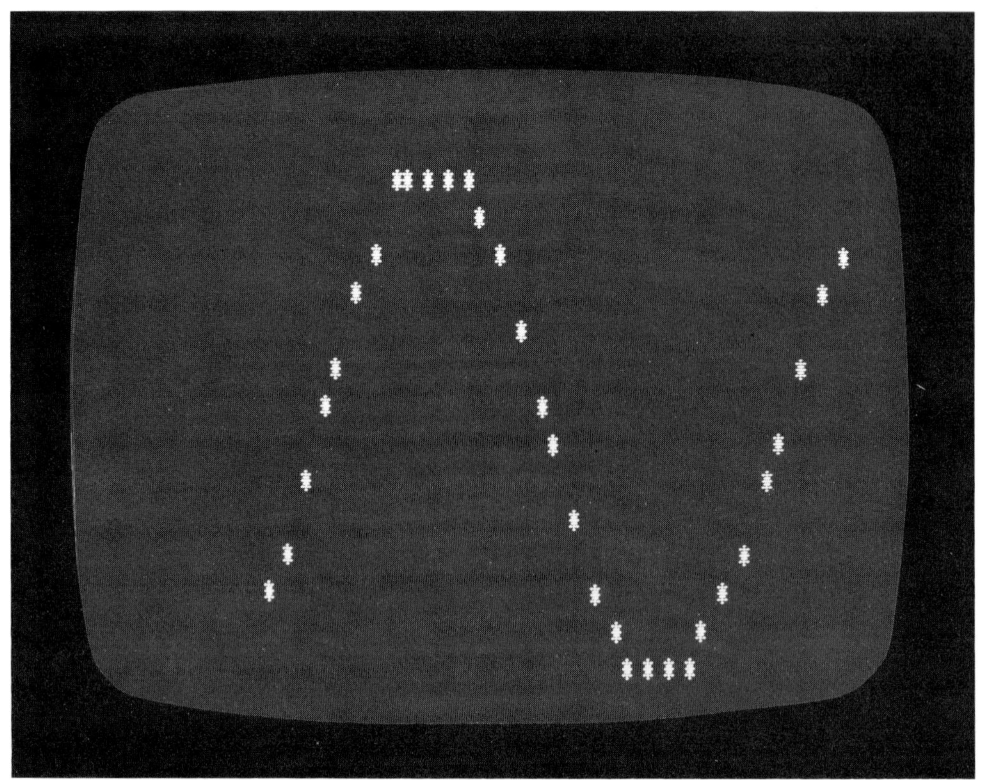

Discussion

- A lot of memory is used to store the table. Each position of the table is an integer value that indicates whether or not that position is on the sine curve.
- Each line of output is produced directly by building a string of mostly blanks and a few asterisks "(*)" from scanning a row of the table.
- The program uses the fact that BASIC sets all variables to 0 initially. This is not a good programming practice, because if the program was to be used as a subroutine and was called more than once, it would "remember" all elements of the table that had been set previously to 1. To make the program more generally useful, you should set each element of the table to zero before each use.

Suggestions

- Try modifying the program so that a composite graph of sines and cosines can be made. You'll have to devise a way to encode three potential symbols; point for sine, point for cosine, and no point at all. What if the sine and cosine intersect? Maybe a fourth symbol could be used to show this occurrence.
- Cause the X-axis and Y-axis to be printed along with the graphs.

Problem 4.2

Display the changing thermal gradient around a rectangular fireplace located at the center of a rectangular room. Imagine a room surrounded by exterior walls on three sides with a Franklin stove in its center. It's a cold, overcast winter day. What is the heat distribution in the room as the exterior of the Franklin stove begins to heat from 70° F to 400° F?

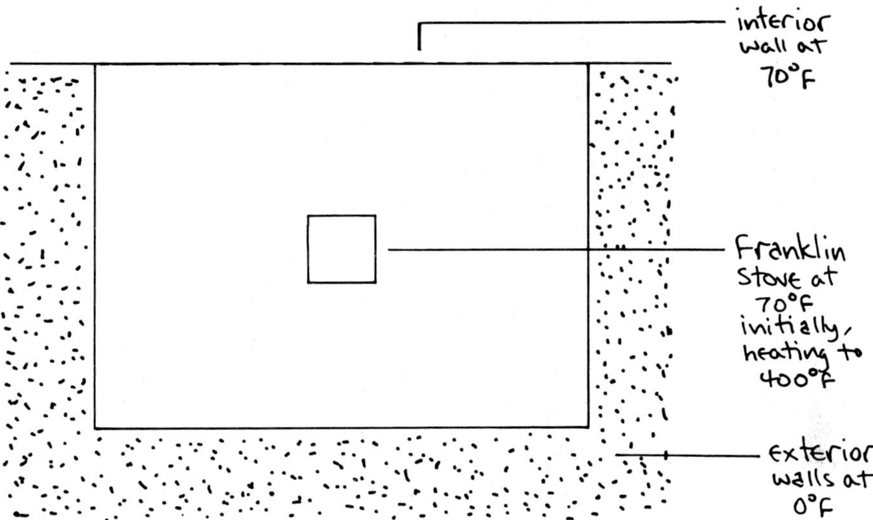

The problem resembles a problem on page 98 of Daniel D. McCracken's *A Guide to FORTRAN Programming,* (Wiley, 1965).

Solution

- Consider the room to be 40 feet long and 30 feet wide. The exterior walls are at a constant 0° F and the interior wall is a constant 70° F.

- Reserve a 30 x 40 integer table X in memory, with X(0,1) to X(0,39) held at a value of 70; X(30,0) to X(30,40), X(0,0) to X(0,30), and X(0,40) to X(30,40) held at a value of 0. These are the walls of the room. The 6-foot wide by 4-foot deep center area is the Franklin stove that starts at 70° F and ends at 400° F.

- Proceed to compute the temperatures between wall and stove, from X(1,1) to X(1,39), then X(2,1) to X(2,39), . . . , through X(29,1) to X(29,39), calculating each point on the basis of its neighbors according to the formula:
  X(I,J)=(X(I-1),J)+X(I,J-1)+X(I+1,J)+X(I,J+1))/4
  This formula calculates the temperature of a point by averaging the temperatures of that point's four neighbors.

- Repeat the computations for as many iterations as the user wishes.

- Convert all numeric values of table X to characters one 64-character line at a time using the chart of symbols below to indicate various temperatures.

Integer value	Symbol
0- 9	A
20- 29	B
40- 49	C
.	.
.	.
.	.
380-389	U
400-409	V

All temperatures in unspecified intervals like 10-19, 30-39, etc., are symbolized with a blank.

- Paint the picture on the screen or line printer one line at a time.

- Repeat the above process increasing the temperature of the Franklin stove by 50 degrees, until it reaches 400 degrees.

- Continue the above for as many iterations as the user wishes or until the output is a picture of the room at equilibrium conditions.

```
10 'filename:"s4p2"
20 '  purpose: graph thermal gradient in a heated room
30 '   author: jps 1/80
40 '
50 CLEAR 300: DEFINT A-Z
60 'set up initial conditions
80 DEPTH=30: WIDTH=40                            'room measurements
90 LL=5/12*WIDTH:      LR=7/12*WIDTH    'stove position
100 LT=5/12*DEPTH:       LB=7/12*DEPTH
110 INPUT "INNER, OUTER WALL TEMPERATURES";IN,OU
115 INPUT "STARTING, LAST, STEP TEMPERATURES OF STOVE";ST,FI,CY
118 INPUT "TOTAL ITERATIONS, NUMBER PER PRINTING CYCLE";IT,Q
120 DIM X(DEPTH,WIDTH), S$(41)
125 LPRINT "INNER=";IN,"OUTER=";OU,"STOVE=";ST"TO"FI"BY"CY
127 LPRINT "ITERATIONS=";IT,"NUMBER/PRINTING CYCLE=";Q
130 FOR I=0 TO 40 STEP 2:  READ S$(I):  NEXT I
140 DATA A, B, C, D, E, F, G, H, I, J, K
145 DATA L, M, N, O, P, Q, R, S, T, U, V, W, X, Y, Z
150 FOR I=1 TO 40 STEP 2:  S$(I)=" ":  NEXT I
```

```
160 'set initial room temperature to random between OU & ST
170 FOR I=1 TO DEPTH-1: FOR J=1 TO WIDTH-1
180   X(I,J)=RND(ST-OU)/10
190 NEXT J,I
200 'set inner wall, bottom outer wall to starting temperatures
210 FOR I=0 TO WIDTH:X(0,I)=IN/10: X(DEPTH,I)=OU/10: NEXT I
220 'set left and right outer walls to starting temperatures
230 FOR I=0 TO DEPTH: X(I,0)=OU/10: X(I,WIDTH)=OU/10: NEXT I
240 'set stove to starting temperature for this cycle
250 FOR S=ST/10 TO FI/10 STEP CY/10
260   LPRINT: LPRINT: LPRINT "STOVE IS AT"S*10"DEGREES",TIME$
270   FOR I=LT TO LB: FOR J=LL TO LR: X(I,J)=S: NEXT J,I
280   CLS
290   FOR N=1 TO IT: I=0: GOSUB 400
300     FOR I=1 TO DEPTH-1
302         'weave calculations back and forth
304         'instead of always left to right
305         IF I/2=INT(I/2) THEN S1=1: S2=WIDTH-1: S3=1
                              ELSE S1=WIDTH-1: S2=1: S3=-1
310       FOR J=S1 TO S2 STEP S3
320           'calculate all inner values.  if stove, bypass
330         IF I>=LT AND I<=LB AND J>=LL AND J<=LR THEN NEXT J
340         X(I,J)=(X(I-1,J)+X(I+1,J)+X(I,J-1)+X(I,J+1)+2)/4
350       NEXT J: GOSUB 400
360     NEXT I: GOSUB 400
370   NEXT N
380 NEXT S
390 GOTO 390
400 'subroutine to graph a single line
410 A$="": FOR K=0 TO WIDTH
420 'the symbol # is reserved for the stove's position
430 IF K>=LL AND K<=LR AND I>=LT AND I<=LB
     THEN A$=A$+"#"   ELSE A$=A$+S$(X(I,K))
440 NEXT K
450 PRINT A$,N;I
460 IF INT(N/Q)=N/Q THEN LPRINT A$,N;I
470 RETURN
500 CLEAR 100
9999 END
```

```
INNER= 70       OUTER= 0        STOVE= 70 TO 400 BY 50
ITERATIONS= 9   NUMBER/PRINTING CYCLE= 3


STOVE IS AT 70 DEGREES           00/00/00 00:35:18
A                                       A         3  0
A CCCCCCCCCCCCCCCCCCCCCCCCCCCCCCCCCCCCC A         3  1
A BBBBBBBBBBBBBBBBBBBBBBBBBBBBBBBBBBBBB A         3  2
A                                      AA         3  3
AAAAAAAAAAAAAAAAAAAAAAAAAAAAAAAAAAAAAAAAA         3  4
AAAAAAAAAAAAAAAAAAAAAAAAAAAAAAAAAAAAAAAAA         3  5
AAAAAAAAAAAAAAAAAAAAAAAAAAAAAAAAAAAAAAAAA         3  6
AAAAAAAAAAAAAAAAAAAAAAAAAAAAAAAAAAAAAAAAA         3  7
AAAAAAAAAAAAAAAAAAAAAAAAAAAAAAAAAAAAAAAAA         3  8
AAAAAAAAAAAAAAAAAAAAAAAAAAAAAAAAAAAAAAAAA         3  9
AAAAAAAAAAAAAAA          AAAAAAAAAAAAAAAA         3 10
AAAAAAAAAAAAAA B CCCCCC B AAAAAAAAAAAAAAA         3 11
AAAAAAAAAAAAAA  ########  AAAAAAAAAAAAAAA         3 12
AAAAAAAAAAAAA BC########C AAAAAAAAAAAAAAA         3 13
AAAAAAAAAAAAA BC########CB AAAAAAAAAAAAAA         3 14
AAAAAAAAAAAAA BC########CB AAAAAAAAAAAAAA         3 15
AAAAAAAAAAAAA BC########CB AAAAAAAAAAAAAA         3 16
AAAAAAAAAAAAA BC########CB AAAAAAAAAAAAAA         3 17
AAAAAAAAAAAAA B CCCCCCCC   AAAAAAAAAAAAAA         3 18
AAAAAAAAAAAAA  BBBBBBBBB  AAAAAAAAAAAAAAA         3 19
AAAAAAAAAAAAAAA           AAAAAAAAAAAAAAA         3 20
AAAAAAAAAAAAAAAAAAAAAAAAAAAAAAAAAAAAAAAAA         3 21
AAAAAAAAAAAAAAAAAAAAAAAAAAAAAAAAAAAAAAAAA         3 22
AAAAAAAAAAAAAAAAAAAAAAAAAAAAAAAAAAAAAAAAA         3 23
AAAAAAAAAAAAAAAAAAAAAAAAAAAAAAAAAAAAAAAAA         3 24
AAAAAAAAAAAAAAAAAAAAAAAAAAAAAAAAAAAAAAAAA         3 25
AAAAAAAAAAAAAAAAAAAAAAAAAAAAAAAAAAAAAAAAA         3 26
AAAAAAAAAAAAAAAAAAAAAAAAAAAAAAAAAAAAAAAAA         3 27
AAAAAAAAAAAAAAAAAAAAAAAAAAAAAAAAAAAAAAAAA         3 28
AAAAAAAAAAAAAAAAAAAAAAAAAAAAAAAAAAAAAAAAA         3 29
AAAAAAAAAAAAAAAAAAAAAAAAAAAAAAAAAAAAAAAAA         3 30
```

Discussion

- The previous output shows the effect of starting the room's temperature a 0 degrees, the same temperature as the exterior walls. We arbitrarily started the interior of the room at various random settings between 0 and the temperature of the stove, and while not realistic, it seems to be most effective in reaching equilibrium quickly.

```
INNER= 70        OUTER= 0         STOVE= 70 TO 400 BY 50
ITERATIONS= 9    NUMBER/PRINTING CYCLE= 3


STOVE IS AT 70 DEGREES           00/00/00 00:16:48
A                                       A        3  0
AC DDDDDDDDDDDDDDDDDDDDDDDDDDDDDDDD     A        3  1
A C                                CCCCBA        3  2
AB CCCCCCCCCCCCCCCCCCCCCCCCCCCCCCCCCC   BA       3  3
AB CCCCCCCCCCCCCCCCCCCCCCCCCCCCCCCCCC   BA       3  4
AB CCCCCCCCCCCCCCCCCCCCCCCCCCCCC        BA       3  5
AB CCCCCCCCCCCCCCCCCCCCCCCCCCCCCCCC     BA       3  6
AB CCCCCCCCCCCCCCCCCCCCCCCCCCCCCCCC     BA       3  7
AB CCCCCCCCCCCCCCCCCCCCCCCCCCCCCCCC     BA       3  8
AB  CCCCC   CCCCCCCCCCCCCCCCCCCCCCC     BA       3  9
AB     CC   CCCCCCCCCCCCCCCCCCCCCCCC    BA       3  10
AB     CCC             CCCCCCCCCCC  B A          3  11
AB     CCCCC   D######## CCCCCCCCCCC  B A        3  12
AB    CCCCCC   D######## CCCCCCCCC    BA         3  13
AB   CCCCCCCCC D#########D CCCCCCCCCC  BA        3  14
AB  CCCCCCCCCC D#########D CCCCCCCCCCC  BA       3  15
AB  CCCCCCCCCC D#########D CCCCCCCCCCCC BA       3  16
AB  CCCCCCCCCC D#########D CCCCCCCCCCCC BA       3  17
AB  CCCCCCCCCCCC     DD    CCCCCCCCCCCC BA       3  18
AB CCCCCCCCCCCCCCCCCCCCCCCCC   CCCCCCCC BA       3  19
AB CCCCCCCCCCCCCCCCCCCCCCCCC    CCCCCCC BA       3  20
AB CCCCCCCCCCCCCCCCCC           CCCCCCC BA       3  21
AB CCCCCCCCCCCCCCCCCCCC         CCCCCCC BA       3  22
AB CCCCCCCCCCCCCCCCCCCCC  CCCCCCCCCCCC BA        3  23
AB CCCCCCCCCCCCCCCCCCCCCCCCCCCCCCCCCCC BA        3  24
AB CCCCCCCCCCC  CC    CCCCCCCCCCCCCCCCC BA       3  25
AB CCCCCCCCCC   CC    CCCCCCCCCCCCCCCCC BA       3  26
AB CCCCCCCCCCC  CC    CCCCCCCCCCCCCCC   BA       3  27
AB  CCC        CC                       BA       3  28
A BBBBBBBBBBBBBBBBBBBBBBBBBBBBBBBBBBBBBB A       3  29
AAAAAAAAAAAAAAAAAAAAAAAAAAAAAAAAAAAAAAAAA        3  30
```

- The program was limited to this size room for practical reasons of time. It takes our TRS-80 about 10 minutes to proceed from one graph to the next, with an interval size of 5 iterations.

Suggestions

- Use other symbols to represent temperature, such as:

Temperature	Symbol
0- 9	blank
10-19	.
20-29	:
30-39	;
40-49	-
50-59	=
60-69	1
70-79	I
80-89	L
90-99	T
.	.
.	.
.	.
400-409	#

A minor modification of this program can yield startingly different results. The modification is based on doing an exact point-by-point calculation of a location's value. This kind of calculation isn't appropriate for thermal gradients, as was the case with the wood-burning stove, but it works for a wide variety of applications in which point values are based on field effects, such as electricity, gravitation, and sound.

Consider a "generator" of such a field located at a point in the middle of a rectangularly shaped area. The field strength at any other point is proportional to the square of the distance away from the generator. Thus a sound is one fourth the volume at 20 feet from a speaker as it is 10 feet away. If there are two speakers located in the rectangular area, the intensity of the sound at any point is the sum of the sound from the two speakers. It is easy to determine the distance to each of the speakers by use of the Pythagorean theorem ($c^2=a^2+b^2$). Then the process of summing the individual intensities, taking into account their distances and original intensities, yields the total amount of sound at a selected point. Repeat this process for all points on the grid, and represent point intensities by graphical means. The effect is a "picture" of the sound sources and their acoustic "fields".

The same process can be used to picture any physical field phenomenon, such as gravitational "wells" around planets and ionic field strengths.

An excellent discussion and example of this method of graphing can be found in *BASIC and the Personal Computer* by Dwyer and Critchfield, (Addison-Wesley, 1978), pages 304-306.

Problem 4.3

Display the point-by-point ionic field strength that surrounds each of up to five electrical sources. Each source can be positive or negative in relation to the background field strength. Each source will have a strength from -2 to +2. Pictorially, a negative field will be represented as a series of digits and characters ranging from 9 through 0 to such characters as /, !, +, *, . . . , %, and @. A positive field will be represented as a series of letters, from A to Z. Field areas closest to background will be represented as 9s or As.

Solution

```
10 'filename:"s4p3"
20 ' purpose: to graph electric charges
30 '   author: jps 2/80
40 CLEAR 200
45 DIM A$(52)
50 DATA 35,64,36,42,38,37,94,91,93,95,43,34,40,44,33
60 DATA 47,48,49,50,51,52,53,54,55,56,57
70 FOR I=1 TO 26: READ A: A$(I)=CHR$(A): NEXT I
80 FOR I=27 TO 52: A$(I)=CHR$(I+38): NEXT I
90 '
100 N=5: A(1)=15: B(1)=12: A(2)=18: B(2)=50: A(3)=50
110 B(3)=35: A(4)=70: B(4)=15: A(5)=70: B(5)=45
120 GOTO 180
130 CLS: INPUT "HOW MANY CHARGES";N
140 FOR I=1 TO N
150    PRINT "TYPE X AND Y POSITIONS OF CHARGE";I;
160    INPUT A(I),B(I)
170 NEXT I
180 F=SQR(3)/2
190 FOR I=1 TO N: A(I)=A(I)*F: NEXT I
200 C(1)=1: C(2)=1: C(3)=-2: C(4)=-1: C(5)=1: GOTO 240
210 PRINT "TYPE IN THE SIZE OF EACH CHARGE.  USE 3 FOR 3Q"
220 FOR I=1 TO N
230    PRINT "CHARGE ";I;: INPUT C(I): NEXT I
235 F=SQR(3)/2
240 FOR J=1 TO 121 STEP 2
250    X=J*F
260 FOR Y=1 TO 61
270    GOSUB 1000
280    Z=(V+1)*26
290    IF Z<1 THEN B$=" ": GOTO 320
300    IF Z>52 THEN B$="@": GOTO 320
310    IF Z>INT(Z)+.5 THEN B$=" " ELSE B$=A$(Z)
320    LPRINT B$;
330    NEXT Y
340 LPRINT: NEXT J
350 GOTO 350
```

```
1000 'SUBROUTINE TO CALCULATE FIELD STRENGTH
1010 V=0
1020 FOR I=1 TO N
1030 X1=X-A(I): Y1=Y-B(I)
1040 R=SQR(X1*X1+Y1*Y1)
1050 IF R>0 THEN V=V+C(I)/R ELSE V=10000: RETURN
1060 NEXT I
1070 RETURN
9999 END
```

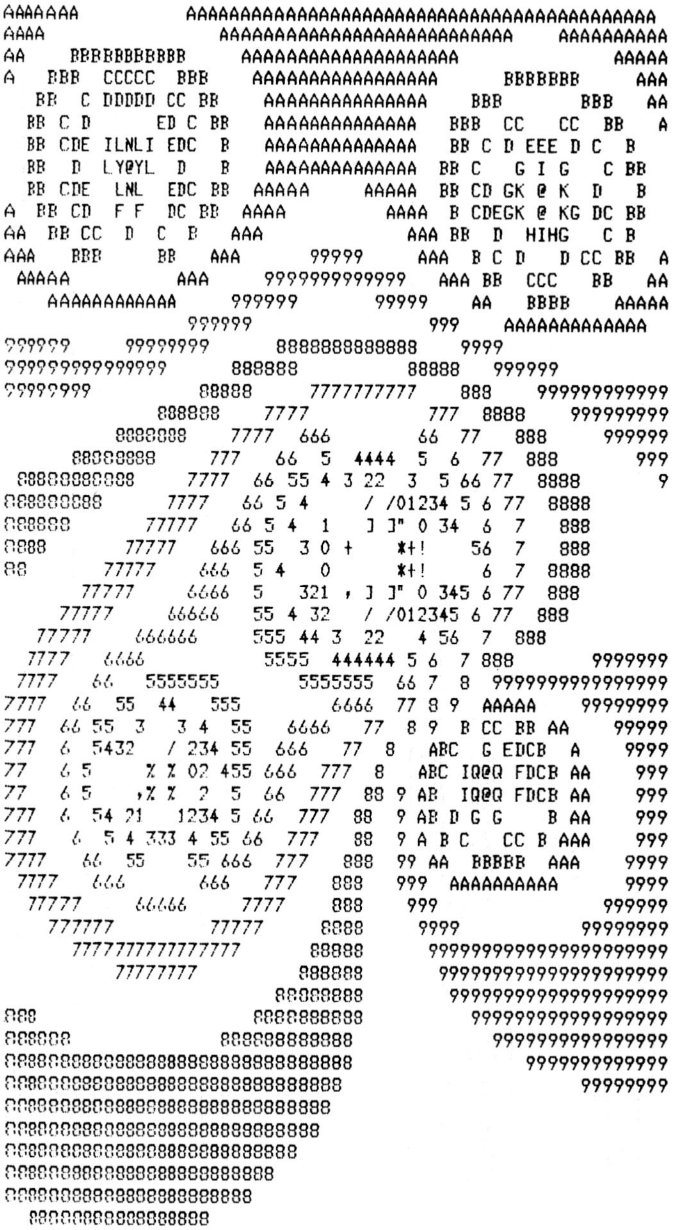

```
AAAAAAA          AAAAAAAAAAAAAAAAAAAAAAAAAAAAAAAAAAAAAAAAAAA
AAAA                AAAAAAAAAAAAAAAAAAAAAAAAAAA    AAAAAAAAAA
AA    BBBBBBBBBBB    AAAAAAAAAAAAAAAAAAAA                AAAAA
A   BBB  CCCCC  BBB    AAAAAAAAAAAAAAAAA      BBBBBBB     AAA
   BB  C DDDDD CC BB    AAAAAAAAAAAAAAA    BBB        BBB   AA
  BB C D      ED C BB   AAAAAAAAAAAAAA   BBB  CC    CC  BB   A
  BB CDE ILNLI EDC  B   AAAAAAAAAAAAAA   BB C D EEE D C  B
  BB  D  LY@YL  D   B   AAAAAAAAAAAAAA  BB C   G I G   C BB
  BB CDE  LNL  EDC BB  AAAAA     AAAAA  BB CD GK @ K  D   B
A  BB CD  F F  DC BB  AAAA            AAAA  B CDEGK @ KG DC BB
AA  BB CC  D  C  B   AAA                AAA BB  D  HIHG   C B
AAA   BBB     BB   AAA       99999     AAA  B C D   D CC BB  A
 AAAAA         AAA     9999999999999   AAA BB  CCC    BB   AA
   AAAAAAAAAAAA     999999       99999    AA   BBBB    AAAAA
                 999999                  999   AAAAAAAAAAAAA
999999     99999999     8888888888888     9999
999999999999999     888888          88888   999999
99999999         88888     7777777777     888     999999999999
                888888    7777            777  8888    999999999
             8888888    7777  666          66  77   888     999999
         88888888    777   66  5  4444  5  6  77  888        999
  88888888888     7777  66 55 4 3 22  3  5 66 77  8888        9
888888888      7777   66 5 4      / /01234 5 6 77  8888
888888      77777   66 5 4  1   ] ]" 0 34  6  7   888
8888      77777   666 55  3 0 +    *+!    56  7   888
88      77777   666  5 4   0       *+!     6  7  8888
     77777    6666  5   321 , ] ]" 0 345 6 77  888
    77777    66666   55 4 32   / /012345 6 77  888
  77777    666666    555 44 3  22   4 56  7  888
  7777   6666         5555  444444 5 6  7 888           9999999
 7777   66   5555555        5555555  66 7  8  9999999999999999
7777  66  55  44   555         6666  77 8 9  AAAAA     99999999
777  66 55  3   3 4  55   6666   77  8 9  B CC BB AA     99999
777  6  5432   / 234 55  666   77  8   ABC  G EDCB  A    9999
77   6 5     % % 02 455 666  777  8   ABC IQ@Q FDCB AA    999
77   6 5    ,% %  2  5  66  777  88 9 AB  IQ@Q FDCB AA    999
777  6  54 21   1234 5 66  777  88  9 AB D G G   B AA    999
777   6  5 4 333 4 55 66  777   88  9 A B C   CC B AAA    999
7777   66  55    55 666  777   888  99 AA  BBBBB  AAA    9999
 7777   666        666   777   888   999  AAAAAAAAAA     9999
  77777     66666     7777    888    999                999999
    777777         77777     8888     9999            99999999
      7777777777777777      88888      9999999999999999999999
          77777777         888888       999999999999999999999
                          88888888       99999999999999999999
888                     8888888888        999999999999999999
888888              88888888888888          9999999999999999
88888888888888888888888888888888888            99999999999999
8888888888888888888888888888888                    99999999
888888888888888888888888888888
888888888888888888888888888
88888888888888888888888888
8888888888888888888888
888888888888888888888
  88888888888888888
```

Discussion

- Notice that the conversational portion of the program has been bypassed by the statements at 100-120 and 180-200. This was done so that a test could be run with 5 charges located on the rectangular area.

- Beware! This program is a number-crunching sloth. You must have patience with the slowness of the output. It is quite extraordinary looking when complete.

Suggestions

- Rewrite the program to display other field relationships. To increase the range of intensity from -2 and +2 to, say, -10 and +10, change line 180 to
  180 F=SQR(3)/10

- To change the characters that represent the various intensities, rewrite the DATA statements in lines 50 and 60 and the loops in 70 and 80. They are presently written to use 52 ASCII characters.

Problem 4.4

Display the varying concentrations of up to six ionic species that may coexist in a solution of varying acidity. Solving this classic problem in analytic chemistry will provide a chemist with the ability to determine at a glance what the "soup" of acid contains at a particular level of acidity, or pH. Without such a graphical aid, the chemist must rely on rather complex and time-consuming calculations to obtain the same information.

Solution

```
10 'filename: "g4p4"
20 '  purpose: chemical soup graphing
30 '   author: jpg 9/80
40 '
50 CLEAR 4000
60 DIM G$(26),PK(6),K(6),A(6),Y(6)
70 W=71: WI=5          'Set up width to 71 cols, intervals to 5
80 INPUT "Which included acid from the DATA stmts"; K
90 FOR J=1 TO K: READ A$,N: Y(0)=1
100    FOR I=1 TO N: READ PK(I)
110 '             Get ionization constants, cumulative products
120      K(I)=10[(-PK(I)): Y(I)=K(I)*Y(I-1)
130 '             Note the left bracket prints for an up-arrow
140    NEXT I
150 NEXT J
160 LPRINT: LPRINT
170 LPRINT TAB(5); CHR$(1); A$     'Double-wide
180 LPRINT TAB(5); CHR$(2); "the";N;"pKs are:";
190 FOR I=1 TO N: LPRINT TAB(I*10); PK(I);: NEXT I
200 LPRINT: LPRINT
```

```
210 '       Prepare the background grid
220 '           First, blank out inner strings
230 FOR I=2 TO 25: G$(I)=STRING$(W-2,32): NEXT I
240 '           Then dot the outer, interval strings
250 FOR I=1 TO 26 STEP 5: G$(I)=STRING$(W-2,"."): NEXT I
260 '           Then dot left, right, center columns
270 FOR I=1 TO 26
280   G$(I)="."+LEFT$(G$(I),34)+"."+RIGHT$(G$(I),34)+"."
290 NEXT I
300 'Go through pH range
310 '           calculate H-ion concentration
320 FOR PH=0 TO 14 STEP .2:  PRINT PH;: H=10[(-PH): D=0
330 '           Calculate H-ion cumulative products, denom.
340   FOR I=0 TO N: Z(I)=H[(N-I)*Y(I): D=D+Z(I): NEXT I
350 '           Calculate Alpha value (activity of subspecies)
360   FOR I=0 TO N: A(I)=Z(I)/D
370 '          Calculate vertical displacement V (which string)
380 '           and horizontal displacement B
390     V=A(I)*25+1.5: B=PH*WI+1
400 '           Substitute appropriate digit
410 '             in proper position of proper string
420     MID$(G$(V),B,1)=CHR$(48+I)
430   NEXT I
440 NEXT PH
450 PRINT
460 T=1.2       'T is vertical concentration marker 0 to 1.0
470 FOR I=26 TO 1 STEP -1
480   IF INT((I-1)/5)*5<>I-1 THEN 520
490     T=T-.2
500       IF T<.2 THEN T=0
510     LPRINT T;
520   LPRINT TAB(7); G$(I)
530 NEXT I
540 LPRINT " pH=->";
550 FOR I=0 TO 14: LPRINT TAB(I*WI+7);I;: NEXT I
560 LPRINT: STOP
1000 '***** data statements with acid names, pKs
1010 DATA "Ethylene Diamine Tetra-acetic Acid (EDTA)"
1020 DATA 4, 2.00, 2.67, 6.16, 10.26
1030 DATA "Arsenic Acid", 3, 2.22, 6.98, 11.4
1040 DATA "Carbonic Acid", 2, 6.35, 10.33
1050 DATA "Citric Acid", 3, 3.13, 4.76, 6.40
1060 DATA "Malic Acid", 2, 3.40, 5.05
1070 DATA "Oxalic Acid", 2, 1.27, 4.27
1080 DATA "Phosphoric Acid", 3, 2.15, 7.20, 12.4
1090 DATA "Pyrophosphoric Acid", 4, .85, 1.96, 6.54, 8.44
1100 DATA "Salicylic Acid", 2, 2.97, 13.0
1110 DATA "Tartaric Acid", 2, 3.04, 4.37
1120 DATA "DCTA", 4, 2.40, 3.52, 6.12, 11.7
9999 END
```

```
       Arsenic Acid
          the 3 pKs are: 2.22  6.98  11.4

1      000.................111111.................22222................33333.
       .  000           11      11        .   222     222           333     .
       .     0        11          11      .  2            2        3        .
       .      0                           . 2              2      3         .
       .              1              1    .                                 .
.8     ........0.....1................1.....2...............2....3...........
       .                                  .                                 .
       .        0   1                  1  .2                 2  3           .
       .                                  .                                 .
       .         0                        2                                 .
.6     ............1....................1.....................2.3............
       .                                  .                                 .
       .          0                      2.                                 .
       .          1                      1.                    3            .
       .                                  .                                 .
.4     ............0....................2.....................3.2............
       .         1                        1                                 .
       .                                  .                                 .
       .        1   0                  2  .1                 3   2          .
       .                                  .                                 .
.2     ........1.....0................2.....1...............3.....2..........
       .              0              2    .                                 .
       .      1                           .  1             3       2        .
       .     1          00          22    .   1           3         2       .
       .  111             00      22      .    111     333          222     .
0      333333333333333333333333333333333333333333333333111111111111111122222.
pH=->   0    1    2    3    4    5    6    7    8    9    10   11  12  13  14
```

Carbonic Acid

the 2 pKs are: 6.35 10.33

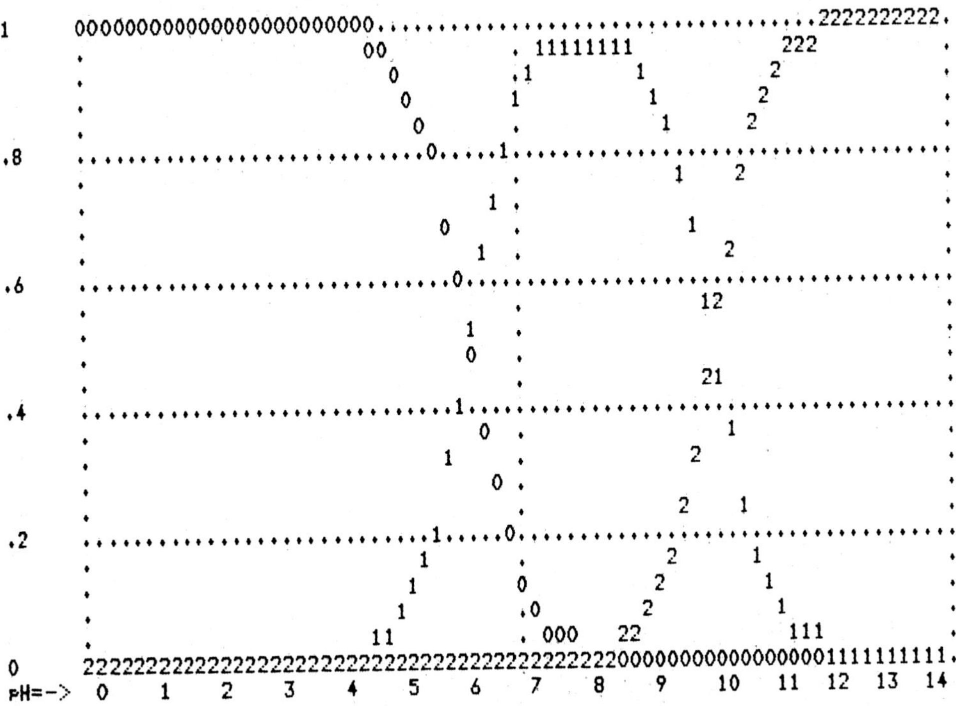

Malic Acid

the 2 pKs are: 3.4 5.05

```
1      000000000.........................222222222222222222222222222222222222222.
       .        000                     22  .                                    .
       .            0                  2    .                                    .
       .             0                2     .                                    .
       .                             2      .                                    .
.8     ...............0...........................................................
       .                    111     2       .                                    .
       .               0       1            .                                    .
       .                   1       2        .                                    .
       .                       1            .                                    .
.6     .................0.1.......2...............................................
       .                                    .                                    .
       .                         1          .                                    .
       .                 1       2          .                                    .
       .                                    .                                    .
.4     .................1.........1...............................................
       .                  0    2            .                                    .
       .                           1        .                                    .
       .               1   0                .                                    .
       .                       2            .                                    .
.2     ...............1.....0.......1.............................................
       .                      2      1      .                                    .
       .             1       2        1     .                                    .
       .            1       2 0        1    .                                    .
       .        111       22   0        11  .                                    .
0      2222222222222222222.....000000000111111111111111111111111111111111111111111.
pH=->   0    1    2    3    4    5    6    7    8    9    10   11   12   13   14
```

Pyrophosphoric Acid

the 4 pKs are: .85 1.96 6.54 8.44

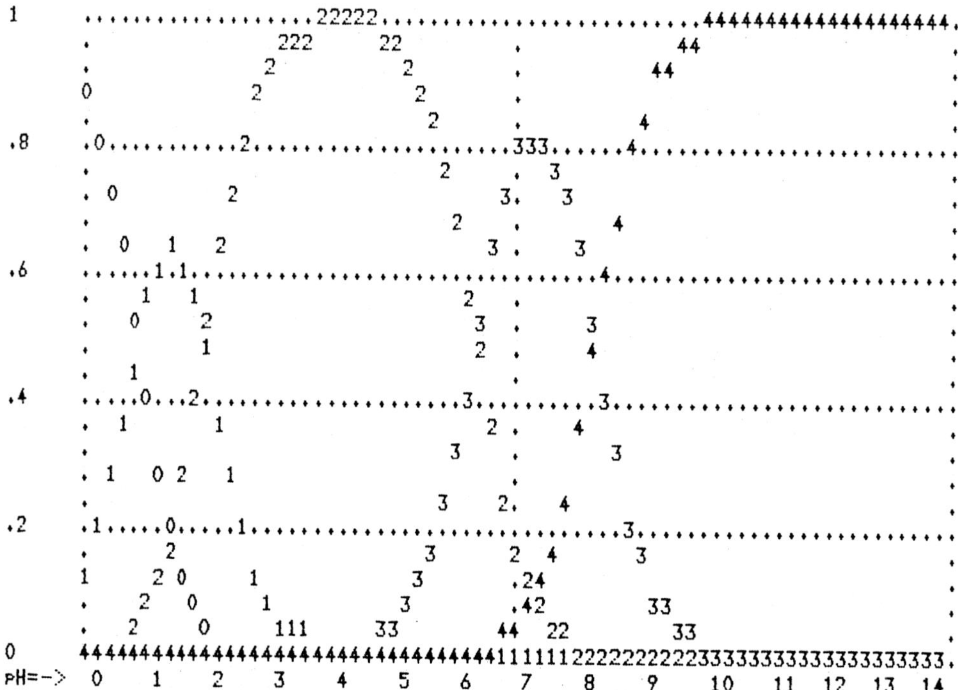

Discussion

- A wide variety of disciplines are plagued with experimental conditions such as these. Interfering signals in electronics, competing species in genetics, varying levels of soil conditioners, fertilizers and hybrids in agriculture—all lend themselves to this graphing technique. The calculations for for each application are different, but the terminal result is the same: The experimenter wants a graph of competing, interfering, or mutually affecting species.

Suggestions

- RUN this program with various acids to get a feel for the way pKs affect competing species. Here is a list of acids and their pKs for you to try.

Name	pK1	pK2	pK3	pK4
Arsenic acid	2.22	6.98	11.4	
Carbonic acid	6.35	10.33		
Citric acid	3.13	4.76	6.40	
Malic acid	3.40	5.05		
Oxalic acid	1.27	4.27		
Phosphoric acid	2.15	7.20	12.4	
Pyrophosphoric acid	0.85	1.96	6.54	8.44
Salicylic acid	2.97	13.0		
Tartaric acid	3.04	4.37		
EDTA	2.00	2.67	6.16	10.26
DCTA	2.40	3.52	6.12	11.7

- Add a table-printing feature to this program that prints out the concentrations of all species present at each pH.

Problem 4.5

Produce a chart on the printer that displays blocks of all printable characters so that an enterprising programmer can scan it to pick out likely candidates for future density gradient graphs. Each block is to be 5 characters tall and 8 characters wide, and separated from its neighboring blocks by 8 spaces. Above each block is to be printed the ASCII code value which that character represents.

Solution

```
10 'filename:"s4p5"
20 '  purpose: produce a chart to show character densities
30 '   author: jdr 8/80
40 '
50 I=32
60 FOR L=1 TO 4
70     FOR K=1 TO 6
80         LPRINT I,I+1,I+2,I+3
90         FOR J=1 TO 5
100            LPRINT STRING$(8,I), : LPRINT STRING$(8,I+1),
110            LPRINT STRING$(8,I+2), : LPRINT STRING$(8,I+3)
120        NEXT J
130        LPRINT : LPRINT
140        I=I+4
150    NEXT K
160    FOR K=1 TO 8
170        LPRINT
180    NEXT K
190 NEXT L
9999 END
```

```
32          33          34          35
            !!!!!!!!    """"""""    ########
            !!!!!!!!    """"""""    ########
            !!!!!!!!    """"""""    ########
            !!!!!!!!    """"""""    ########
            !!!!!!!!    """"""""    ########

36          37          38          39
$$$$$$$$    %%%%%%%%    &&&&&&&&    ''''''''
$$$$$$$$    %%%%%%%%    &&&&&&&&    ''''''''
$$$$$$$$    %%%%%%%%    &&&&&&&&    ''''''''
$$$$$$$$    %%%%%%%%    &&&&&&&&    ''''''''
$$$$$$$$    %%%%%%%%    &&&&&&&&    ''''''''

40          41          42          43
((((((((    ))))))))    ********    ++++++++
((((((((    ))))))))    ********    ++++++++
((((((((    ))))))))    ********    ++++++++
((((((((    ))))))))    ********    ++++++++
((((((((    ))))))))    ********    ++++++++

44          45          46          47
,,,,,,,,    --------    ........    ////////
,,,,,,,,    --------    ........    ////////
,,,,,,,,    --------    ........    ////////
,,,,,,,,    --------    ........    ////////
,,,,,,,,    --------    ........    ////////

48          49          50          51
00000000    11111111    22222222    33333333
00000000    11111111    22222222    33333333
00000000    11111111    22222222    33333333
00000000    11111111    22222222    33333333
00000000    11111111    22222222    33333333

52          53          54          55
44444444    55555555    66666666    77777777
44444444    55555555    66666666    77777777
44444444    55555555    66666666    77777777
44444444    55555555    66666666    77777777
44444444    55555555    66666666    77777777
```

```
 56          57          58          59
88888888    99999999    ::::::::    ;;;;;;;;
88888888    99999999    ::::::::    ;;;;;;;;
88888888    99999999    ::::::::    ;;;;;;;;
88888888    99999999    ::::::::    ;;;;;;;;
88888888    99999999    ::::::::    ;;;;;;;;

 60          61          62          63
<<<<<<<<    ========    >>>>>>>>    ????????
<<<<<<<<    ========    >>>>>>>>    ????????
<<<<<<<<    ========    >>>>>>>>    ????????
<<<<<<<<    ========    >>>>>>>>    ????????
<<<<<<<<    ========    >>>>>>>>    ????????

 64          65          66          67
@@@@@@@@    AAAAAAAA    BBBBBBBB    CCCCCCCC
@@@@@@@@    AAAAAAAA    BBBBBBBB    CCCCCCCC
@@@@@@@@    AAAAAAAA    BBBBBBBB    CCCCCCCC
@@@@@@@@    AAAAAAAA    BBBBBBBB    CCCCCCCC
@@@@@@@@    AAAAAAAA    BBBBBBBB    CCCCCCCC

 68          69          70          71
DDDDDDDD    EEEEEEEE    FFFFFFFF    GGGGGGGG
DDDDDDDD    EEEEEEEE    FFFFFFFF    GGGGGGGG
DDDDDDDD    EEEEEEEE    FFFFFFFF    GGGGGGGG
DDDDDDDD    EEEEEEEE    FFFFFFFF    GGGGGGGG
DDDDDDDD    EEEEEEEE    FFFFFFFF    GGGGGGGG

 72          73          74          75
HHHHHHHH    IIIIIIII    JJJJJJJJ    KKKKKKKK
HHHHHHHH    IIIIIIII    JJJJJJJJ    KKKKKKKK
HHHHHHHH    IIIIIIII    JJJJJJJJ    KKKKKKKK
HHHHHHHH    IIIIIIII    JJJJJJJJ    KKKKKKKK
HHHHHHHH    IIIIIIII    JJJJJJJJ    KKKKKKKK

 76          77          78          79
LLLLLLLL    MMMMMMMM    NNNNNNNN    OOOOOOOO
LLLLLLLL    MMMMMMMM    NNNNNNNN    OOOOOOOO
LLLLLLLL    MMMMMMMM    NNNNNNNN    OOOOOOOO
LLLLLLLL    MMMMMMMM    NNNNNNNN    OOOOOOOO
LLLLLLLL    MMMMMMMM    NNNNNNNN    OOOOOOOO
```

~~~
80          81          82          83
PPPPPPPP    QQQQQQQQ    RRRRRRRR    SSSSSSSS
PPPPPPPP    QQQQQQQQ    RRRRRRRR    SSSSSSSS
PPPPPPPP    QQQQQQQQ    RRRRRRRR    SSSSSSSS
PPPPPPPP    QQQQQQQQ    RRRRRRRR    SSSSSSSS
PPPPPPPP    QQQQQQQQ    RRRRRRRR    SSSSSSSS

84          85          86          87
TTTTTTTT    UUUUUUUU    VVVVVVVV    WWWWWWWW
TTTTTTTT    UUUUUUUU    VVVVVVVV    WWWWWWWW
TTTTTTTT    UUUUUUUU    VVVVVVVV    WWWWWWWW
TTTTTTTT    UUUUUUUU    VVVVVVVV    WWWWWWWW
TTTTTTTT    UUUUUUUU    VVVVVVVV    WWWWWWWW

88          89          90          91
XXXXXXXX    YYYYYYYY    ZZZZZZZZ    [[[[[[[[
XXXXXXXX    YYYYYYYY    ZZZZZZZZ    [[[[[[[[
XXXXXXXX    YYYYYYYY    ZZZZZZZZ    [[[[[[[[
XXXXXXXX    YYYYYYYY    ZZZZZZZZ    [[[[[[[[
XXXXXXXX    YYYYYYYY    ZZZZZZZZ    [[[[[[[[

92          93          94          95
\\\\\\\\    ]]]]]]]]    ↑↑↑↑↑↑↑↑    ________
\\\\\\\\    ]]]]]]]]    ↑↑↑↑↑↑↑↑    ________
\\\\\\\\    ]]]]]]]]    ↑↑↑↑↑↑↑↑    ________
\\\\\\\\    ]]]]]]]]    ↑↑↑↑↑↑↑↑    ________
\\\\\\\\    ]]]]]]]]    ↑↑↑↑↑↑↑↑    ________

96          97          98          99
````````    aaaaaaaa    bbbbbbbb    cccccccc
````````    aaaaaaaa    bbbbbbbb    cccccccc
````````    aaaaaaaa    bbbbbbbb    cccccccc
````````    aaaaaaaa    bbbbbbbb    cccccccc
````````    aaaaaaaa    bbbbbbbb    cccccccc

100         101         102         103
dddddddd    eeeeeeee    ffffffff    gggggggg
dddddddd    eeeeeeee    ffffffff    gggggggg
dddddddd    eeeeeeee    ffffffff    gggggggg
dddddddd    eeeeeeee    ffffffff    gggggggg
dddddddd    eeeeeeee    ffffffff    gggggggg
~~~

104	105	106	107
hhhhhhhh hhhhhhhh hhhhhhhh hhhhhhhh hhhhhhhh	iiiiiiii iiiiiiii iiiiiiii iiiiiiii iiiiiiii	jjjjjjjj jjjjjjjj jjjjjjjj jjjjjjjj jjjjjjjj	kkkkkkkk kkkkkkkk kkkkkkkk kkkkkkkk kkkkkkkk
108	**109**	**110**	**111**
llllllll llllllll llllllll llllllll llllllll	mmmmmmmm mmmmmmmm mmmmmmmm mmmmmmmm mmmmmmmm	nnnnnnnn nnnnnnnn nnnnnnnn nnnnnnnn nnnnnnnn	oooooooo oooooooo oooooooo oooooooo oooooooo
112	**113**	**114**	**115**
pppppppp pppppppp pppppppp pppppppp pppppppp	qqqqqqqq qqqqqqqq qqqqqqqq qqqqqqqq qqqqqqqq	rrrrrrrr rrrrrrrr rrrrrrrr rrrrrrrr rrrrrrrr	ssssssss ssssssss ssssssss ssssssss ssssssss
116	**117**	**118**	**119**
tttttttt tttttttt tttttttt tttttttt tttttttt	uuuuuuuu uuuuuuuu uuuuuuuu uuuuuuuu uuuuuuuu	vvvvvvvv vvvvvvvv vvvvvvvv vvvvvvvv vvvvvvvv	wwwwwww wwwwwww wwwwwww wwwwwww wwwwwww
120	**121**	**122**	**123**
xxxxxxxx xxxxxxxx xxxxxxxx xxxxxxxx xxxxxxxx	yyyyyyyy yyyyyyyy yyyyyyyy yyyyyyyy yyyyyyyy	zzzzzzzz zzzzzzzz zzzzzzzz zzzzzzzz zzzzzzzz	{{{{{{{{ {{{{{{{{ {{{{{{{{ {{{{{{{{ {{{{{{{{
124	**125**	**126**	**127**
|||||||| |||||||| |||||||| |||||||| ||||||||	}}}}}}}} }}}}}}}} }}}}}}}} }}}}}}}} }}}}}}}}	~~~~~~~~ ~~~~~~~~ ~~~~~~~~ ~~~~~~~~ ~~~~~~~~	

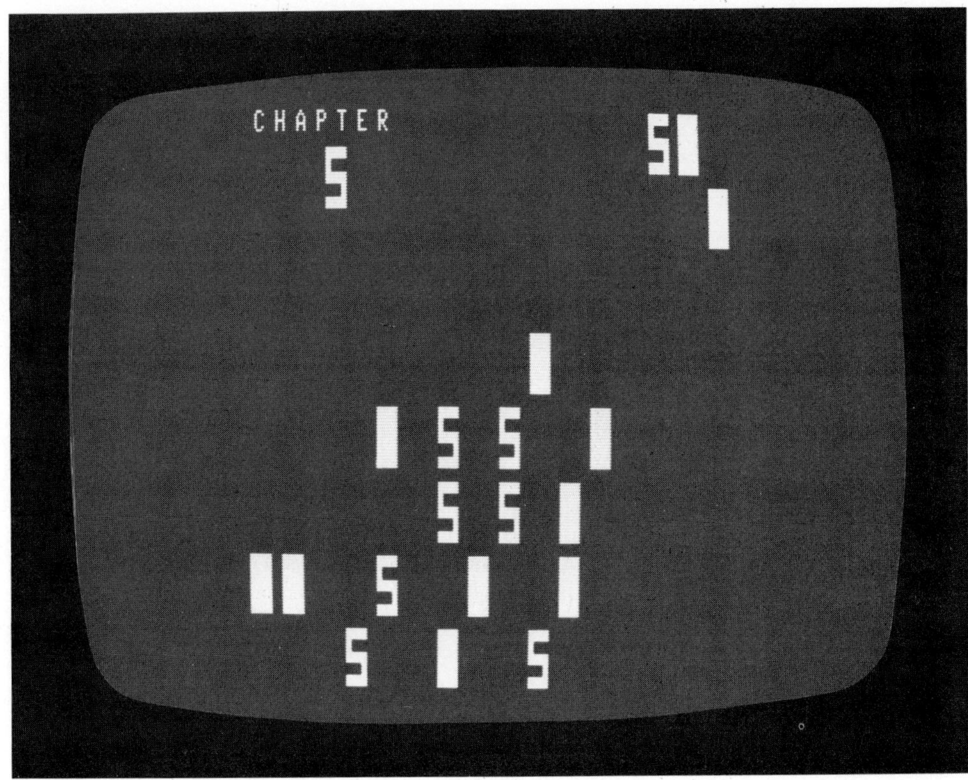

Table-Driven Pictures

Many graphic designs can be contained within a program as DATA statements whose values represent an encoded version of the picture or design. The program READs the DATA values and performs the decoding necessary to reconstruct the graphic design.

Problem 5.1

Draw an expanded digit 1 on the screen.

Solution

Store the sketch of the digit into a 2-dimensional table in which the first column represents the starting position in a line of output of a string of asterisks. The second column of the table specifies the length of the string.

```
10 'filename:"s5p1"
20 ' purpose: draw expanded digit 1, coded by position & length
30 '   author: jdr 8/80
40 '
50 DEFINT A-Z : DIM D(14,2)
60 FOR I=1 TO 14
70    READ D(I,1),D(I,2)
80 NEXT I
90 DATA 23,3,22,4,22,4,22,4,24,2,24,2,24,2,24,2
100 DATA 23,6,22,8,22,8,22,8,22,8,23,6
110 FOR I=1 TO 14
120    PRINT TAB(D(I,1));STRING$(D(I,2),"*")
130 NEXT I
140 END
```

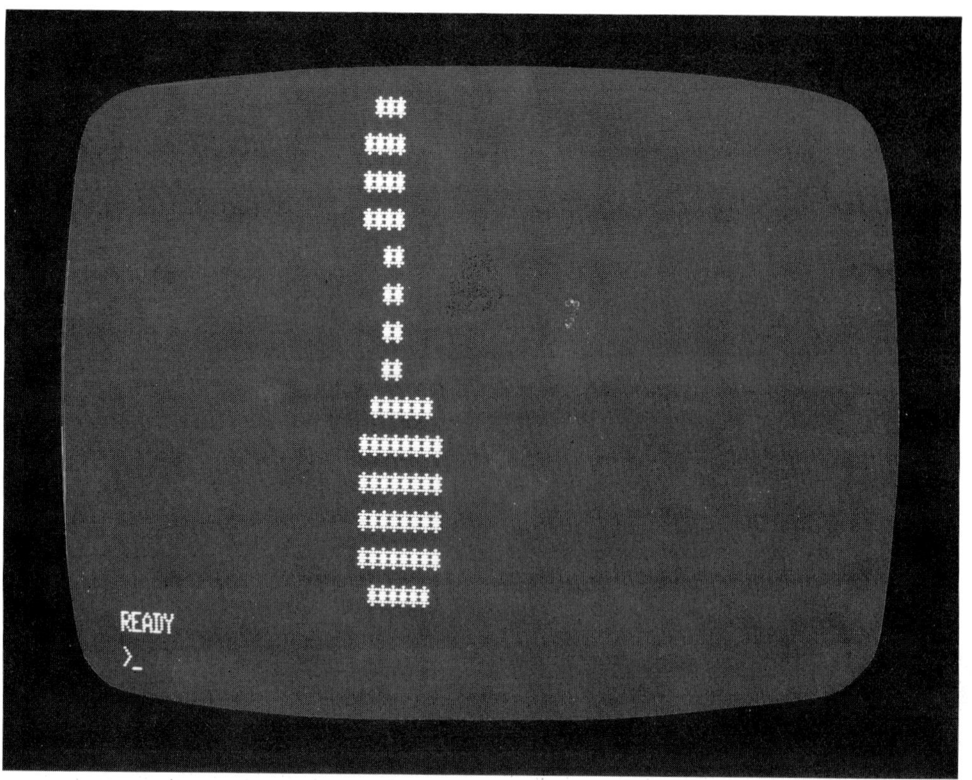

Discussion

- The graph of a single digit, as in this case, suggests the many such designs that could be produced this way.

- You can expand the technique that this example shows by incorporating a repetition factor, wherein there are three values associated with a PRINT statement:
  (1) number of PRINT statements of this format,
  (2) starting position for the string,
  (3) length of the string.

- In order to fully generalize this technique, two more pieces of information could be added to the encoding information:
  (1) indicator of whether this PRINT line is finished or is to be continued,
  (2) what character is to be used in the string.

Suggestions

- Modify the program by implementing the ideas in the discussion points above. Cause the program to draw an enlarged digit 0.

- Modify the program so that the user can select the position where the digit is to be placed on the screen.

- Create graphic symbols and make up DATA statements that could be used by your program for display on the screen.

Problem 5.2 Draw an expanded digit 1 on the screen.

Solution Encode the sketch of the digit into a series of binary numbers, with zeros and ones representing the absence or presence of a character. For example, each line of a sketch of the digit 1

```
 xxx
xxxx
xxxx
xxxx
  xx
  xx
  xx
  xx
 xxxxxx
xxxxxxxx
xxxxxxxx
xxxxxxxx
xxxxxxxx
 xxxxxx
```

can be encoded into binary by using a binary digit 1 to represent an x and a binary digit 0 to represent a blank. The result would be the 14 8-bit binary numbers

```
01110000
11110000
11110000
11110000
00110000
00110000
00110000
00110000
01111110
11111111
11111111
11111111
11111111
01111110
```

Convert each of the binary numbers to its decimal equivalent. Remember that the binary number system uses each place to represent a power of two. The rightmost position corresponding to 2 to the zero power or 1, the next being 2 to the first power or 2, the next being 2 to the second power or 4, and so on. Thus the binary numbers above equal the decimal numbers

```
112
240
240
240
```

48
48
48
48
123
255
255
255
255
123

All the program needs to do then is decode the decimal numbers (convert them back to binary) and cause an asterisk to correspond to a 1 and a blank to correspond to a 0.

```
10 'filename:"s5p2"
20 '  purpose: draw expanded digit 1, coded in binary
30 '   author: jdr 8/80
40 '
50 DEFINT A-Z : CLEAR 200 : DIM D(14),X$(14)
60 FOR I=1 TO 14
70     READ D(I)
80 NEXT I
90 DATA 112,240,240,240,48,48,48,48
100 DATA 126,255,255,255,255,126
110 FOR I=1 TO 14
120     C=D(I)
130     X$(I)=""
140     FOR J=1 TO 8
150         Q=INT(C/2)
160         R=C-2*Q
170         IF R=1
              THEN X$(I)="*"+X$(I)
              ELSE X$(I)=" "+X$(I)
180         C=Q
190     NEXT J
200 NEXT I
210 FOR I=1 TO 14
220     PRINT TAB(22);X$(I)
230 NEXT I
240 END
```

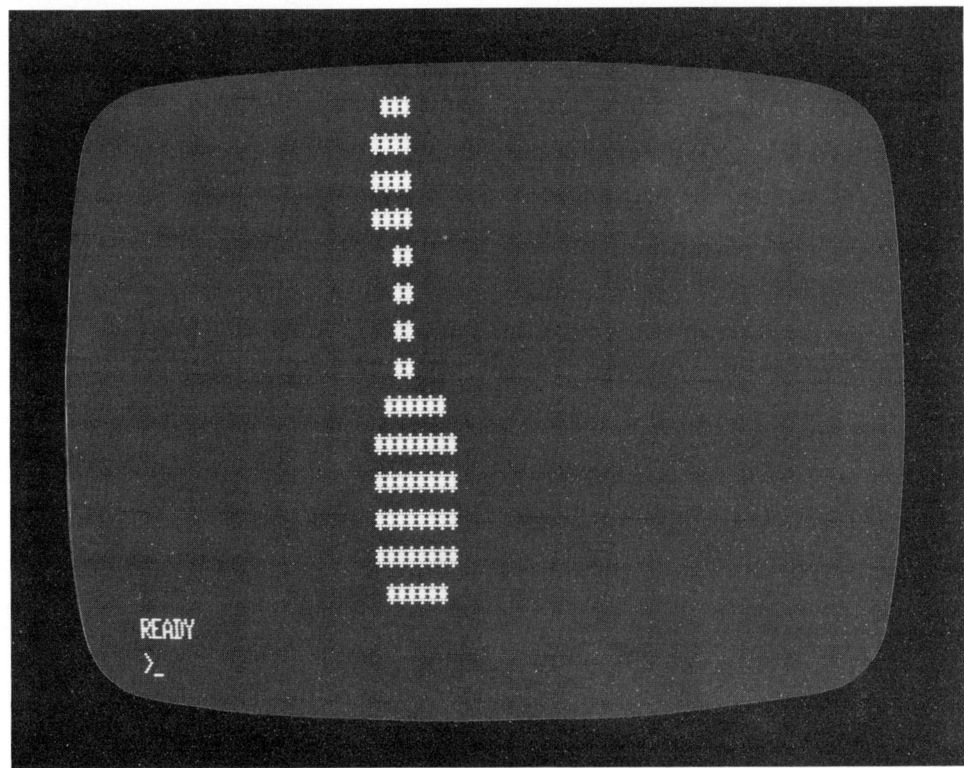

Discussion

- Because of the internal representation of integers in the TRS-80, we are able to code each line of the figure in binary if its width is less than sixteen characters wide. Of course, wider pictures could use two or more numbers to represent each line of the picture.

- Many other kinds of designs can be easily represented this way. For example, an alphabet or other set of graphic symbols could be coded and thus displayed in a manner similar to that used in this program.

Suggestions

- Alter the program so that the one becomes twice as fat when displayed, but don't change any of the encoded data values.

- Alter the program so that the user can specify the position of the number on the screen. Also, let the user specify the character used to sketch the figure.

- Design a corporate logo or other simple figure and place the encoded information in DATA statements and alter the program to output it.

Problem 5.3 Draw the silhouette of a witch.

Solution

```
10 'filename:"s5p3"
20 '  purpose: draw a silhouette of a witch
30 '   author: sps 9/79
40 '
50 LPRINT CHR$(31) '  convert printer to 16.5 cpi
60 CLEAR 500 '  make room for strings
70 READ A$ '  get next piece of data
80 IF A$="END" THEN 9999
90 '    check for a new line
100 IF A$="B" THEN LPRINT: LPRINT TAB(21); : GOTO 70
110 '    check for the code for spaces (S##)
120 IF LEFT$(A$,1)="S" THEN
      LPRINT STRING$(VAL(MID$(A$,2))," "); : GOTO 70
130 LPRINT STRING$(VAL(A$),"%");
140 GOTO 70
150 DATA B,S44,2,B,S43,4,B,S43,5,B,S44,6,B,S45,5,B,S45,
6,B,S46,6,B,S46,7,S7,2,B,S45,9,S5,3,B,S45,16,B,S45,15,
B,S45,14,B,S42,17,B,S40,20,B,S40,21,B,S43,16,B,S34,26,
B,S31,28,B,S28,28,B,S26,30,B,S24,32,B
160 DATA S22,34,B,S20,36,B,S18,39,B,S16,43,B,S15,46,B,S14,
54,B,S10,65,S3,3,B,S5,74,B,79,B,S1,77,B,S2,23,S3,45,B,S8,14,
S6,44,B,S28,36,S3,4,B,S28,37,B,S28,36,B,S29,34,B,S30,32,B,S30,
32,B,S32,30,B,S37,24,B,S29,2,S2,27,B,S25,34,B
170 DATA S14,5,S1,12,S2,24,B
180 DATA S8,23,S2,24,S9,3,B,28,S3,26,S3,10,B,25,S4,40,B,S1,
21,S4,40,B,S3,15,S4,39,B,S3,14,S4,24,B,S4,9,S4,23,B,S6,5,S3,
23,B,S6,3,S3,22,B,S6,2,S4,16,B,S14,8
190 DATA END
9999 END
```

Discussion

- This program is a variation on many of the ideas presented in the previous programs.

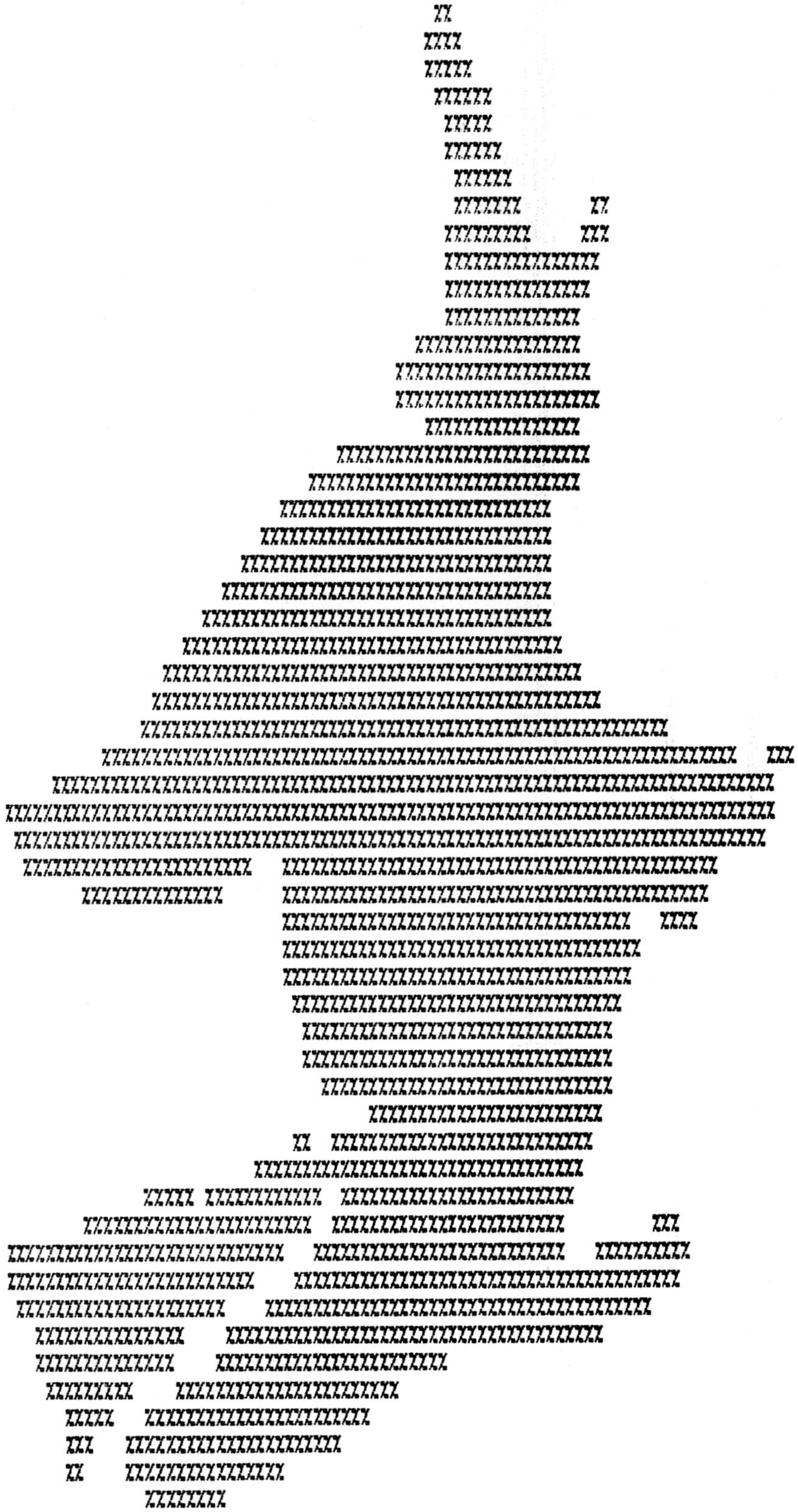

As we near completion of this chapter and the discussion of line printer graphics in general, we will introduce another method for encoding a picture description that will provide a generalized program upon which many other programs can be based to generate graphic designs of all kinds.

The method used to code a picture or design is based on the fact that all pictures produced on a video screen or line printer are formed from single characters or straight lines composed of characters. If a grid is introduced over the picture like that shown below, then the picture or design can be reduced to a set of pairs of end points of a bunch of straight lines.

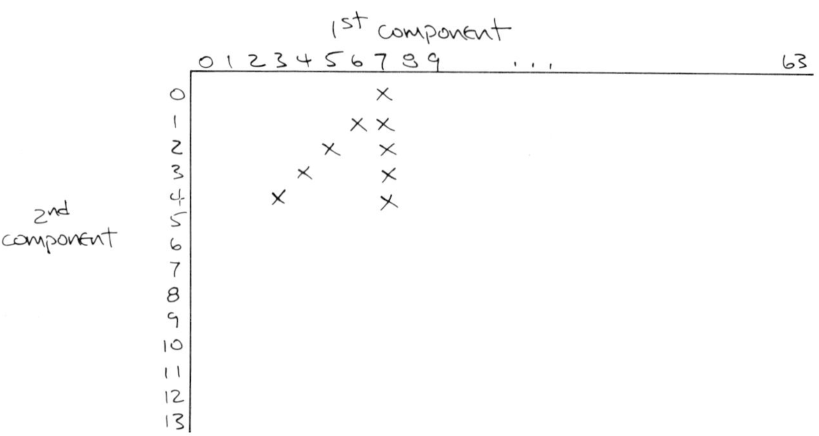

As an example, the figure in the grid is composed of two straight lines. The first has end points (3,4) and (7,0). The second has end points (7,0) and (7,4). If we were to draw the straight lines connecting these end points and fill in the middle points, the figure shown in the drawing would be created. That is the basis of this method: Reduce the drawing to end points of a straight line. The plot the endpoints and all points on the line in between.

The expanded digit 1 of programs G5P1 and G5P2 could be coded as:

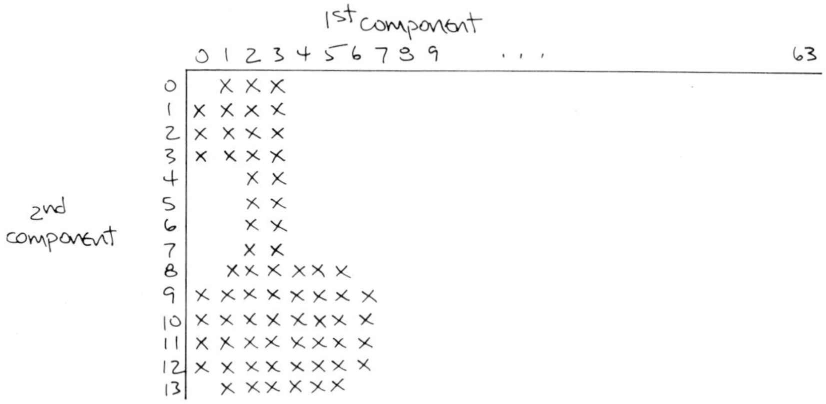

```
                     1st component
              0 1 2 3 4 5 6 7 8 9   . . .   63
             ------------------------------------
           0 |  X X X
           1 |X X X X
           2 |X X X X
           3 |X X X X
           4 |    X X
2nd        5 |    X X
component  6 |    X X
           7 |    X X
           8 |  X X X X X X
           9 |X X X X X X X X
          10 |X X X X X X X X
          11 |X X X X X X X X
          12 |X X X X X X X X
          13 |  X X X X X X
```

(0,1) to (0,3)
(1,0) to (1,3)
(2,0) to (2,7)
(3,0) to (3,7)
(1,8) to (6,8)
(0,9) to (7,9)
(0,10) to (7,10)
(0,11) to (7,11)
(0,12) to (7,12)
(1,13) to (6,13)

A further compression of this encoding scheme would be to combine the two numbers of each end point into a single number without loss of information. Since the second number will be at most 2 digits, the end point (7,10) could be expressed as the single number 710 with the understanding that the rightmost two digits of such a number represent the vertical grid position or second component. The horizontal grid position or first component is the part of the number left when the rightmost two digits are removed. With such a compression scheme, the expanded digit 1 could be encoded as the series of numbers:

1,3,100,103,200,207,300,307,108,608,9,709,
10,710,11,711,12,712,113,613

Notice that each pair of numbers are the end points of a line to be drawn. Also notice that the first two numbers (1 and 3) would be more recognizable as 001 and 003, but the leading zeros are redundant when we normally write numbers and were left off with no loss of information.

Problem 5.4

Draw an expanded digit 1 on the video screen using the straight line coding method.

Solution

```
10 'filename:"s5p4"
20 ' purpose: draw expanded digit 1, coded as straight lines
30 '  author: jdr 8/80
40 '
50 CLS
60 INPUT "input position of picture on screen";XINC,YINC
70 INPUT "input characters to be used in drawing";CHAR$
80 CHAR$=LEFT$(CHAR$,10)
90 GOSUB 1000 'draw the picture
100 IF INKEY$="" THEN 100
110 STOP
```

```
1000 'subroutine to draw picture on screen
1010 CLS
1020 READ N 'number of straight lines to draw in picture
1030 FOR L=1 TO N
1040    READ E,C,D
1050    X1=INT(C/100) : Y1=C-100*X1
1060    X2=INT(D/100) : Y2=D-100*X2
1080 X1=X1+XINC : Y1=Y1+YINC 'relocate coordinates
1090 X2=X2+XINC : Y2=Y2+YINC
1100 IF X1>63 OR X2>63 OR Y1>15 OR Y2>15
       THEN PRINT "picture will not fit, cannot continue" :
            RETURN
1110 IF X1=X2 THEN 1270
1120 IF Y1=Y2 THEN 1310
1130 M=(Y2-Y1)/(X2-X1) 'calculate slope of line
1140 B=Y1-M*X1 'calculate y-intercept
1150 IF M>0
       THEN IF M<=1 THEN 1220 ELSE 1170
       ELSE IF M>=-1 THEN 1220 ELSE 1160
1160 T=Y1 : Y1=Y2 : Y2=T 'slope between -1 and -infinity
1170 FOR J=Y1 TO Y2 'slope between 1 and infinity
1180    I=INT((J-B)/M+0.5)
1190    PRINT@64*J+I,MID$(CHAR$,E+1,1);
1200 NEXT J
1210 GOTO 1340
1220 FOR I=X1 TO X2 'slope between -1 and 1
1230    J=INT(M*I+B+0.5)
1240    PRINT@64*J+I,MID$(CHAR$,E+1,1);
1250 NEXT I
1260 GOTO 1340
1270 FOR J=Y1 TO Y2 'no slope, vertical line
1280    PRINT@64*J+X1,MID$(CHAR$,E+1,1);
1290 NEXT J
1300 GOTO 1340
1310 FOR I=X1 TO X2 'zero slope, horizontal line
1320    PRINT@64*Y1+I,MID$(CHAR$,E+1,1);
1330 NEXT I
1340 NEXT L
1350 RETURN
2000 DATA 10,0,1,3,0,100,103,0,200,207,0,300,307,0,108,608
2010 DATA 0,9,709,0,10,710,0,11,711,0,12,712,0,113,613
9999 END
```

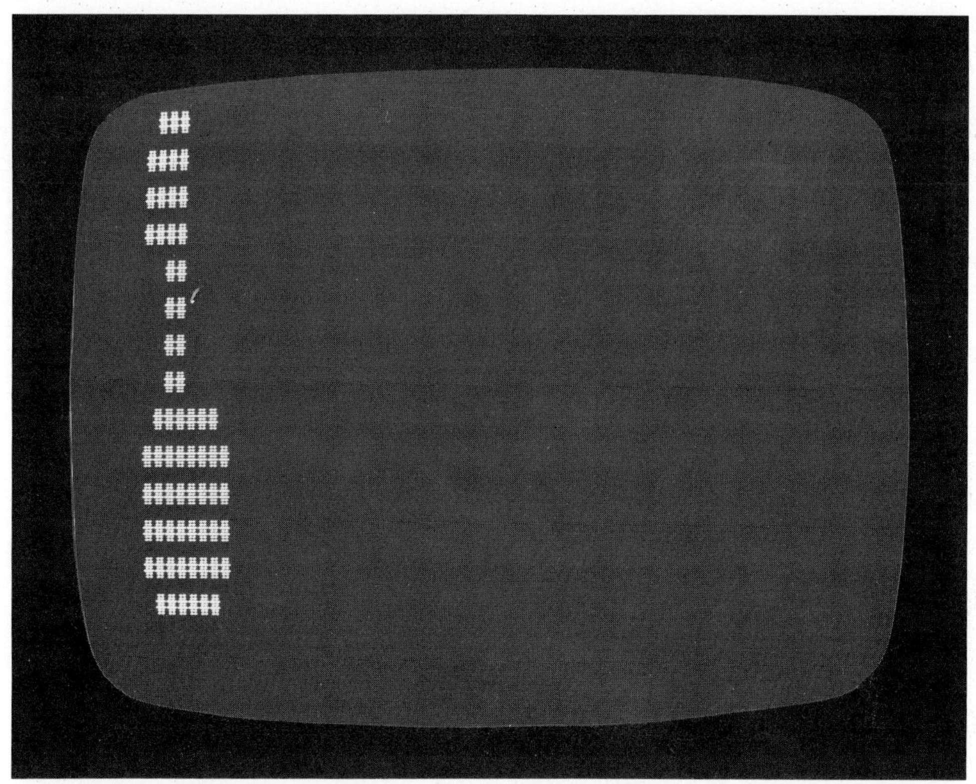

###
####
####
####
##
##
##
##
######
########
########
########
########
######

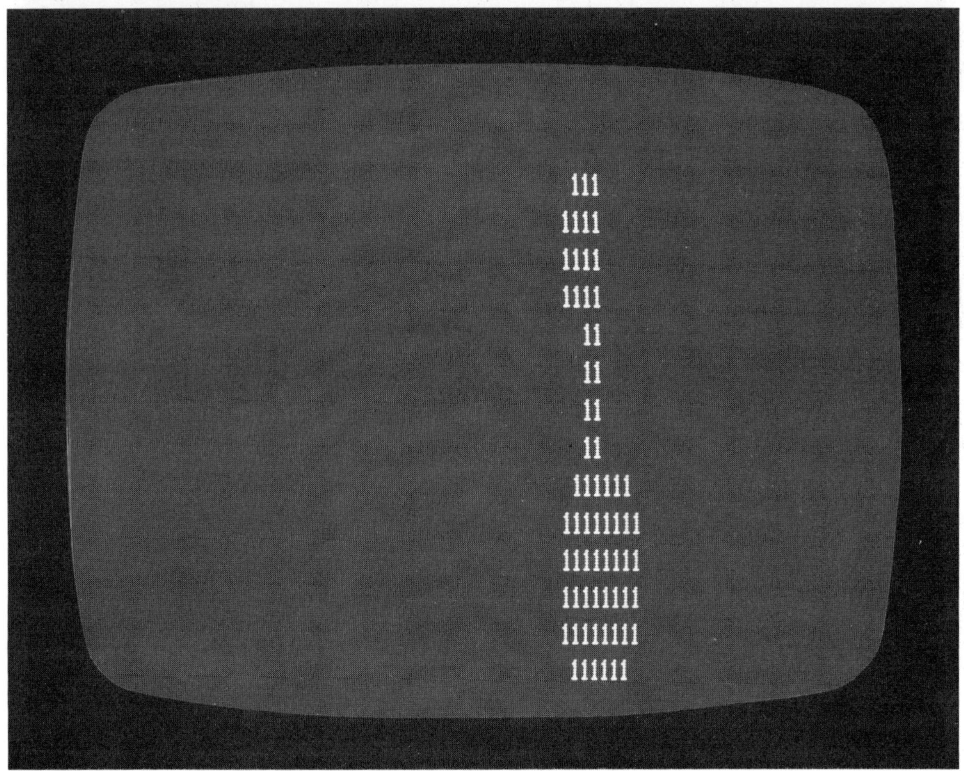

111
1111
1111
1111
11
11
11
11
111111
11111111
11111111
11111111
11111111
111111

Discussion

- The number zero has been inserted in front of each pair of numbers that represents the end points of a straight line. Its purpose is to specify which character is to be used when drawing the straight line. The effect here is minimal since the same character is used to draw the entire picture. But as will be shown in the next program, this number will not always be zero and will provide for flexibilty in the characters used to draw the picture.

- The picture can be placed anywhere on the screen because when the picture was coded we located it in the upper left-hand corner. The program reads in XINC and YINC values which are added to each point to relocate it on the screen.

- It is necessary that the two numbers representing the end points of a line are in numeric order; that is, the first is less than or equal to the second. For example, 3 then 307 is okay, but 307 then 3 is not acceptable. Of course, the program could be modified to place them in order.

Problem 5.5

Draw the logo for Bentley College with an optional user's initials to be embedded within it.

Solution

The previous program with changes only to the DATA statements, will be used to draw the logo.

```
10 'filename:"s5p5"
20 ' purpose: draw Bentley College logo with users initials
30 '   author: jdr 8/80
40 '
50 CLS
60 INPUT "input position of picture on screen";XINC,YINC
70 INPUT "input characters to be used in drawing";CHAR$
80 CHAR$=LEFT$(CHAR$,10)
90 GOSUB 1000 'draw the picture
100 IF INKEY$="" THEN 100
110 STOP
```

```
1000 'subroutine to draw picture on screen
1010 CLS
1020 READ N 'number of straight lines to draw in picture
1030 FOR L=1 TO N
1040    READ E,C,D
1050    X1=INT(C/100) : Y1=C-100*X1
1060    X2=INT(D/100) : Y2=D-100*X2
1080 X1=X1+XINC : Y1=Y1+YINC 'relocate coordinates
1090 X2=X2+XINC : Y2=Y2+YINC
1100 IF X1>63 OR X2>63 OR Y1>15 OR Y2>15
       THEN PRINT "picture will not fit, cannot continue" :
            RETURN
1110 IF X1=X2 THEN 1270
1120 IF Y1=Y2 THEN 1310
1130 M=(Y2-Y1)/(X2-X1) 'calculate slope of line
1140 B=Y1-M*X1 'calculate y-intercept
1150 IF M>0
       THEN IF M<=1 THEN 1220 ELSE 1170
       ELSE IF M>=-1 THEN 1220 ELSE 1160
1160 T=Y1 : Y1=Y2 : Y2=T 'slope between -1 and -infinity
1170 FOR J=Y1 TO Y2 'slope between 1 and infinity
1180    I=INT((J-B)/M+0.5)
1190    PRINT@64*J+I,MID$(CHAR$,E+1,1);
1200 NEXT J
1210 GOTO 1340
1220 FOR I=X1 TO X2 'slope between -1 and 1
1230    J=INT(M*I+B+0.5)
1240    PRINT@64*J+I,MID$(CHAR$,E+1,1);
1250 NEXT I
1260 GOTO 1340
1270 FOR J=Y1 TO Y2 'no slope, vertical line
1280    PRINT@64*J+X1,MID$(CHAR$,E+1,1);
1290 NEXT J
1300 GOTO 1340
1310 FOR I=X1 TO X2 'zero slope, horizontal line
1320    PRINT@64*Y1+I,MID$(CHAR$,E+1,1);
1330 NEXT I
1340 NEXT L
1350 RETURN
2000 DATA 31,0,0,4700,0,1,14,0,101,114,0,4601,4614,0,4701,4714
2010 DATA 0,15,4715,0,1005,1705,0,806,1906,0,607,612,0,707,712
2020 DATA 0,807,812,0,907,912,0,1807,1812,0,1907,1912
2030 DATA 0,2007,2012,0,2107,2112,0,613,2113,0,3002,3702
2040 DATA 0,2803,3903,0,2604,2612,0,2704,2712,0,2804,2812
2050 DATA 0,2904,2912,0,3804,3812,0,3904,3912,0,4004,4012
2060 DATA 0,4104,4112,0,2613,4113,1,302,302,2,402,402,3,502,502
9999 END
```

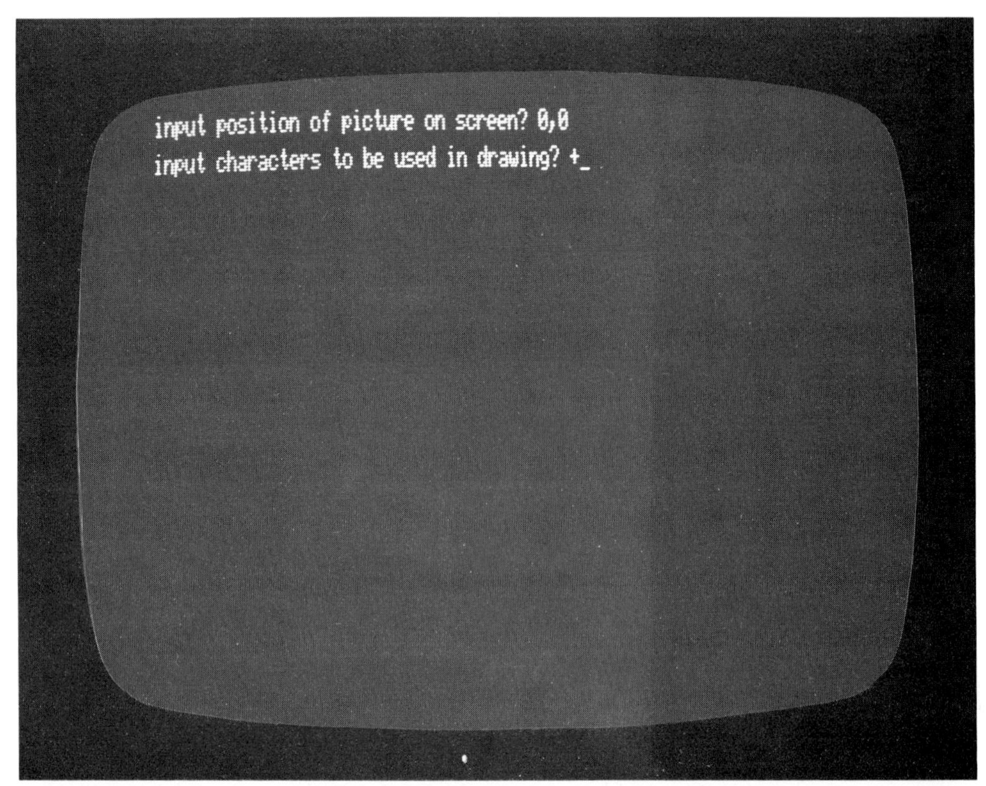
input position of picture on screen? 0,0
input characters to be used in drawing? +_

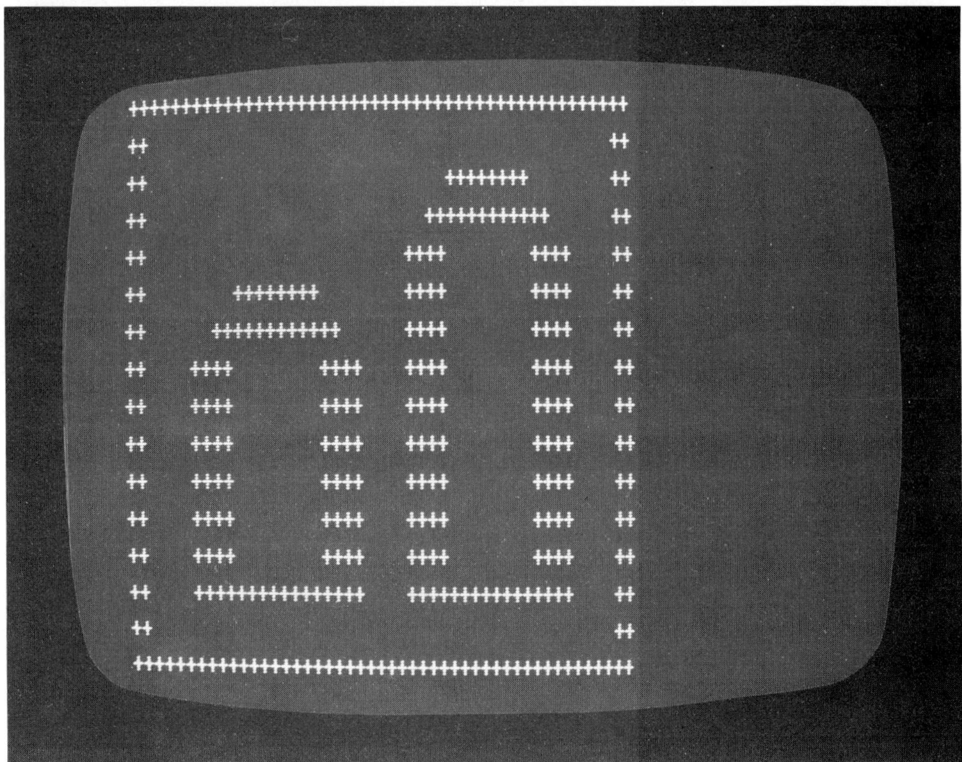

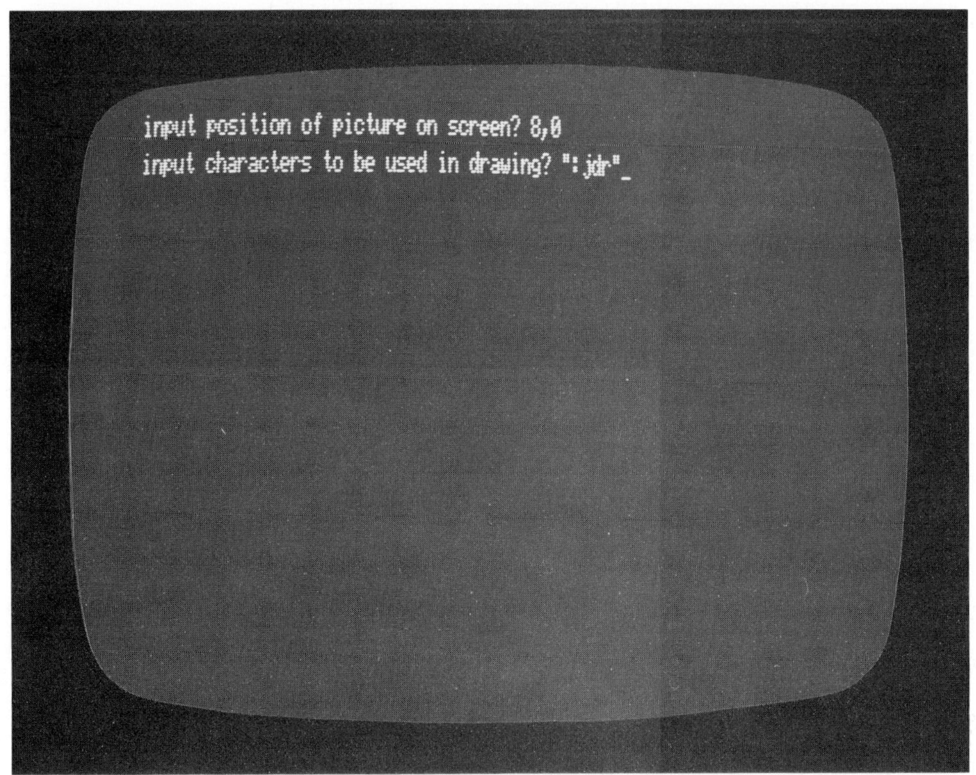
input position of picture on screen? 8,0
input characters to be used in drawing? ":jdr"_

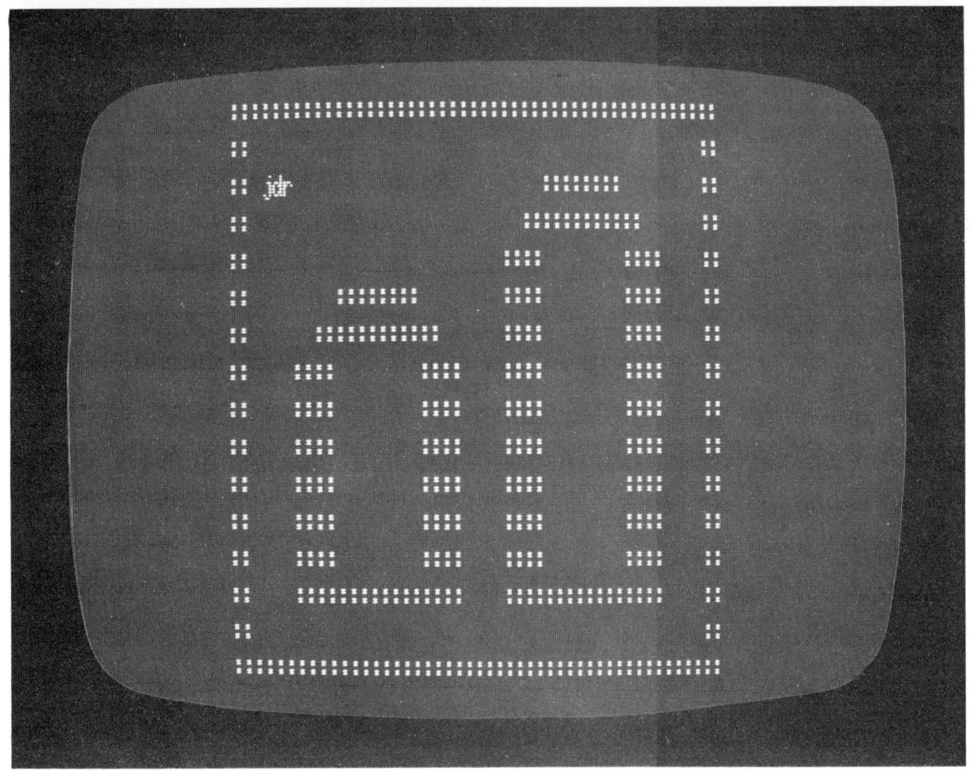
jdr

Discussion

- The digit zero isn't in front of each pair of end points. The last 3 pairs have the digits 1, 2, and 3 in front. This means that four characters will be used in drawing the picture. The same character will be used for drawing most of the picture, but the last three lines will be drawn using different characters.

- The last three pairs of end points are strange. Both end points of the line are the same. This means that the line is really just a point, which is a special case of the more general line. The line drawing portion of the subroutine will handle this properly.

- Notice that the input to this program is the character to be used to draw the Bentley College logo followed by the user's initials. If the users initials are missing, then the last three lines are plotted with blanks.

Suggestions

- Investigate the broad generality of this program by using it to draw a number of different pictures in various positions on the screen. The only changes to the program will be in the DATA statements.

Problem 5.6

Draw the Bentley College logo on the line printer.

Solution

```
10 'filename:"s5p6"
20 ' purpose: draw Bentley College logo on line printer
30 '   author: jdr 8/80
40 '
50 CLEAR 8000 : DIM P$(64) : CLS
51 FOR I=0 TO 63
53     P$(I)=STRING$(64,32)
55 NEXT I
60 INPUT "input position of picture on printer";XINC,YINC
70 INPUT "input characters to be used in drawing";CHAR$
80 CHAR$=LEFT$(CHAR$,10)
90 GOSUB 1000 'draw the picture
100 IF INKEY$="" THEN 100
110 STOP
```

```
1000 'subroutine to draw picture on screen
1010 CLS
1020 READ N 'number of straight lines to draw in picture
1030 FOR L=1 TO N
1040    READ E,C,D
1050    X1=INT(C/100) : Y1=C-100*X1
1060    X2=INT(D/100) : Y2=D-100*X2
1080 X1=X1+XINC : Y1=Y1+YINC 'relocate coordinates
1090 X2=X2+XINC : Y2=Y2+YINC
1100 IF X1>63 OR X2>63 OR Y1>63 OR Y2>63
       THEN PRINT "picture will not fit, cannot continue" :
            RETURN
1110 IF X1=X2 THEN 1270
1120 IF Y1=Y2 THEN 1310
1130 M=(Y2-Y1)/(X2-X1) 'calculate slope of line
1140 B=Y1-M*X1 'calculate y-intercept
1150 IF M>0
       THEN IF M<=1 THEN 1220 ELSE 1170
       ELSE IF M>=-1 THEN 1220 ELSE 1160
1160 T=Y1 : Y1=Y2 : Y2=T 'slope between -1 and -infinity
1170 FOR J=Y1 TO Y2 'slope between 1 and infinity
1180    I=INT((J-B)/M+0.5)
1190    MID$(P$(J),I+1,1)=MID$(CHAR$,E+1,1)
1200 NEXT J
1210 GOTO 1340
1220 FOR I=X1 TO X2 'slope between -1 and 1
1230    J=INT(M*I+B+0.5)
1240    MID$(P$(J),I+1,1)=MID$(CHAR$,E+1,1)
1250 NEXT I
1260 GOTO 1340
1270 FOR J=Y1 TO Y2 'no slope, vertical line
1280    MID$(P$(J),X1+1,1)=MID$(CHAR$,E+1,1)
1290 NEXT J
1300 GOTO 1340
1310 FOR I=X1 TO X2 'zero slope, horizontal line
1320    MID$(P$(Y1),I+1,1)=MID$(CHAR$,E+1,1)
1330 NEXT I
1340 NEXT L
1350 FOR J=0 TO 63
1360    LPRINT P$(J)
1370 NEXT J
1380 RETURN
2000 DATA 31,0,0,4700,0,1,14,0,101,114,0,4601,4614,0,4701,4714
2010 DATA 0,15,4715,0,1005,1705,0,806,1906,0,607,612,0,707,712
2020 DATA 0,807,812,0,907,912,0,1807,1812,0,1907,1912
2030 DATA 0,2007,2012,0,2107,2112,0,613,2113,0,3002,3702
2040 DATA 0,2803,3903,0,2604,2612,0,2704,2712,0,2804,2812
2050 DATA 0,2904,2912,0,3804,3812,0,3904,3912,0,4004,4012
2060 DATA 0,4104,4112,0,2613,4113,1,302,302,2,402,402,3,502,502
9999 END
```

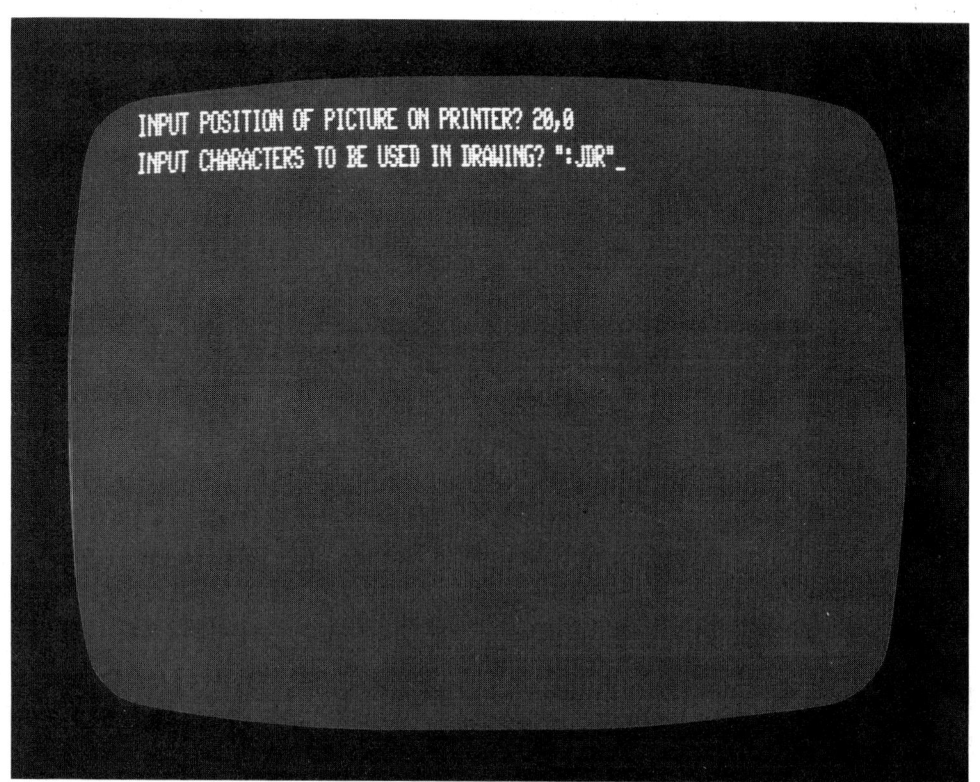

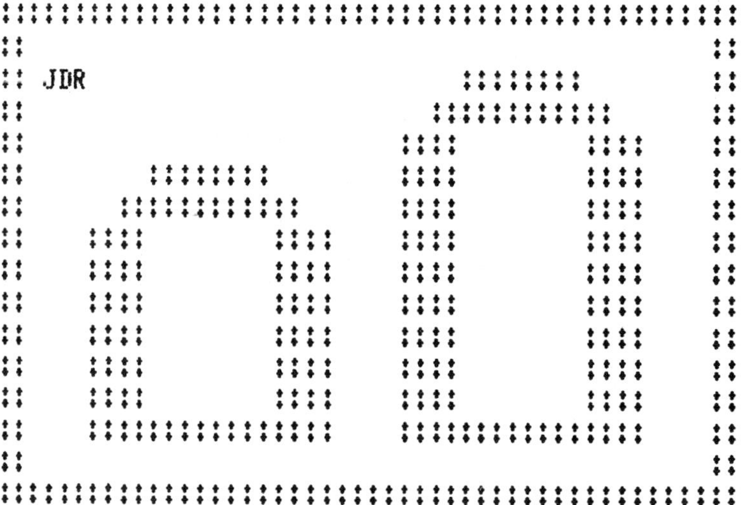

Discussion

- Notice that this is program G5P5 with a few minor changes. The PRINT@s were changed to LET statements using the MID$ function on the *left* of the equal sign. A simple routine to PRINT the strings at the subroutine's end furnishes the output to the printer.

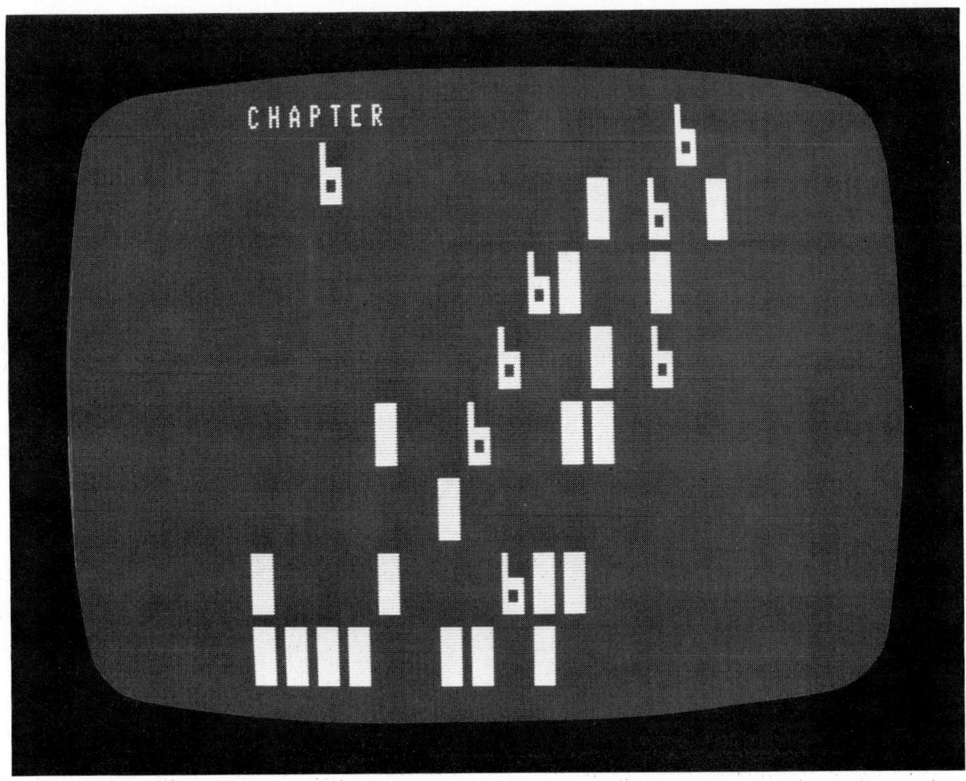

Character Graphics

Character Graphics techniques rely on the use of a few advanced BASIC commands and the graphic character set. This chapter will explore the full range of instructions in the TRS-80's Level II BASIC that is needed for this type of graphics.

PRINT@

The TRS-80 video screen is 64 columns wide and 16 rows deep. All of the 1024 positions are addressable. The positions in the screen's top row are numbered 0 to 63, the second row 64 to 127, the third row 128 to 191, and so on until the last row, which has addresses 960 to 1023.

The PRINT@ statement positions the cursor at the screen location (0 to 1023) defined by the value of the expression immediately following the PRINT@ instruction. When keying the PRINT@ command, be careful to *not* depress the shift key. The shift-@ symbol looks like a @ with no shift, but when the program is run a syntax error will result.

```
    Instruction                     Output
    -----------                     ------

10 PRINT @ 0,"X"                X at the top left of the screen
20 PRINT @ 95,"ZOT"             ZOT centered on the second line
30 PRINT @ 510,"ZOTZOT"         ZOTZOT centered on the screen
40 PRINT @ 1023,"Z";            Z at the bottom right of the screen
```

If the PRINT@ instruction ends with no punctuation, the cursor returns to the beginning of the next line, and this may produce undesirable results. If the address is between 960 and 1023, the string prints on the last line of the screen, then the screen scrolls one line. The effect of a PRINT@960 becomes the same as a PRINT@896, which is not what was intended.

If the PRINT@ instruction ends with a semicolon (;), the result is predictable. We recommend that you always end all PRINT@ instructions with a semicolon.

Problem 6.1 List a table in a variety of ways using the PRINT@ statement.

Solution

```
10 'filename:"s6p1"
20 ' purpose: output table in sundry ways using TAB function
30 '   author: jdr 8/80
40 '
50 DIM P$(15)
60 FOR I=1 TO 15
70     READ P$(I)
80 NEXT I
90 CLS : RANDOM
100 FOR I=1 TO 15
110     PRINT@64*(I-1)+25,P$(I)
120 NEXT I : GOSUB 1000 'pause and clear screen
140 FOR I=1 TO 15
150     PRINT@64*(I-1)+I,P$(I)
160 NEXT I : GOSUB 1000 'pause & clear
180 FOR I=1 TO 15
190     PRINT@64*(I-1)+2*I,P$(I)
200 NEXT I : GOSUB 1000 'pause & clear
220 FOR I=1 TO 15
230     PRINT@64*(I-1)+3*ABS(8-I),P$(I)
240 NEXT I : GOSUB 1000 'pause & clear
260 FOR I=1 TO 15
270     PRINT@64*(I-1)+RND(40),P$(I)
280 NEXT I : GOSUB 1000 'pause & clear
300 FOR I=1 TO 15
310     PRINT@64*(I-1)+40-LEN(P$(I)),P$(I)
320 NEXT I : GOSUB 1000 'pause & clear
340 STOP
350 DATA "puffer","pompano","pickeral","pollock","piranha"
360 DATA "pinfish","platy","porcupine fish","pirarucu","porgy"
370 DATA "pilchard","plaice","perch","plectognath","panchax"
1000 'pause and clear screen subroutine
1010 FOR J=1 TO 200 : NEXT J : CLS : RETURN
9999 END
```

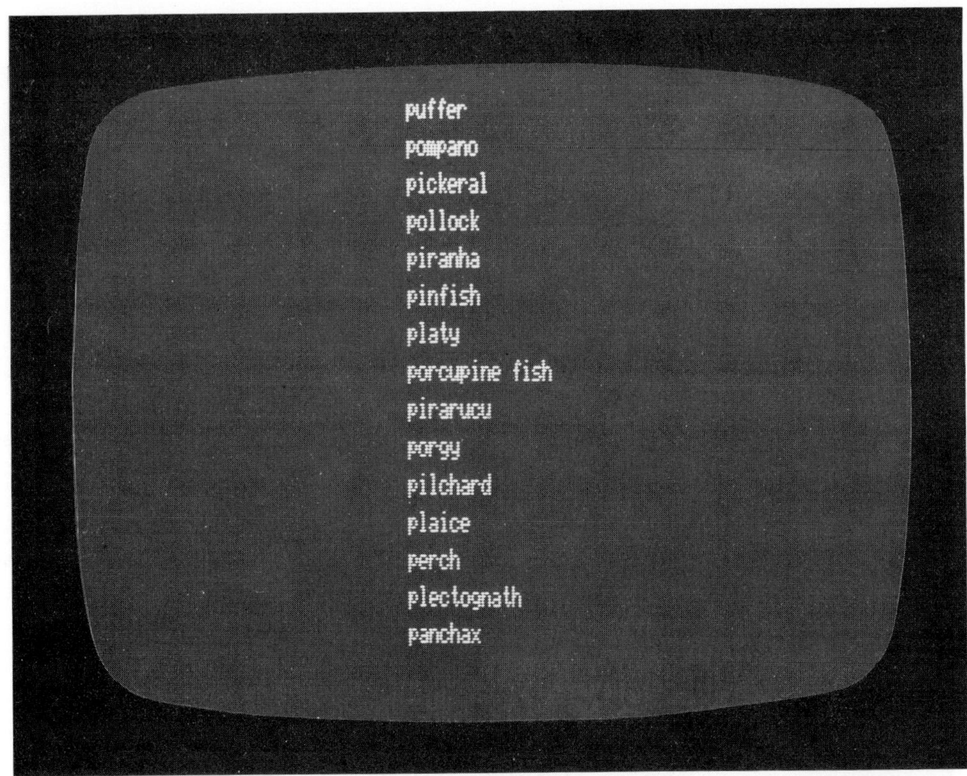
puffer
pompano
pickeral
pollock
piranha
pinfish
platy
porcupine fish
pirarucu
porgy
pilchard
plaice
perch
plectognath
panchax

puffer
pompano
pickeral
pollock
piranha
pinfish
platy
porcupine fish
pirarucu
porgy
pilchard
plaice
perch
plectognath
panchax

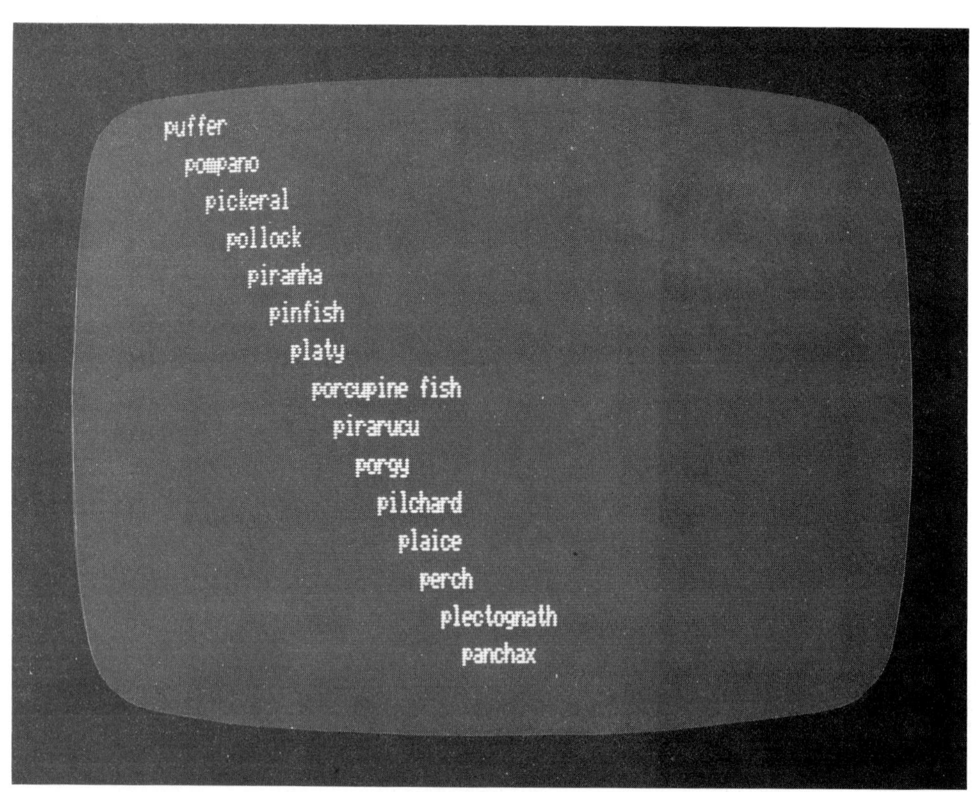
puffer
pompano
pickeral
pollock
piranha
pinfish
platy
porcupine fish
pirarucu
porgy
pilchard
plaice
perch
plectognath
panchax

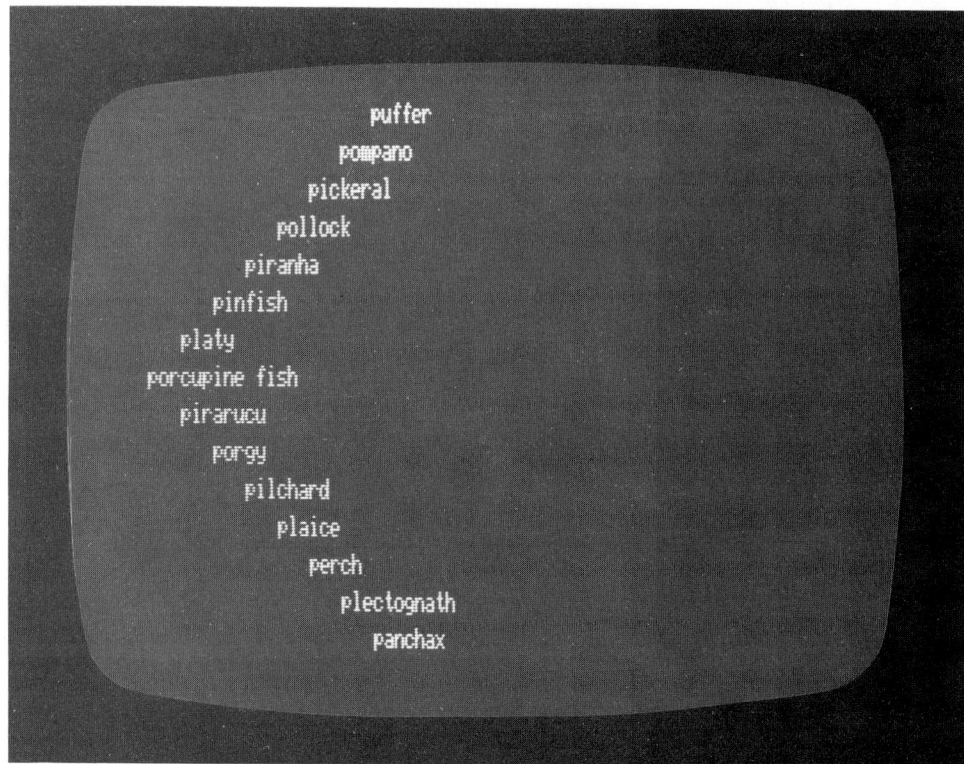
puffer
pompano
pickeral
pollock
piranha
pinfish
platy
porcupine fish
pirarucu
porgy
pilchard
plaice
perch
plectognath
panchax

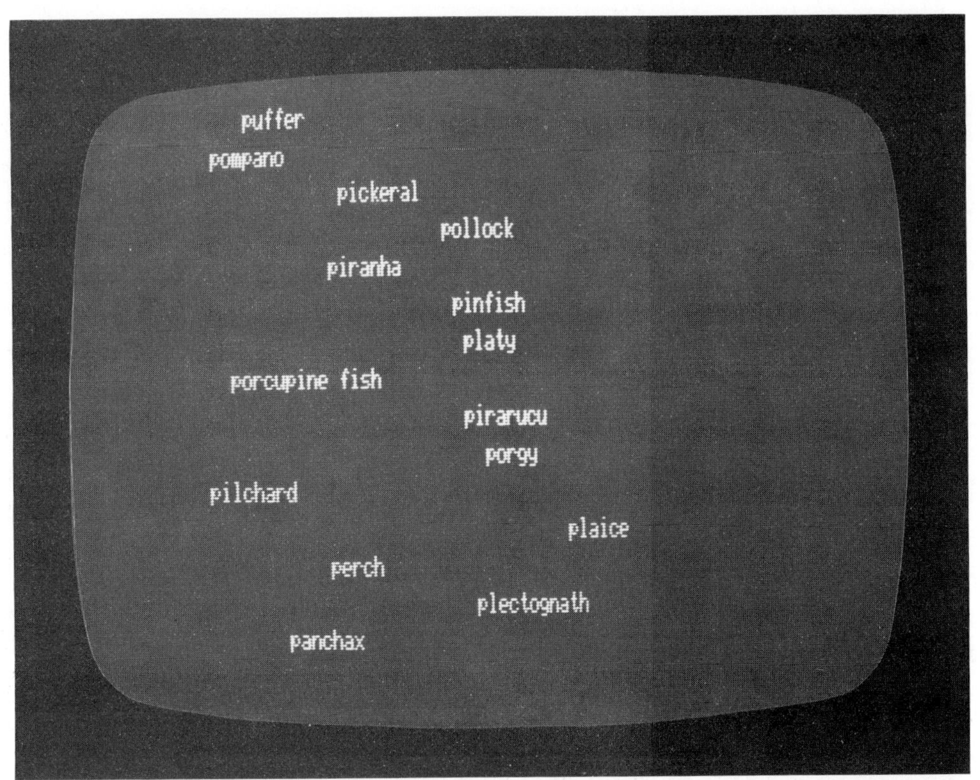
puffer
pompano
pickeral
pollock
piranha
pinfish
platy
porcupine fish
pirarucu
porgy
pilchard
plaice
perch
plectognath
panchax

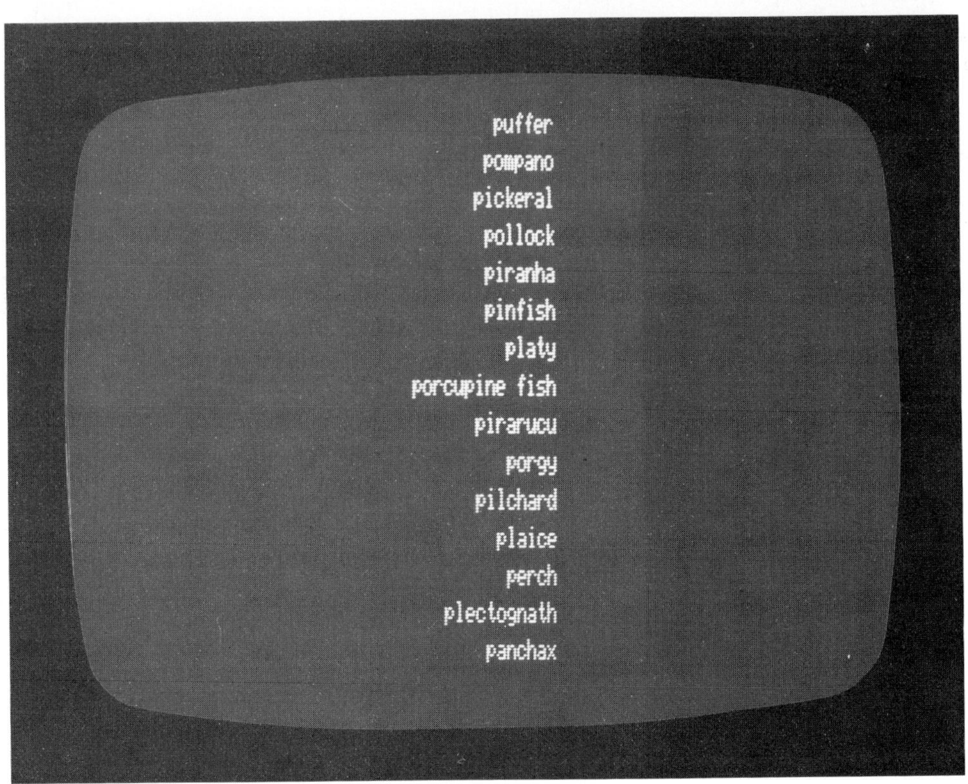
puffer
pompano
pickeral
pollock
piranha
pinfish
platy
porcupine fish
pirarucu
porgy
pilchard
plaice
perch
plectognath
panchax

STRING$

A Level II BASIC function which is useful in graphing is the STRING$ function. This function has two arguments: The first is the number of characters desired, up to 255, and the second is the character itself.

Instruction	Output
10 PRINT STRING$(10,"*")	**********
20 PRINT STRING$(5,CHR$(65))	AAAAA
30 PRINT STRING$(8,CHR$(13))	Cursor moves down 8 lines, positions itself at left of line. CHR$(13) is a carriage/cursor return which is the character produced by the ENTER Key (/EN/).
40 PRINT @960, STRING$(64,"Z");	ZZZ...ZZZ (64 of them) on the bottom of the screen
50 A=128: B$="9": PRINT STRING$(A,B$)	Two rows of 9s

Note: Since the computer builds the string in its memory first, before displaying it, your program may require additional string space to be reserved for it. Use the CLEAR instruction to allow for more string space.

The Character Set

A look at Appendix A reveals that the TRS-80 has a total of 256 possible characters, and the effect of each can be displayed by using the instruction PRINT CHR$(N) where N is a number from 0 to 255. A few of these values of the TRS-80's character code have no effect on the TRS-80, but most do, and they are certainly more numerous than would be necessary for just the alphabet, digits, and special characters that BASIC needs. The table below is a summary of the expanded table in Appendix A.

Code	Function
0-7	None
8-31	Carriage/Cursor Control
32-47	Special Characters
48-57	Digits
58-64	Special Characters
65-90	Alphabet (Upper Case)
91-95	Up, down, left, right arrows
96	Lower Case @
97-122	Alphabet (Lower Case)
123-127	Lower Case of Codes 91-95
128-191	Graphics Characters
192-255	Tabs for 0 to 63 Spaces

Tabulation Codes

The last two groups of codes represent half the possible printable characters, and they deserve special mention. The last 64 codes allow tabbing without the TAB function.

Instruction	Output
10 PRINT CHR$(202);"*"	* in the 10th position
20 A$=CHR$(192+I): PRINT A$;"*"	* in the Ith position

Graphics Codes

The codes from 128 to 191 are graphic characters that are made up of six small rectangles, or *pixels*, arranged in three rows and two columns for each character. Each character entirely fills one of the 1024 print positions on the screen. Each pixel is either on (bright) or off (blank), depending on the code. For example, the graphic character 134 looks like this:

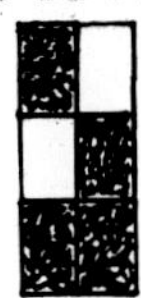

where ▮ is off, and

and ▯ is on.

The result of PRINT CHR$(134) would be the printing of the graphics character shown above.

Graphic to Binary Conversion

Each character code can be thought of as a visual representation of a six-bit binary number from 000000 to 111111, corresponding to all 64 possible combinations of bits. The character's code value can be computed by translating each off pixel to a 0 and each on pixel to a 1. Then the positions of the 1s can be masked into the six-bit binary number. The value of that number plus 128 is equal to the code value.

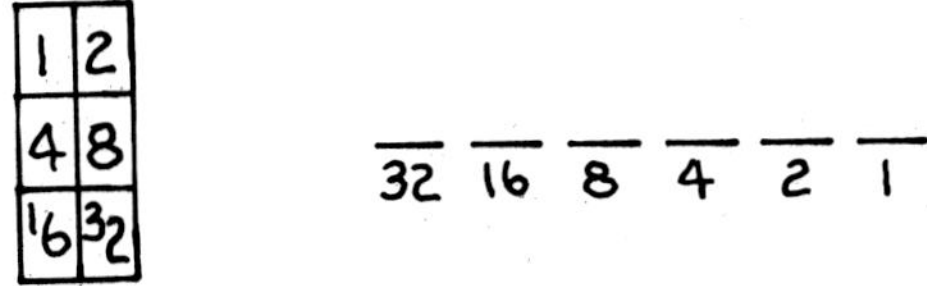

Thus the graphics character whose code is 134 is

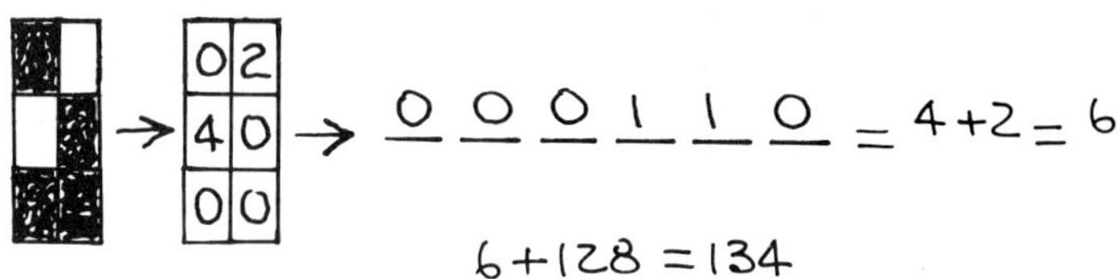

and so the statement PRINT CHR$(134) produces that graphic symbol. The graphic character whose code is 191 is the one in which all pixels are on, resulting in a large rectangle of light.

Problem 6.2

Display the graphics characters on the video screen.

Solution

```
10 'filename:"s6p2"
20 '  purpose: display graphics characters
30 '   author: jdr 7/80
40 '
50 CLEAR 1000
60 CLS
70 DIM A$(64)
80 FOR I=128 TO 191
90    IF I=INT(I/8)*8 THEN PRINT
100   PRINT RIGHT$(STR$(I),3);" ";CHR$(I);"   ";
110 NEXT I
120 IF INKEY$="" THEN 120
130 END
```

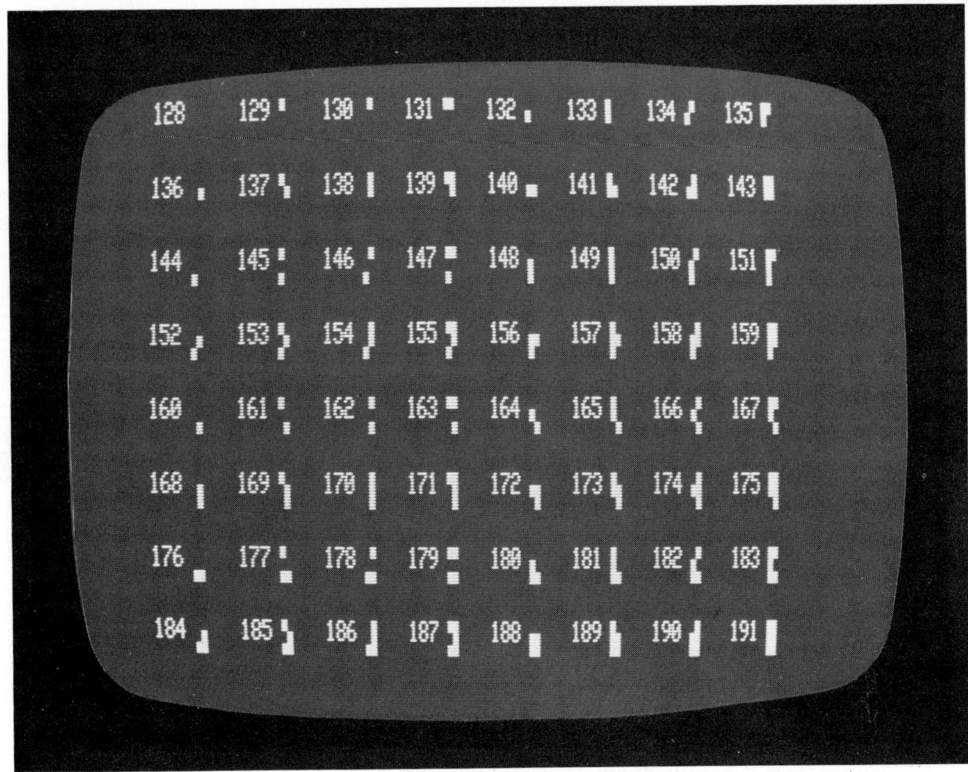

Suggestions

- Investigate the character obtained from CHR$(23). Printing it causes the TRS-80 video screen to go to double-wide character format. Printing CHR$(28) causes return to the normal mode for screen output.
- Modify the program to output the graphic characters in double-wide format.

Problem 6.3

Create a dynamic visual display using the TRS-80 graphics characters.

Solution

```
10 'filename:"s6p3"
20 '  purpose: random pattern of characters
30 '           Battlechar Galactica!
40 '   author: jdr 5/79
50 '
60 CLS
70 FOR I=1 TO 1024
80     PRINT@RND(1024)-1,CHR$(RND(64)+127);
90 NEXT I
100 END
```

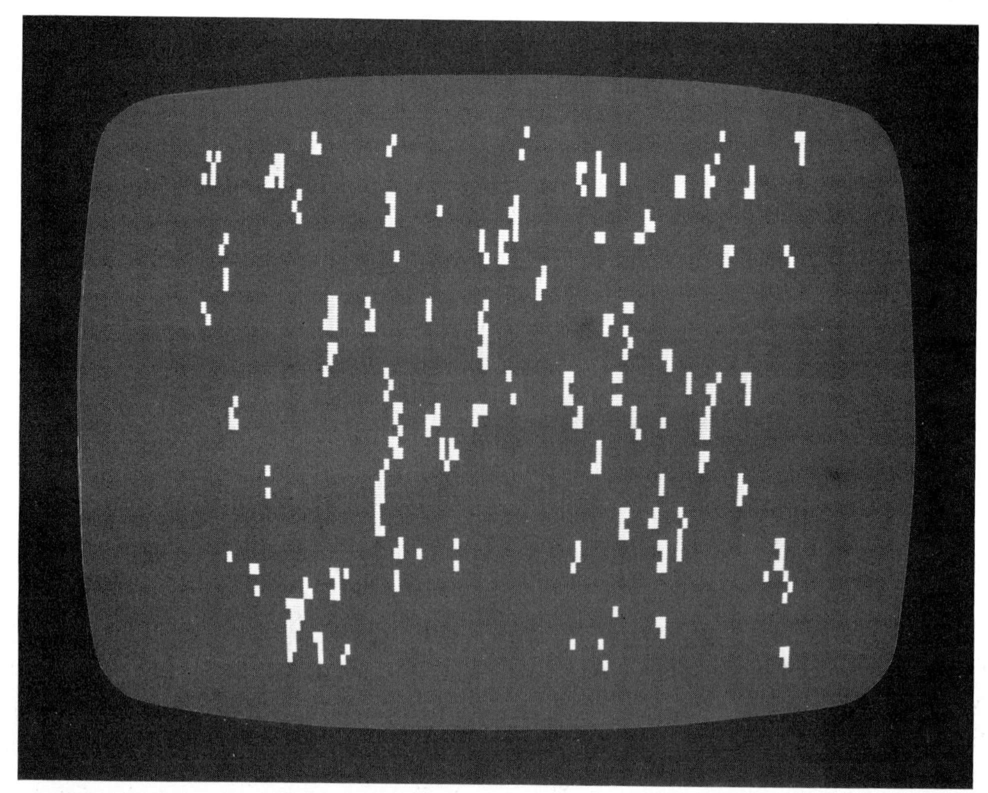

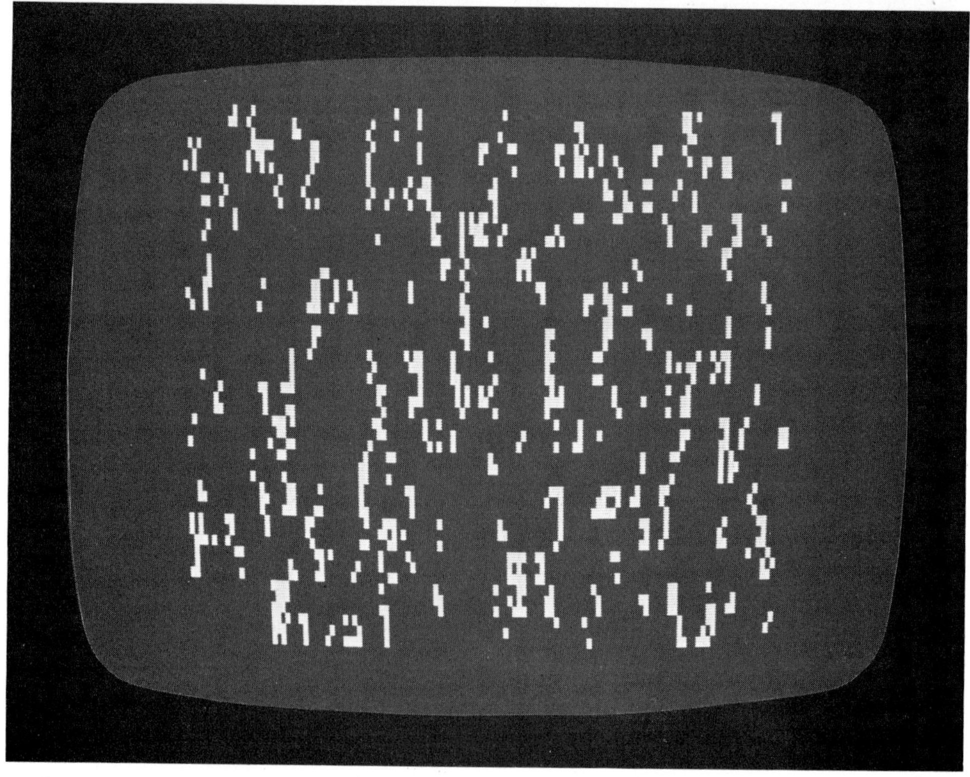

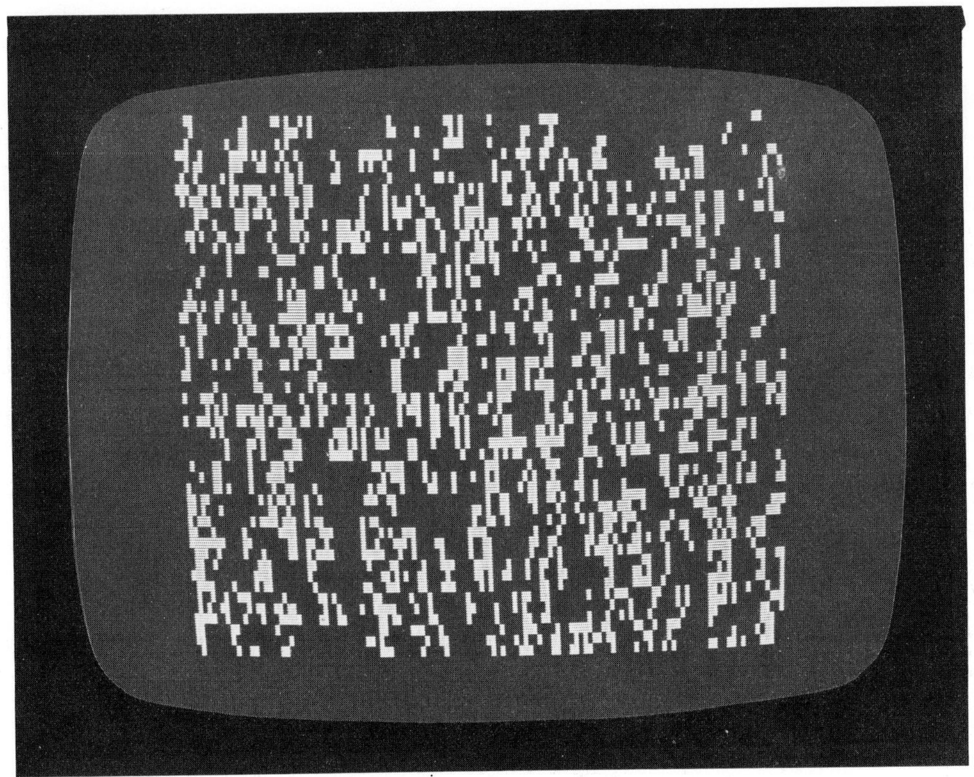

Discussion

- A very simple program can create an attractive visual display.

Suggestions

- Modify the program so that the display uses double-wide graphics characters.
- Modify the program so that it outputs all TRS-80 characters in the display.

Problem 6.4

Write a program that will put a box around a message near the center of the screen.

Solution

```
10 'filename:"s6p4"
20 ' purpose: place a message in a box
30 '  author: jdr 8/80
40 '
50 CLS : CLEAR 300
60 PRINT "input message with less than 60 characters"
70 PRINT@67,"";
80 INPUT T$
85 T$=" "+T$+" "
90 CLS
100 L=INT(64-LEN(T$))/2-1
110 M=448
120 PRINT@M-65+L,STRING$(LEN(T$)+2,CHR$(131));
130 PRINT@M+63+L,STRING$(LEN(T$)+2,CHR$(176));
140 FOR I=1 TO 3
150   K=M+L+64*(I-2)-1
160   PRINT@K,CHR$(170); : PRINT@K+LEN(T$)+1,CHR$(149);
170 NEXT I
180 PRINT@M+L,T$;
190 IF INKEY$="" THEN 190 ELSE 50
200 END
```

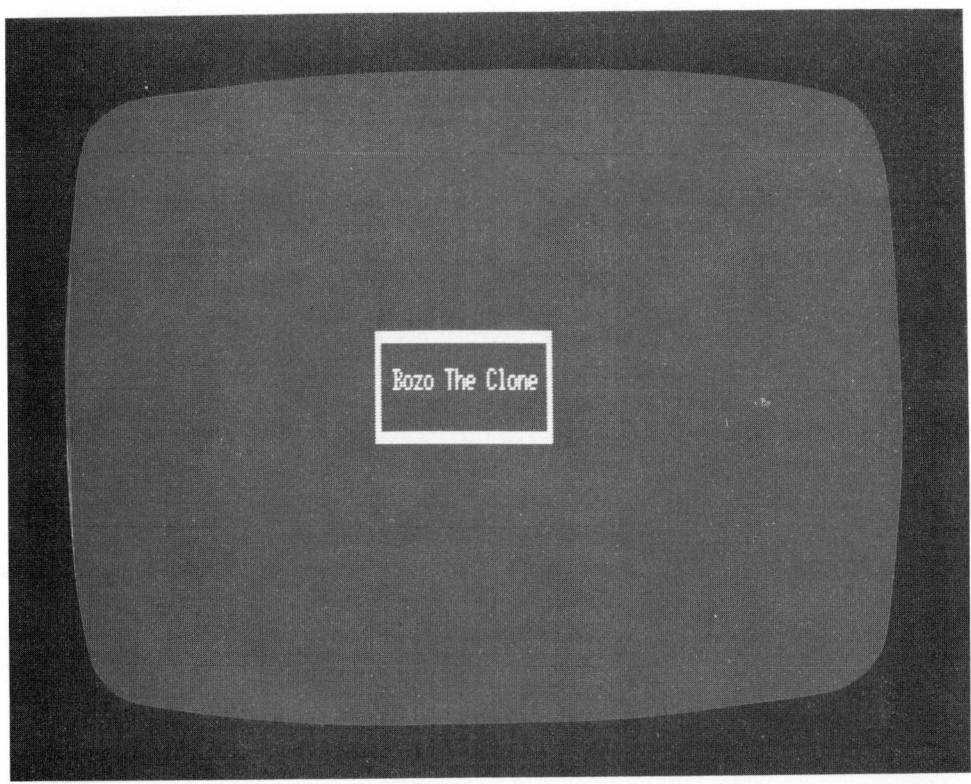
Bozo The Clone

Please do not spit on the COMPUTER !

Discussion

- The variable L points to the position of the screen where the message will be printed.

- Look at the output from program G6P2 to see the characters corresponding to CHR$(131), CHR$(176), CHR$(170), and CHR$(149). They are used here as the top horizontal bar, bottom horizontal bar, left vertical bar, and right vertical bar respectively.

- Notice how the values of the variables M and L are used to position the box and message.

Suggestions

- Write the boxing portion of the program as a subroutine that can be called to box and center a message.

- Generalize the program so that the user can specify the position of the boxed message.

Problem 6.5

Write a program that will display a message as a moving banner similar to the flashing light messages appearing at night on the side of a blimp.

Solution

```
10 'filename:"s6p5"
20 ' purpose: moving banner of characters
30 ' author : jdr 8/80
40 '
45 CLS : CLEAR 1000 : DEFINT A-Z
46 INPUT"input message to be displayed";B$ : Z=25 'speed factor
47 C$="" : FOR I=1 TO 15 : C$=C$+CHR$(128+RND(63))+" " : NEXT I
48 D$=" " : FOR I=1 TO 15 : D$=" "+CHR$(128+RND(63))+D$ : NEXT I
50 CLS
60 B$=STRING$(19,32)+C$+" "+B$+" "+D$+STRING$(19,32)
65 PRINT@528,CHR$(149); : PRINT@549,CHR$(170);
70 I=1 : FOR J=1 TO 1000 : PRINT@529,MID$(B$,I,20);
75 I=I+1 : IF I>LEN(B$)-20 THEN I=1
76 FOR K=1 TO Z : NEXT K : NEXT J
100 END
```

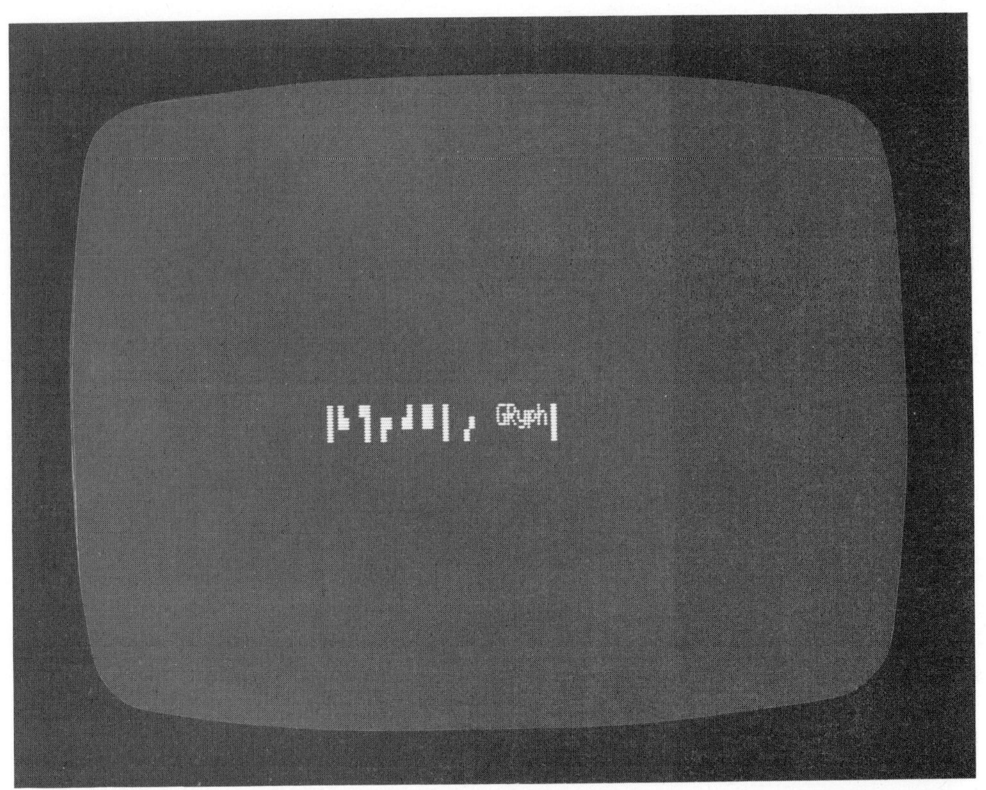
GRyph

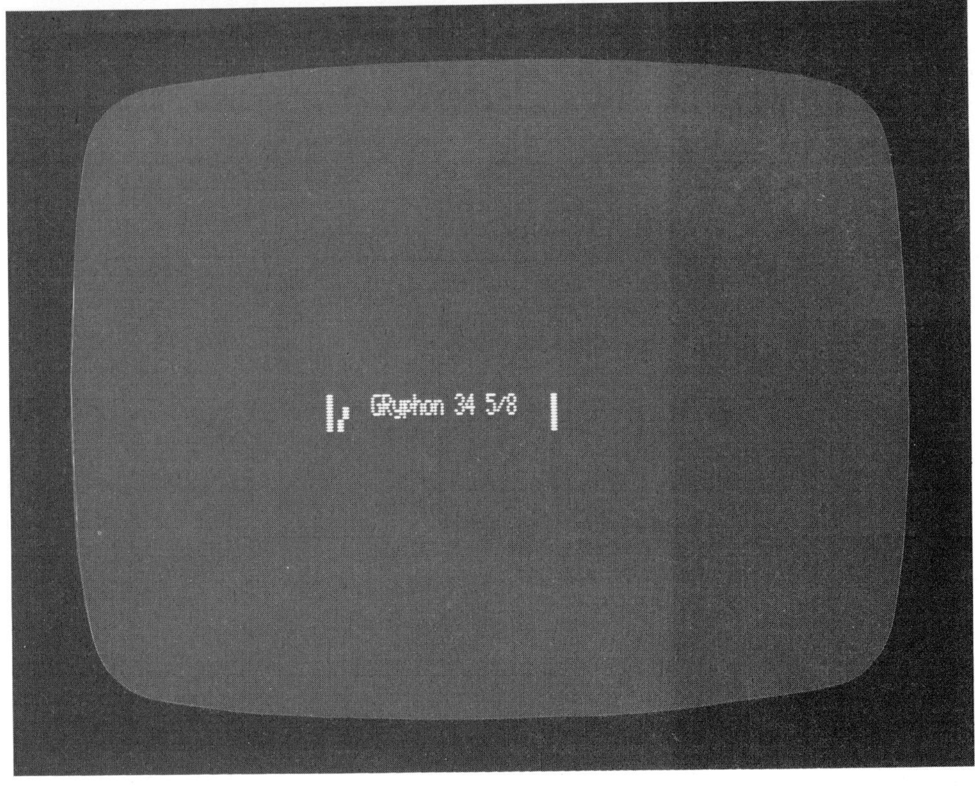
GRyphon 34 5/8

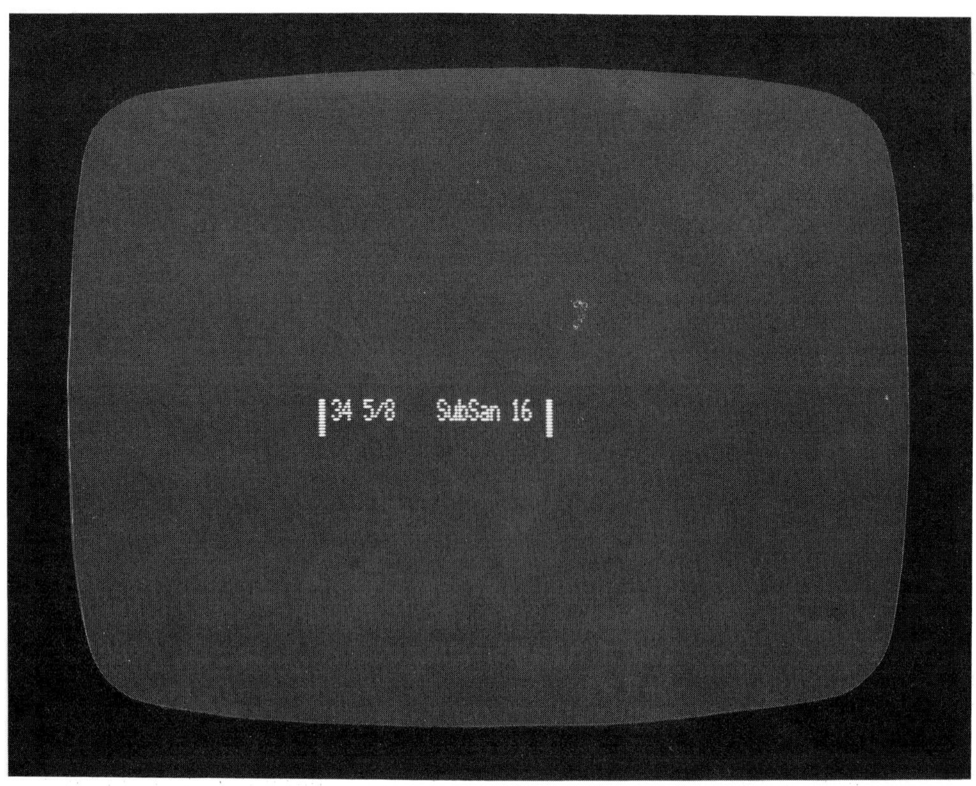

Discussion

- 15 randomly selected graphics characters are affixed to the beginning and the end of the message to be displayed.
- 19 blanks are affixed to the beginning and end of the string to be displayed.
- A 20 character wide window is provided for the message to move through and be displayed.
- The motion is obtained by using the MID$ function to select the 20 characters to be printed by the PRINT@ statement.
- A delay loop is needed to slow the TRS-80 down so that the message can be read.

Suggestions

- Convert the program to a subroutine that can be called to create a moving banner out of a message.
- Modify the program so that the width of the banner is specified by the user of the program.
- Modify the program so that the position of the banner can be specified by the user of the program.
- Convert the program to produce a double-wide banner.

Problem 6.6 Produce a screen full of oversize random digits.

Solution

```
10 'filename:"s6p6"
20 ' purpose: produce screen full of large digits
30 '  author: jdr 6/79
40 '
50 CLS
60 CLEAR 100
70 RANDOM
80 DIM D$(10)
90 E$=CHR$(26)+CHR$(8)+CHR$(8) 'linefeed-backspace-backspace
100 FOR I=1 TO 10
110     A$=""
120     FOR J=1 TO 4
130         READ X
140         A$=A$+CHR$(X)
150         IF J=2 THEN A$=A$+E$
160     NEXT J
170     D$(I)=A$
180 NEXT I
190 DATA 151,171,141,142,175,128,143,143
200 DATA 179,187,141,140,179,181,140,143
210 DATA 149,176,131,143,183,179,140,143
220 DATA 181,176,141,142,131,155,138,128
230 DATA 183,187,141,142,183,187,128,143
240 FOR K=0 TO 60 STEP 3
250     FOR L=K TO 896+K STEP 128
260         C=RND(10)
270         PRINT@L,D$(C);
280     NEXT L
290 NEXT K
300 IF INKEY$="" THEN 300
310 END
```

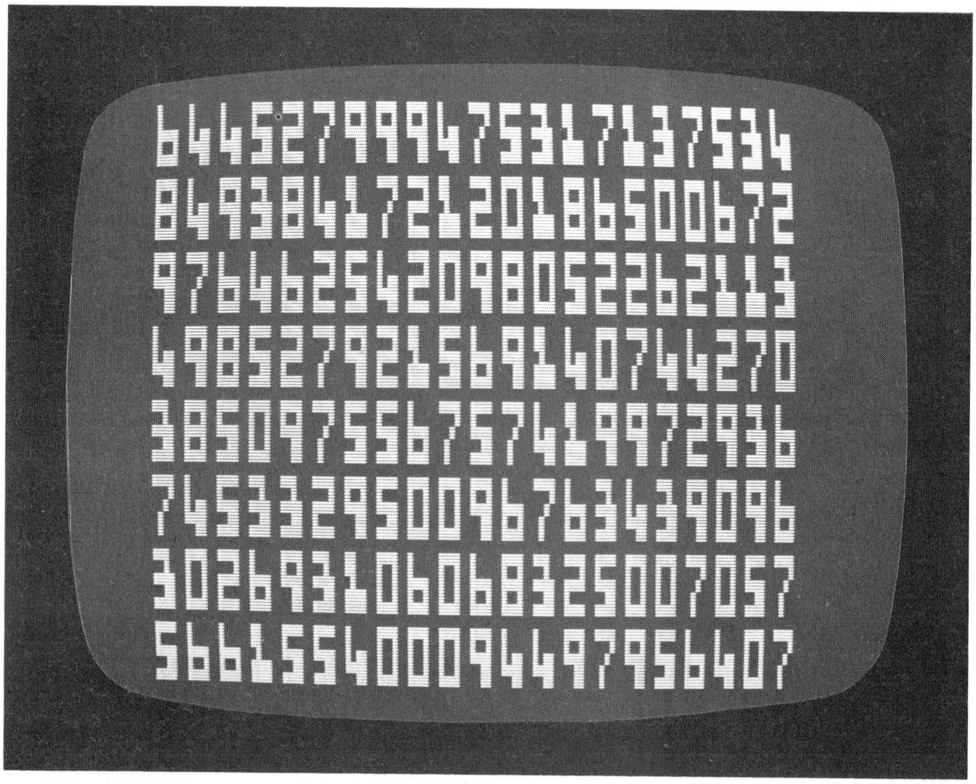

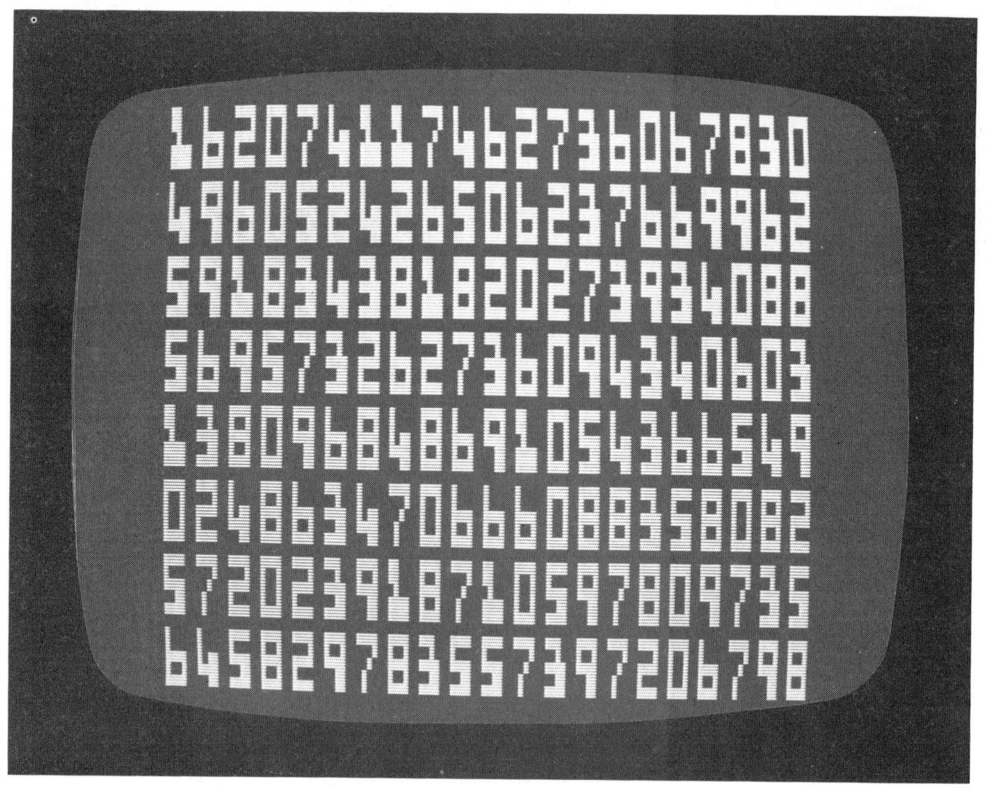

Discussion

- This program couples the table-driven technique with character graphics.

- Notice the speed with which each oversize digit appears on the screen. This is accomplished by concatenating a sequence of linefeed-backspace-backspace characters (CHR$(26)+CHR$(8)+CHR$(8)) in the middle of the four graphics characters that create each large digit.

- The enlarged digit is constructed from 4 graphics characters. For example, the first four numbers in the DATA statements are 151, 171, 141, and 142 are the numbers of the graphic characters used to construct the oversize digit zero. The first two, 151 and 171 are the top of the zero.

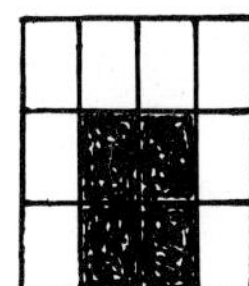

The linefeed+backspace+backspace allows the next two numbers, 141 and 142, to be the bottom of the zero.

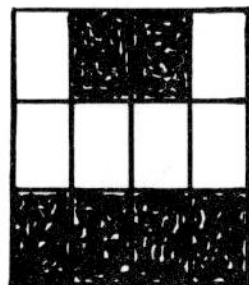

When put together by the program, D$(1) is defined by

D$(1)=CHR$(151)+CHR$(171)+CHR$(26)+CHR$(8)
+CHR$(8)+CHR$(141)+CHR$(142)

and becomes available for printing a large digit zero.

Suggestions

- Modify the DATA statements so that strange symbols instead of digits are displayed.

- Write a program that uses the ideas of the oversize digits to output the value of a numeric variable in oversize form at the center of the screen.

- Modify the program so that the oversize digits disappear one at a time from left to right, top to bottom.

Problem 6.7

Write a program that will display a large-digit digital clock showing hour and minutes in the lower left-hand corner of the screen.

Solution

```
10 'filename:"s6p7"
20 ' purpose: digital clock in lower left screen
30 '   author: jdr 8/80
40 '
50 CLS : CLEAR 300
80 DIM D$(10),T(5)
90 E$=CHR$(26)+CHR$(8)+CHR$(8)
100 FOR I=1 TO 10
110     A$=""
120     FOR J=1 TO 4
130         READ X
140         A$=A$+CHR$(X)
150         IF J=2 THEN A$=A$+E$
160     NEXT J
170     D$(I)=A$
180 NEXT I
190 DATA 151,171,141,142,175,128,143,143
200 DATA 179,187,141,140,179,181,140,143
210 DATA 149,176,131,143,183,179,140,143
220 DATA 181,176,141,142,131,155,138,128
230 DATA 183,187,141,142,183,187,128,143
240 'display time
250 X$=MID$(TIME$,10,5) : GOSUB 1000
260 'continuous check to see if time changes
270 Y$=X$ : X$=MID$(TIME$,10,5)
280 IF X$<>Y$
      THEN GOSUB 1000
      ELSE 270
290 GOTO 250
1000 'digital clock subroutine
1030 J=0
1040 FOR I=1 TO 5
1050     IF I=3 THEN 1080
1060     J=J+1
1070     T(J)=VAL(MID$(X$,I,1))+1
1080 NEXT I
1090 J=1 : K=0 : L=0
1100 FOR I=1 TO 5
1110     IF I=3
            THEN PRINT@902,CHR$(140); :
                 PRINT@966,CHR$(131); : L=L+2
            ELSE K=T(J) : PRINT@896+L,D$(K); :
                 J=J+1 : L=L+3
1120 NEXT I
1130 RETURN
9999 END
```

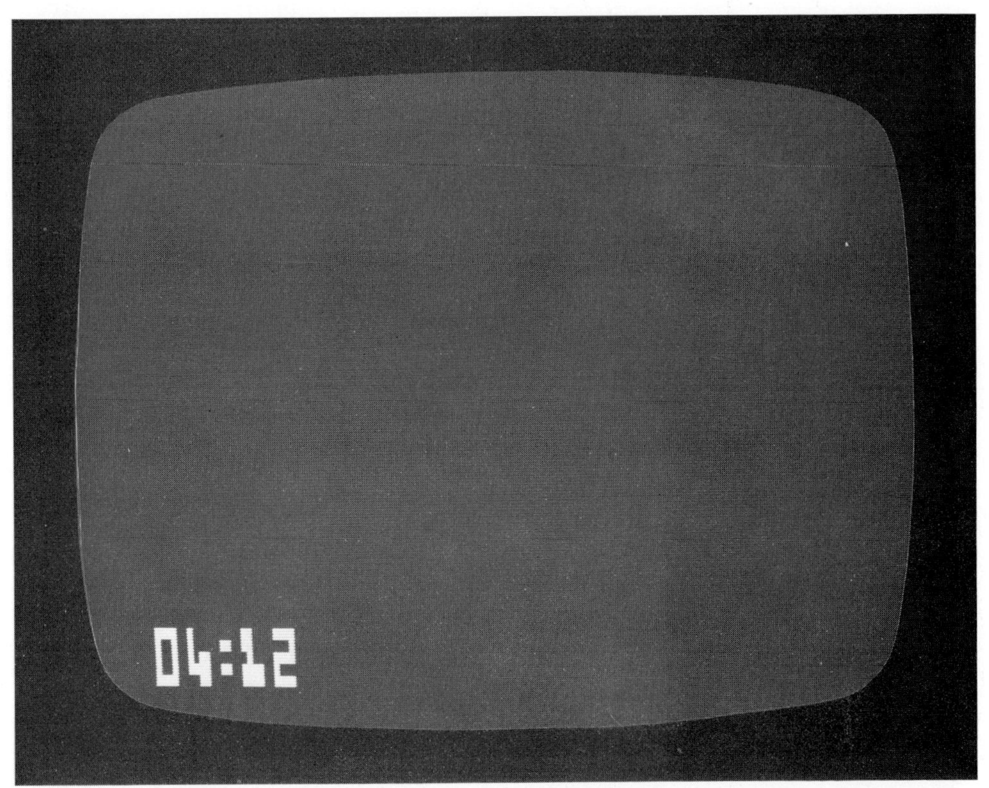
04:12

04:13

Discussion

- The oversize digit routines from program G6P6 are used.
- The function TIME$ returns the date and time established by TRSDOS commands. The last eight characters are the time. The first five of these are 2-digit hour, a colon, and 2-digit minute count. Thus MID$(TIME$,10,5) extracts the required 5 characters from TIME$.

Suggestions

- Modify the program so that the user can specify the position of the clock on the screen.
- Alter the program so that hours, minutes, and seconds are displayed.

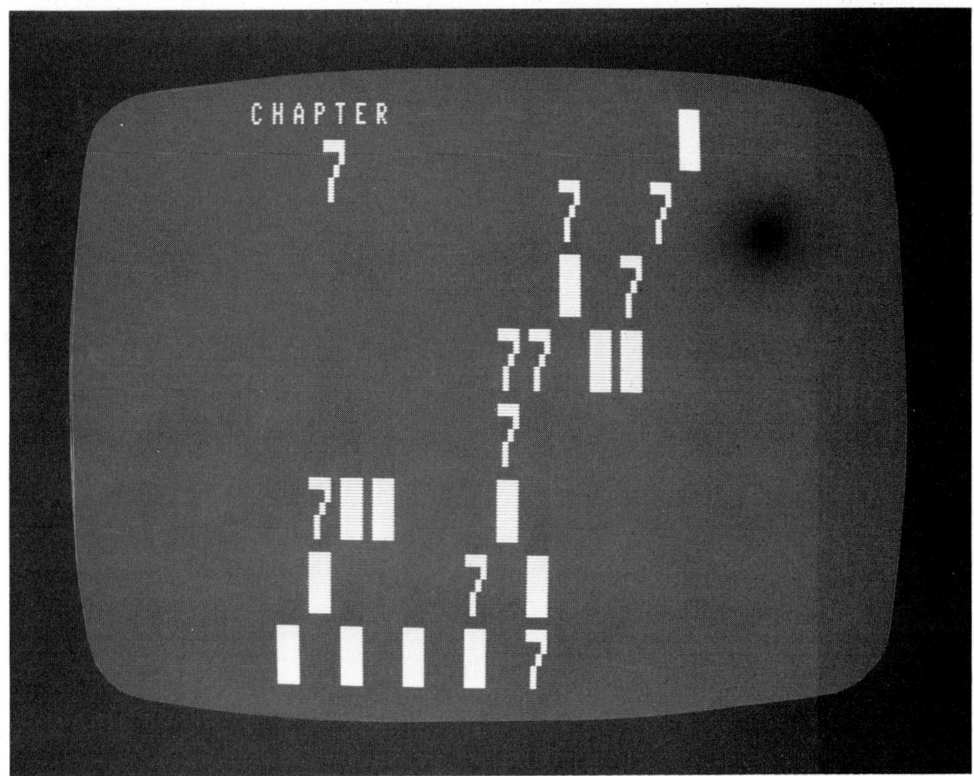

Pixel Graphics

In the previous chapter it was shown that each graphic character is composed of a 3 x 2 rectangle of pixels. The screen, which contains 16 rows and 64 columns of characters, equivalently contains 48 rows and 128 columns of pixels. While the screen address of a character is a single number between 0 and 1023, the screen address of a pixel is a pair of numbers specifying its two-dimensional position or coordinates on the screen. A programmer can address a single pixel with X and Y coordinates, using the column numbers 0 to 127 for X and the row numbers 0 to 47 for Y. See figure 7.1.

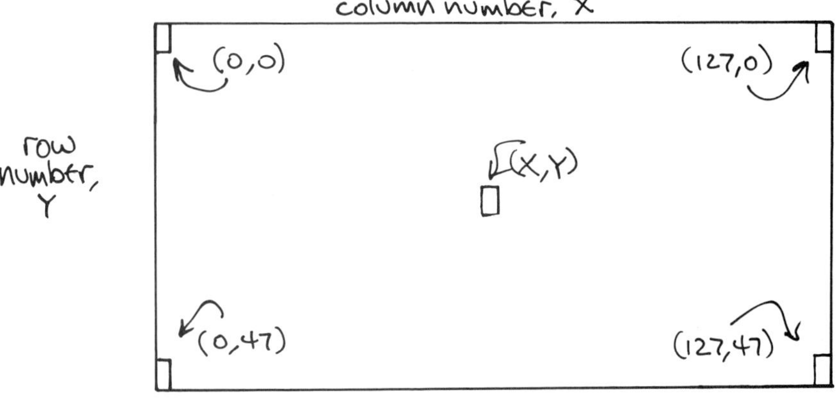

Figure 7.1 Pixel Addressing

SET

The SET command turns on the pixel whose screen address is in X,Y coordinate form in parentheses immediately following the word SET.

Instruction	Output
10 SET(0,0)	Upper left pixel is turned on
20 SET(2,4)	Second pixel on fourth row
30 SET(127,47)	Last pixel on 47th row
40 SET(0,47)	Bottom left pixel
50 SET(127,0)	Top right pixel
60 POKE 15360, 128+21	See text below
70 SET(0,0): SET(0,1): SET(0,2)	See text below

The last two statements above have the same effect, except that the POKE is much faster. Both light up the top left pixels like this:

RESET

The RESET command turns off the pixel whose screen address is in X,Y coordinate form.

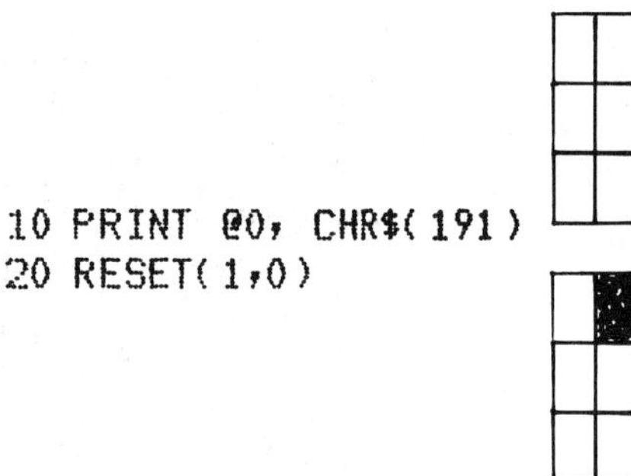

```
10 PRINT @0, CHR$(191)
20 RESET(1,0)
```

POINT

The POINT function returns a zero (false) if the pixel at the X,Y coordinates that make up its argument is off, and a -1 (true) if that pixel is on. Thus it is useful when testing if a particular spot is on or off.

```
10 IF POINT(0,0) THEN RESET(0,0)

20 IF POINT(X,Y) THEN SET(X+1,Y+1): RESET(X,Y)
```

Problem 7.1

Write a program to draw a line using pixel graphics. The user is to input the X,Y coordinates of the two end points.

Solution

```
10 'filename:"s7p1"
20 ' purpose: draw a straight line given two end points
30 '  author: jdr 8/80
40 '
50 INPUT "input X,Y coordinates of end point 1"; X1,Y1
60 INPUT "input X,Y coordinates of end point 2"; X2,Y2
70 IF 100*X1+Y1 > 100*X2+Y2
     THEN T=X1 : X1=X2 : X2=T : T=Y1 : Y1=Y2 : Y2=T
80 GOSUB 1000 'draw the line
90 IF INKEY$="" THEN 90
100 STOP
1000 'subroutine to draw picture on screen
1010 CLS
1100 IF X1>127 OR X2>127 OR Y1>47 OR Y2>47
       THEN PRINT "line will not fit, cannot continue" :
            RETURN
1110 IF X1=X2 THEN 1270
1120 IF Y1=Y2 THEN 1310
1130 M=(Y2-Y1)/(X2-X1) 'calculate slope of line
1140 B=Y1-M*X1 'calculate y-intercept
1150 IF M>0
       THEN IF M<=1 THEN 1220 ELSE 1170
       ELSE IF M>=-1 THEN 1220 ELSE 1160
1160 T=Y1 : Y1=Y2 : Y2=T 'slope between -1 and -infinity
1170 FOR J=Y1 TO Y2 'slope between 1 and infinity
1180    I=INT((J-B)/M+0.5)
1190    SET(I,J)
1200 NEXT J
1210 GOTO 1340
1220 FOR I=X1 TO X2 'slope between -1 and 1
1230    J=INT(M*I+B+0.5)
1240    SET(I,J)
1250 NEXT I
1260 GOTO 1340
1270 FOR J=Y1 TO Y2 'no slope, vertical line
1280    SET(X1,J)
1290 NEXT J
1300 GOTO 1340
1310 FOR I=X1 TO X2 'zero slope, horizontal line
1320    SET(I,Y1)
1330 NEXT I
1340 RETURN
9999 END
```

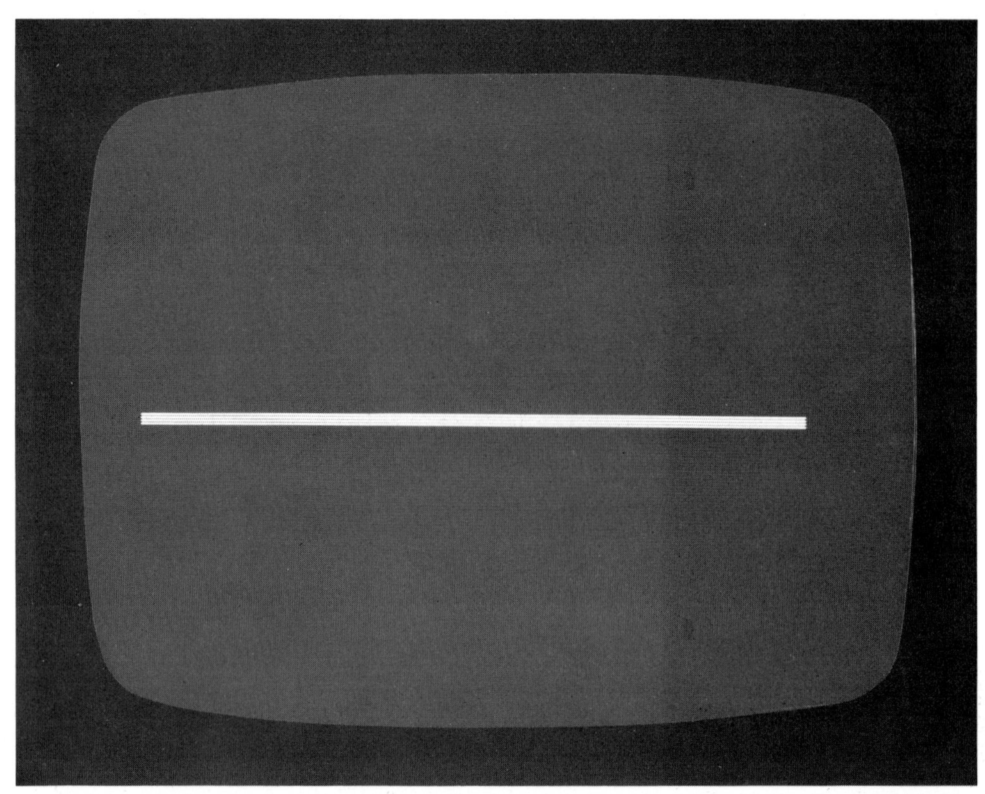

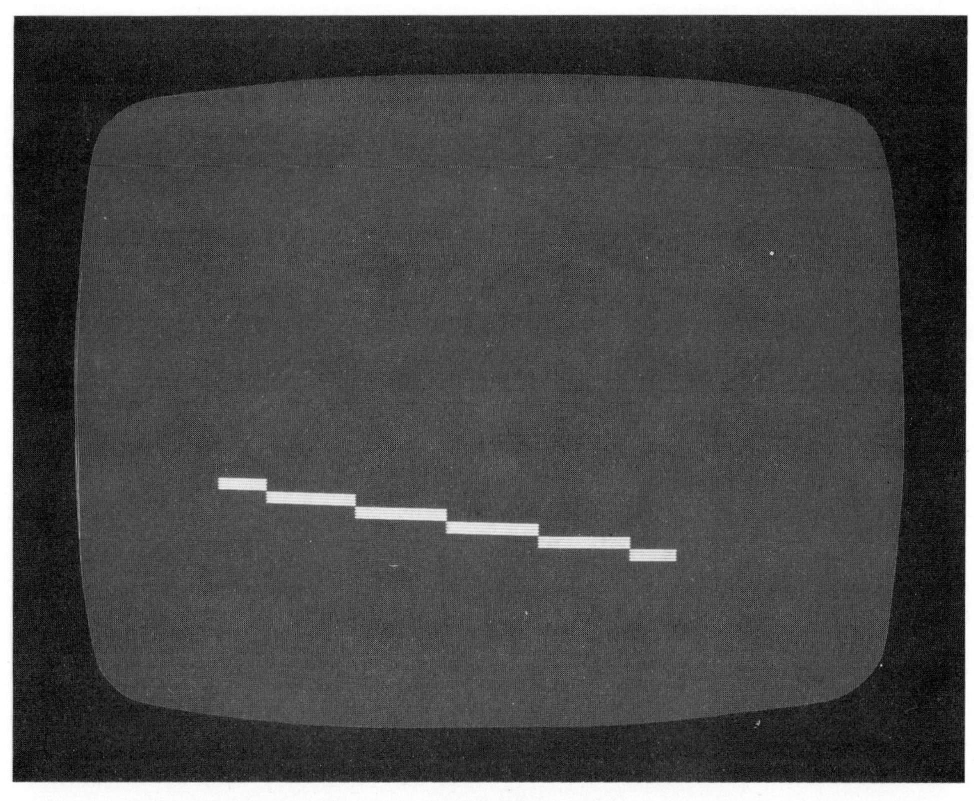

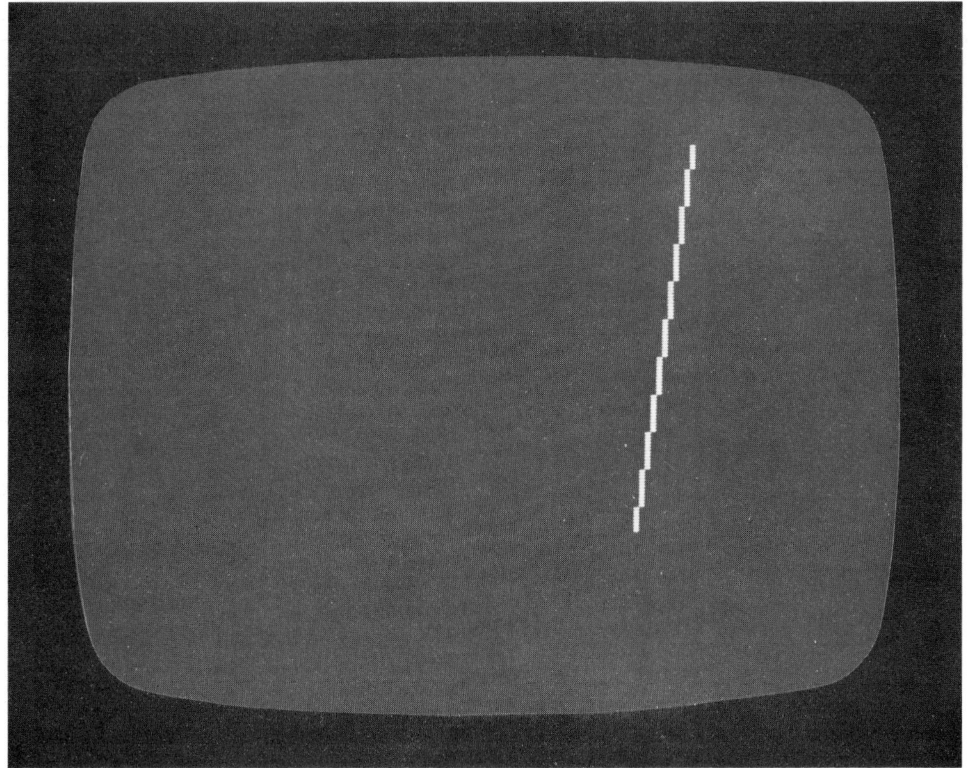

Discussion

- The subroutine used to draw the line is basically the same as that in program G5P4 with all PRINT@ statements replaced with appropriate SET commands.
- The two points are ordered in line 70 so that the drawing of the line can proceed from left to right on the screen.

Problem 7.2

Draw a circle centered at a point X,Y with radius R.

Solution

```
10 'filename:"s7p2"
20 ' purpose: draw a circle
30 '   author: jdr 8/80
40 '
50 INPUT "input X,Y coordinates of circle's center";X1,Y1
60 INPUT "input radius of circle";R
70 CLS : E=128/48
80 FOR T=0 TO 6.3 STEP 1/(R+R)
90    X=INT(E*R*COS(T)+X1+0.5)
100   Y=INT(R*SIN(T)+Y1+0.5)
110   SET(X,Y)
120 NEXT T
130 IF INKEY$="" THEN 130
9999 END
```

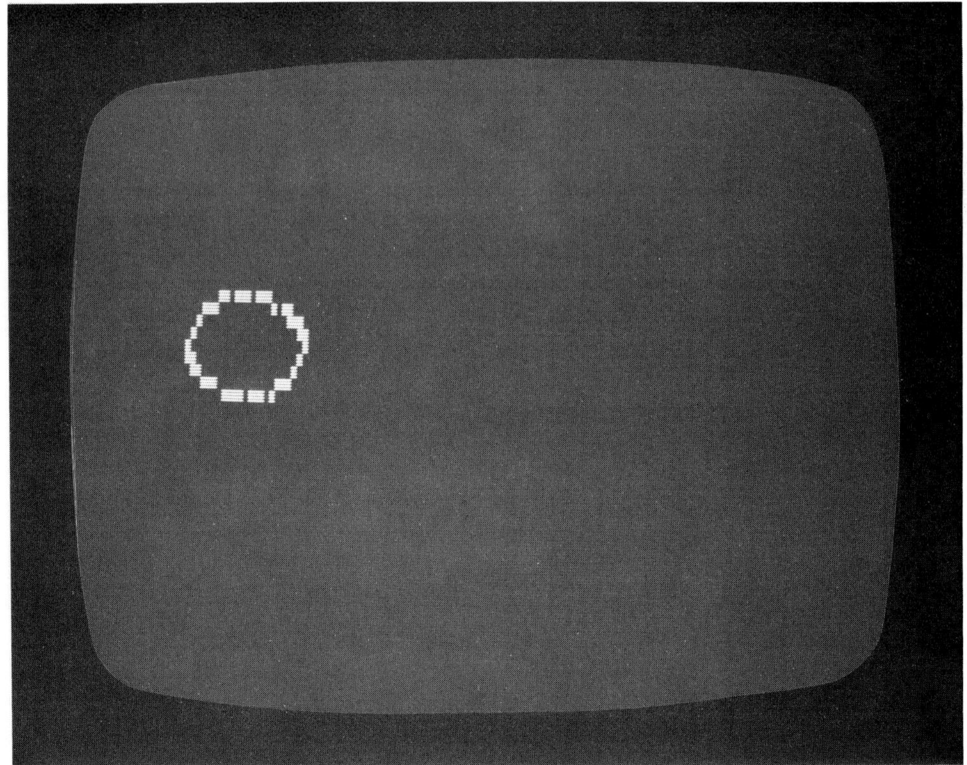

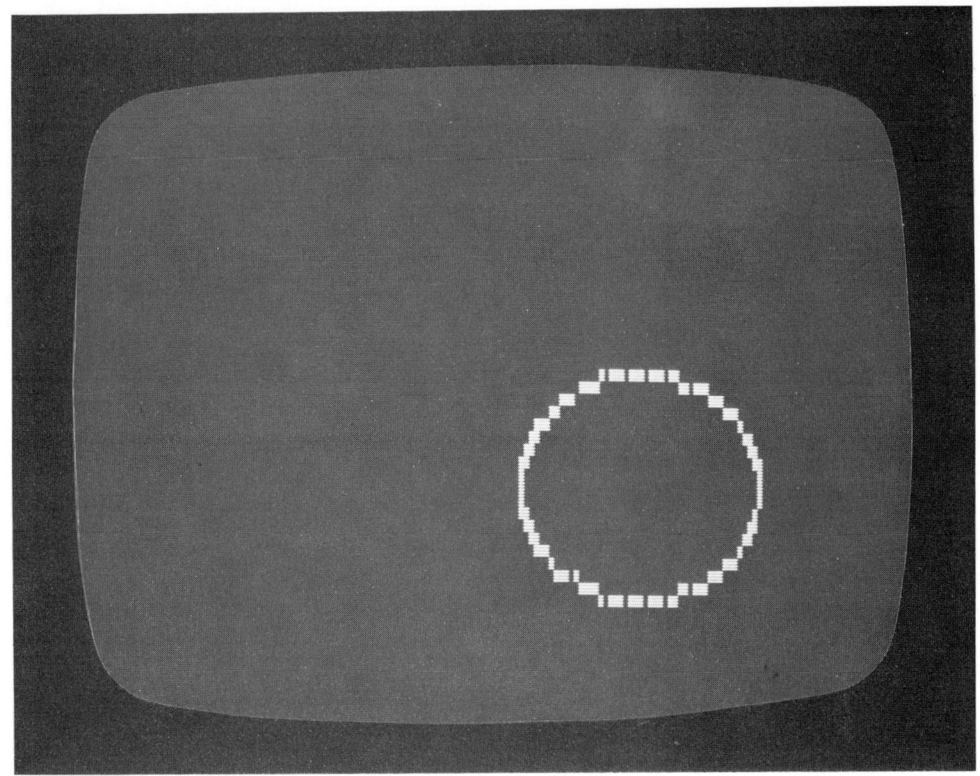

Discussion

- The polar coordinate form for the equation of a circle is used.
- Since pixels are not square, the variable E was used to help overcome inherent distortion.

Suggestions

- Modify the program so that there is a multiplier variable in front of R*SIN(T) as well as R*COS(T). By varying these values, ellipses can be drawn.
- Write a program that draws circles at randomly chosen points on the screen. The radius of each circle can be selected at random also.

Problem 7.3

Draw an outline of the state of Massachusetts using pixel graphics.

Solution

```
10 'filename:"s7p3"
20 ' purpose: draw picture of Massachusetts
30 ' author : jdr 8/80
40 '
50 XINC=35 : YINC=4 : A$="Chelmsford" : X=50 : Y=1 : S=0
70 GOSUB 1000
152 GOSUB 6000
155 RESTORE
160 IF INKEY$="" THEN GOTO 160 ELSE GOTO 45
1000 'subroutine to draw picture on screen
1010 CLS
1020 READ N 'number of straight lines to draw in picture
1030 FOR L=1 TO N
1040    READ C,D
1050    X1=INT(C/100) : Y1=C-100*X1
1060    X2=INT(D/100) : Y2=D-100*X2
1080 X1=X1+XINC : Y1=Y1+YINC 'relocate coordinates
1090 X2=X2+XINC : Y2=Y2+YINC
1100 IF X1>127 OR X2>127 OR Y1>47 OR Y2>47
        THEN PRINT "picture will not fit, cannot continue" :
            RETURN
1110 IF X1=X2 THEN 1270
1120 IF Y1=Y2 THEN 1310
1130 M=(Y2-Y1)/(X2-X1) 'calculate slope of line
1140 B=Y1-M*X1 'calculate y-intercept
1150 IF M>0
        THEN IF M<=1 THEN 1220 ELSE 1170
        ELSE IF M>=-1 THEN 1220 ELSE 1160
1160 T=Y1 : Y1=Y2 : Y2=T 'slope between -1 and -infinity
1170 FOR J=Y1 TO Y2 'slope between 1 and infinity
1180    I=INT((J-B)/M+0.5)
1190    SET(I,J) '
1200 NEXT J
1210 GOTO 1340
1220 FOR I=X1 TO X2 'slope between -1 and 1
1230    J=INT(M*I+B+0.5)
1240    SET(I,J)
1250 NEXT I
1260 GOTO 1340
1270 FOR J=Y1 TO Y2 'no slope, vertical line
1280    SET(X1,J)
1290 NEXT J
1300 GOTO 1340
1310 FOR I=X1 TO X2 'zero slope, horizontal line
1320    SET(I,Y1)
1330 NEXT I
```

```
1340 IF S=1 RETURN
1345 NEXT L
1350 RESTORE : S=1
1360 RETURN
4000 DATA 42,110,602,111,702,802,4602,112,4712,1613,1713
4010 DATA 4701,4801,4900,5600,5701,5702,6203,6203,5802,6302
4020 DATA 5904,6104,5605,5905,5506,5507,5608,6008,6009,6110
4030 DATA 6210,6412,6513,6614,6714,7514,7110,7110,7209,7409
4040 DATA 7310,7510,7511,7511,7611,7914,7415,7815,7816,7816
4050 DATA 6616,7416,6315,6517,6417,6417,6015,6315,5916,5916
4060 DATA 5616,5816,5316,5518,5116,5216,5418,5418,4915,5015
4070 DATA 4714,4814,4613,4713,6320,6920,6419,6619,6919,6919
4080 DATA 7421,7821,7720,7820
6000 'draw line from town name to position in map
6010 X1=8 : Y1=43 : X2=X+XINC : Y2=Y+YINC
6020 PRINT@960,A$; : SET(X2,Y2) : GOSUB 1130
6024 FOR J=1 TO 100
6025    FOR I=1 TO 100 : NEXT I : RESET (X2,Y2)
6026    FOR I=1 TO 100 : NEXT I : SET (X2,Y2)
6027 NEXT J
6030 RETURN
9999 END
```

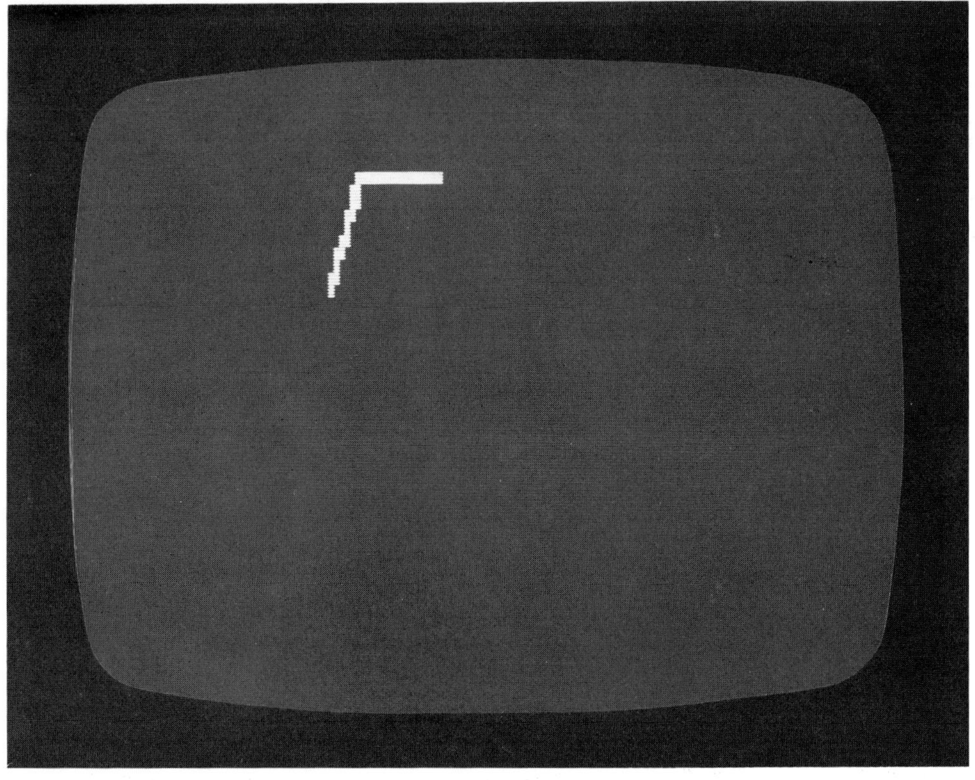

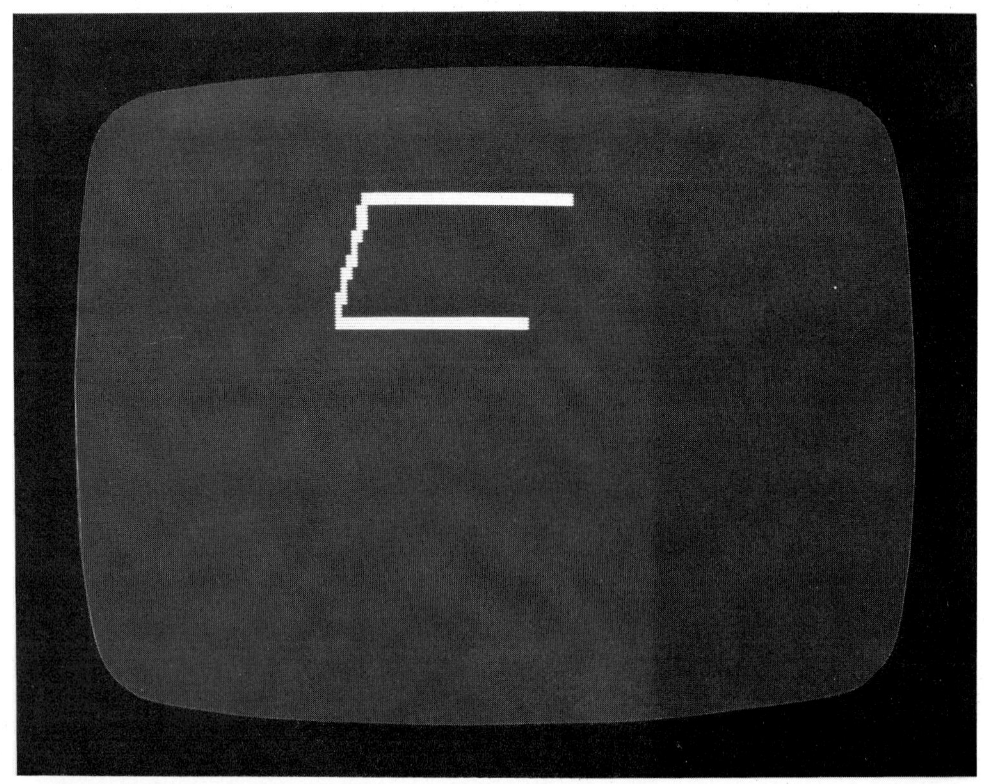

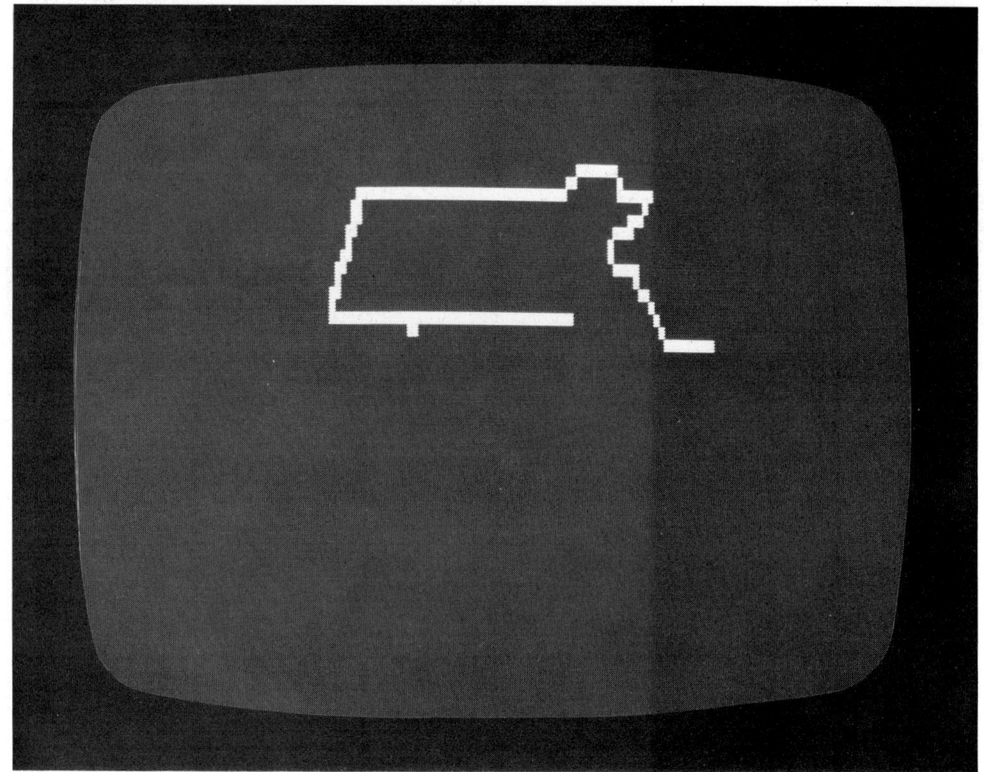

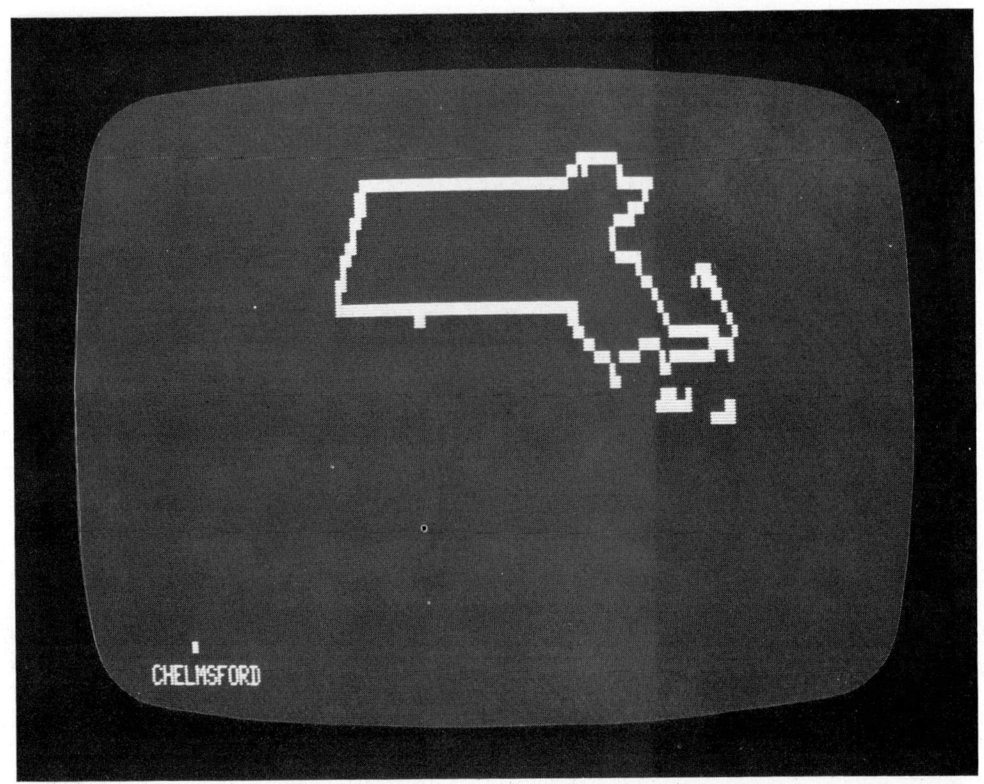
CHELMSFORD

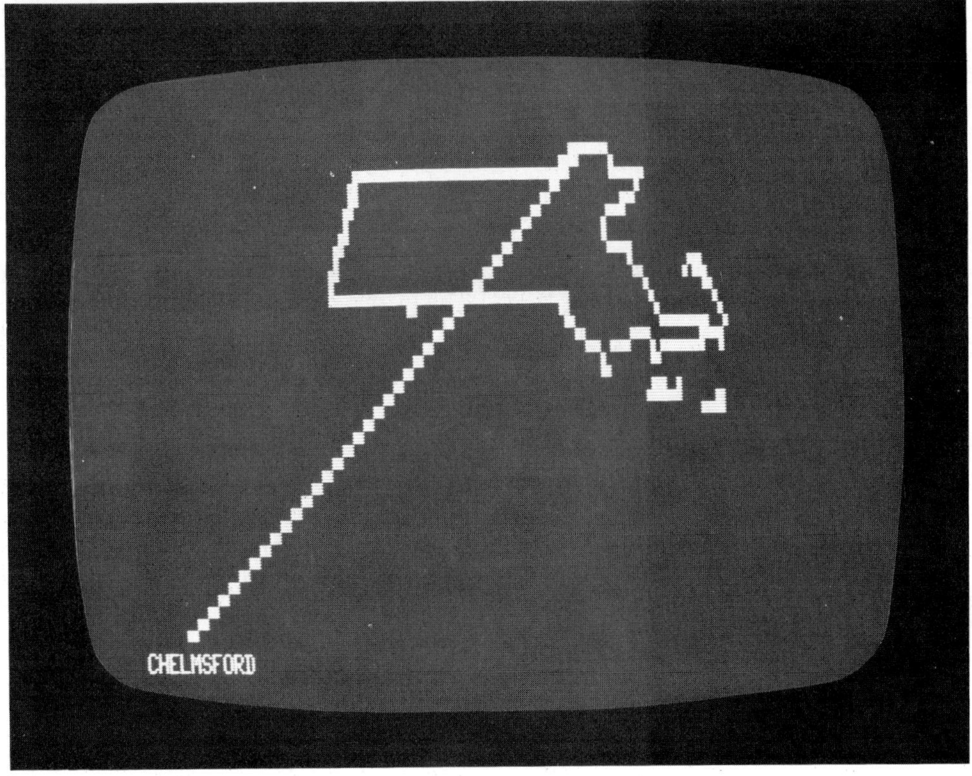
CHELMSFORD

Discussion

- Again, the basic line drawing subroutine that has been used in previous programs appears at lines 1000 and beyond with SET commands doing the drawing on the screen.
- The DATA statements provide end points of the lines that are drawn to form the picture.
- As an extra flourish, the town of Chelmsford is singled out for special identification.
- Finally with panache, the position of the town blinks on and off.

Suggestions

- Modify the program to give the user a menu of cities to choose from, with the program then drawing a line from the town's name to its position in the state.
- Modify the program so that the town name is printed above the town's position, so that a vertical line can connect the town name and the pixel locating the town's position.

Problem 7.4

Write a program that will produce a smile face at a position on the screen specified by the user.

Solution

```
10 'filename:"s7p4"
20 ' purpose: smile face w/ mobility
30 ' author : jdr 8/80
40 '
45 CLS
50 INPUT"input position of picture";XINC,YINC
60 GOSUB 1000
155 RESTORE
160 IF INKEY$="" THEN GOTO 160 ELSE GOTO 45
1000 'subroutine to draw picture on screen
1010 CLS
1020 READ N 'number of straight lines to draw in picture
1030 FOR L=1 TO N
1040     READ C,D
1050     X1=INT(C/100) : Y1=C-100*X1
1060     X2=INT(D/100) : Y2=D-100*X2
1080 X1=X1+XINC : Y1=Y1+YINC 'relocate coordinates
1090 X2=X2+XINC : Y2=Y2+YINC
1100 IF X1>127 OR X2>127 OR Y1>47 OR Y2>47
       THEN PRINT "picture will not fit, cannot continue" :
            RETURN
1110 IF X1=X2 THEN 1270
1120 IF Y1=Y2 THEN 1310
```

```
1130 M=(Y2-Y1)/(X2-X1) 'calculate slope of line
1140 B=Y1-M*X1 'calculate y-intercept
1150 IF M>0
       THEN IF M<=1 THEN 1220 ELSE 1170
       ELSE IF M>=-1 THEN 1220 ELSE 1160
1160 T=Y1 : Y1=Y2 : Y2=T 'slope between -1 and -infinity
1170 FOR J=Y1 TO Y2 'slope between 1 and infinity
1180    I=INT((J-B)/M+0.5)
1190    SET(I,J)
1200 NEXT J
1210 GOTO 1340
1220 FOR I=X1 TO X2 'slope between -1 and 1
1230    J=INT(M*I+B+0.5)
1240    SET(I,J)
1250 NEXT I
1260 GOTO 1340
1270 FOR J=Y1 TO Y2 'no slope, vertical line
1280    SET(X1,J)
1290 NEXT J
1300 GOTO 1340
1310 FOR I=X1 TO X2 'zero slope, horizontal line
1320    SET(I,Y1)
1330 NEXT I
1340 NEXT L
1350 RETURN
4000 DATA 25,1200,1202,1300,1302,3000,3002,3100,3102,7,9
4010 DATA 107,109,4207,4209,4307,4309,209,210,309,310,4009,4010
4020 DATA 4109,4110,410,411,510,511,3810,3811,3910,3911,611,611
4030 DATA 711,711,3611,3611,3711,3711,612,1112,3212,3712
4040 DATA 813,1513,2813,3513,1214,3114
9999 END
```

Discussion

- Notice the similarity between this and the previous program. The generality of this approach for producing graphics is quite astonishing.

Suggestions

- Modify the program so that a circle delineating the head is drawn around the eyes and smile.

Problem 7.5 Write a program that turns the computer into a stand up comedian who does impressions.

Solution

```
10 'filename:"s7p5"
20 ' purpose: stand up comedian doing impersonations
30 ' author : jdr 8/80
40 '
41 DIM W$(15),C$(15)
42 FOR I=1 TO 15
43    READ W$(I),C$(I)
44 NEXT I
45 RANDOM
46 CLS
50 XINC=0 : YINC=12
51 PRINT@26,"And now, heeeeeres John Binary ..."
52 FOR I=1 TO 375 : NEXT I
60 GOSUB 1000 'draw smile face
61 FOR Q=1 TO 15 : PRINT@25,"for my ";
62    IF Q=1 THEN PRINT@32,"first";
              ELSE IF Q=15 THEN  PRINT@32,"last";
                               ELSE PRINT@36," "; : PRINT@32,"next";
63    PRINT@POS(0)+1,"impression ...";
64    PRINT@94,W$(Q);
65 FOR I=1 TO 375 : NEXT I
76 A$=C$(Q)
77 A$=A$+CHR$(191)
80 GOSUB 7000
170 PRINT@94,STRING$(33,32) : FOR I=1 TO 350 : NEXT I : NEXT Q
175 PRINT@25,STRING$(33,32); : FOR I=1 TO 500 : NEXT I
180 PRINT@25,"thank you ..."
185 FOR I=1 TO 1525+RND(1000) : NEXT I
190 PRINT@271," "; : PRINT@262," "; : FOR I=1 TO 50 : NEXT I
200 PRINT@271,CHR$(191); : PRINT@262,CHR$(191);
210 IF INKEY$="" THEN 185
220 STOP
1000 'subroutine to draw picture on screen
1010 CLS
1020 READ N 'number of straight lines to draw in picture
1030 FOR L=1 TO N
1040    READ C,D
1050    X1=INT(C/100) : Y1=C-100*X1
1060    X2=INT(D/100) : Y2=D-100*X2
1080 X1=X1+XINC : Y1=Y1+YINC 'relocate coordinates
1090 X2=X2+XINC : Y2=Y2+YINC
1100 IF X1>127 OR X2>127 OR Y1>47 OR Y2>47
     THEN PRINT "picture will not fit, cannot continue" :
          RETURN
1110 IF X1=X2 THEN 1270
1120 IF Y1=Y2 THEN 1310
```

```
1130 M=(Y2-Y1)/(X2-X1) 'calculate slope of line
1140 B=Y1-M*X1 'calculate y-intercept
1150 IF M>0
       THEN IF M<=1 THEN 1220 ELSE 1170
       ELSE IF M>=-1 THEN 1220 ELSE 1160
1160 T=Y1 : Y1=Y2 : Y2=T 'slope between -1 and -infinity
1170 FOR J=Y1 TO Y2 'slope between 1 and infinity
1180    I=INT((J-B)/M+0.5)
1190    SET(I,J)
1200 NEXT J
1210 GOTO 1340
1220 FOR I=X1 TO X2 'slope between -1 and 1
1230    J=INT(M*I+B+0.5)
1240    SET(I,J)
1250 NEXT I
1260 GOTO 1340
1270 FOR J=Y1 TO Y2 'no slope, vertical line
1280    SET(X1,J)
1290 NEXT J
1300 GOTO 1340
1310 FOR I=X1 TO X2 'zero slope, horizontal line
1320    SET(I,Y1)
1330 NEXT I
1340 NEXT L
1350 RETURN
3990 DATA "Arnold Palmer","444","Little Orphan Annie","ooo"
3991 DATA "Orson Welles","###","Jimmy The Greek","%%%"
3992 DATA "Rona Barrett","'!'","3-year-old child","? ?"
3993 DATA "a math teacher","1+1","a math student","= 3"
3994 DATA "Bozo the Clown","+x+","Gloria Steinem","= ="
3995 DATA "NBC censor","* *","Dean Martin","J&B"
3996 DATA "Irma La Douce","$ $","Hush Hefner","T&A"
3997 DATA "librarian in Boston's combat zone",".oO"
4000 DATA 25,1200,1202,1300,1302,3000,3002,3100,3102,7,9
4010 DATA 107,109,4207,4209,4307,4309,209,210,309,310,4009,4010
4020 DATA 4109,4110,410,411,510,511,3810,3811,3910,3911,611,611
4030 DATA 711,711,3611,3611,3711,3711,612,1112,3212,3712
4040 DATA 813,1513,2813,3513,1214,3114
7000 'impersonation subroutine
7010 FOR I=1 TO 4 : X$=MID$(A$,I,1)
7020    PRINT@262,X$; : PRINT@271,X$;
7030    FOR J=1 TO 150
7040    NEXT J
7045    IF I=3 THEN FOR J=1 TO 150 : NEXT J
7050 NEXT I
7060 RETURN
9999 END
```

for my first impression ...
Arnold Palmer

for my first impression ...
Arnold Palmer
4
4

for my next impression ....
Bozo the Clown

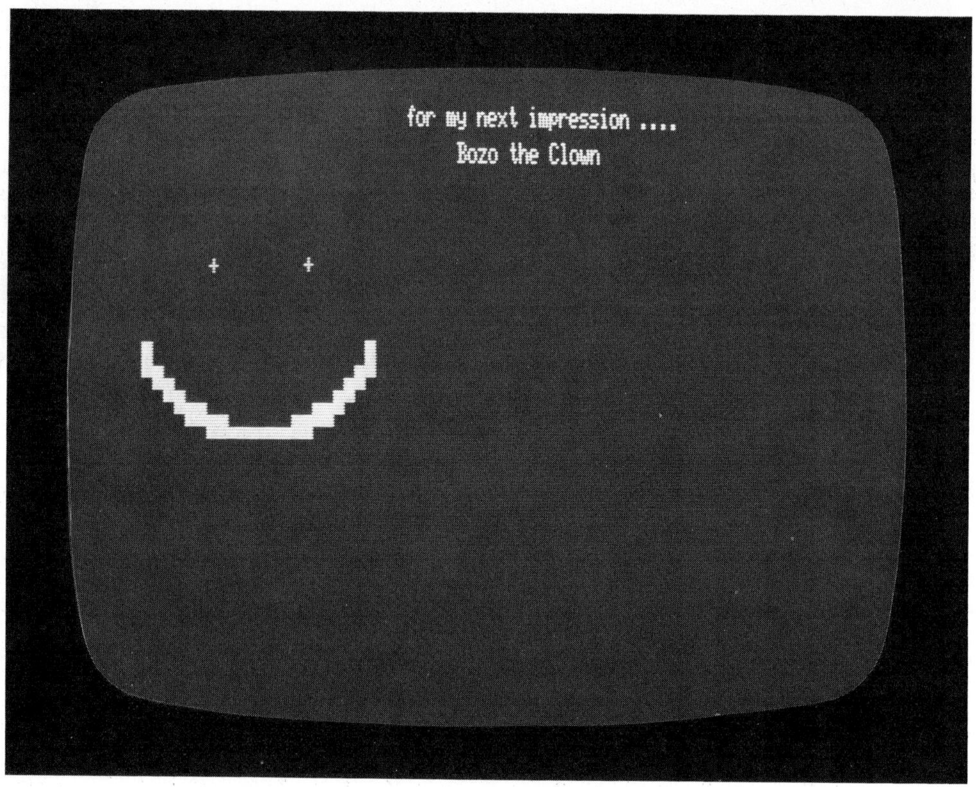
for my next impression ....
Bozo the Clown

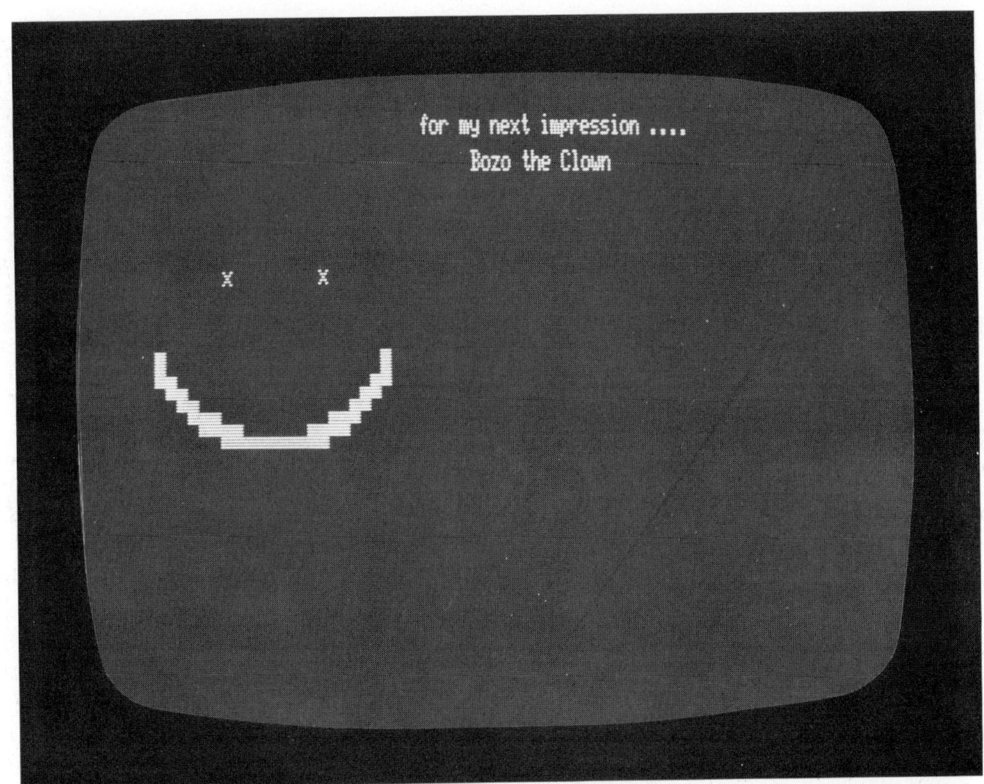
for my next impression ....
Bozo the Clown
x x

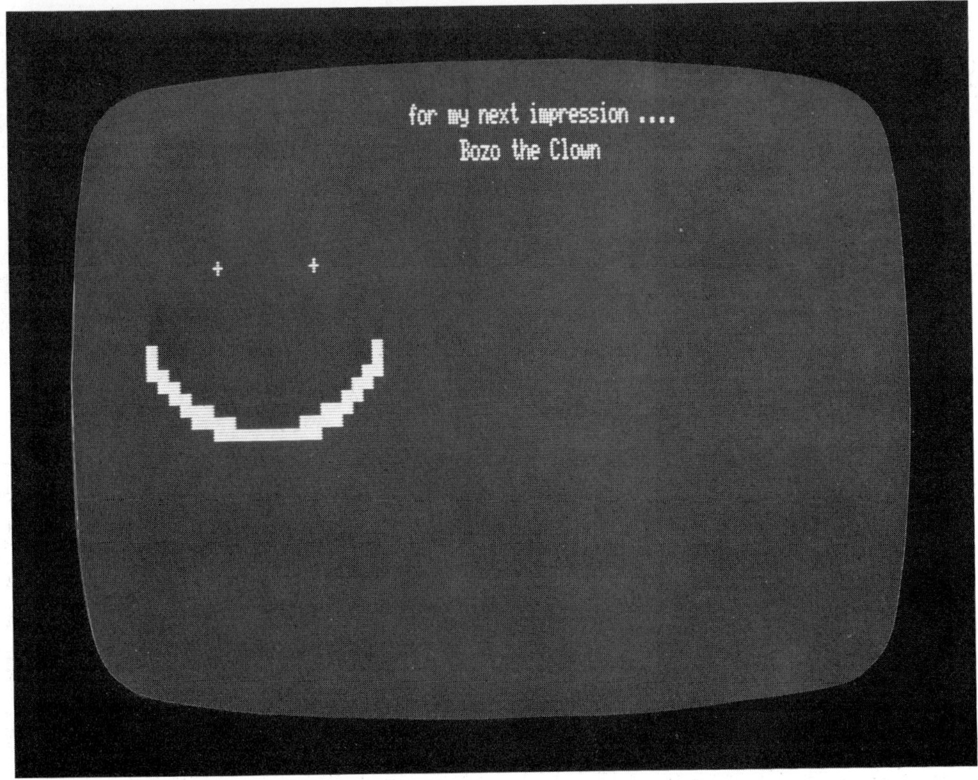
for my next impression ....
Bozo the Clown
+ +

for my last impression ....
librarian in Boston's combat zone

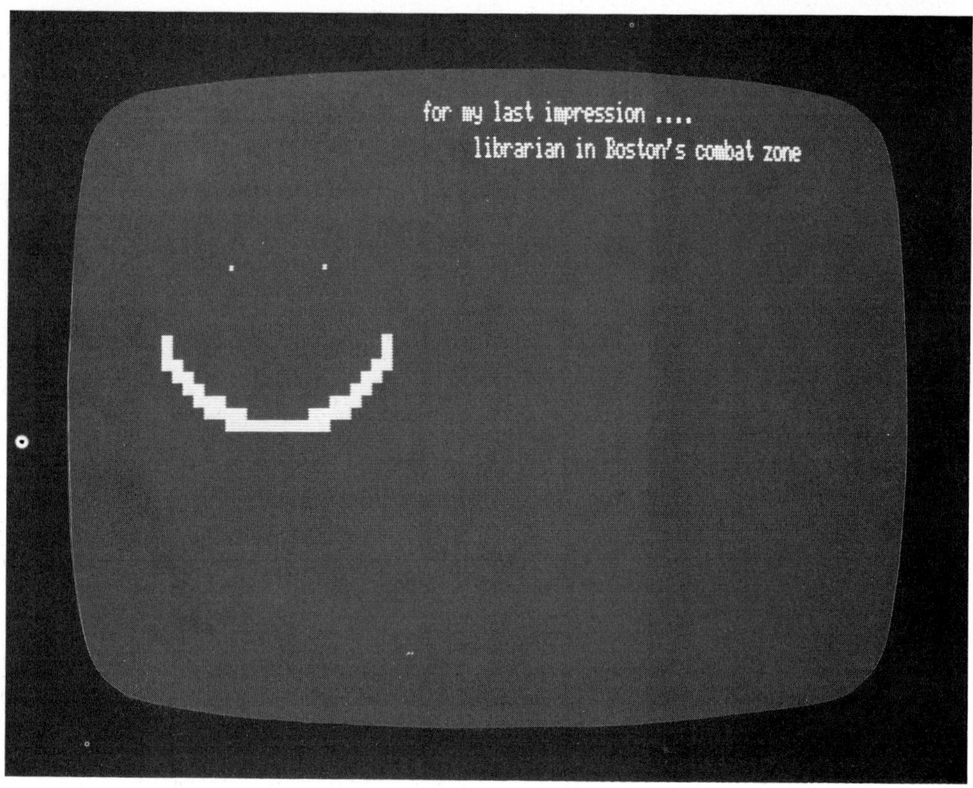
for my last impression ....
librarian in Boston's combat zone

for my last impression ....
librarian in Boston's combat zone
0 0

for my last impression ....
librarian in Boston's combat zone
0 0

Discussion

- The program performs 15 impressions.
- Notice the simple motion that the eyes give the smile face.
- This program is a crude beginning to what might be called cartooning.
- The stand up comic's name is John Binary. Of course, his idol is John Byner.

Suggestions

- Turn the smile-faced impressionist of this program into a comedian that delivers short, snappy one-liners. His name could be Grinny Youngman. "Take my computer – please!"

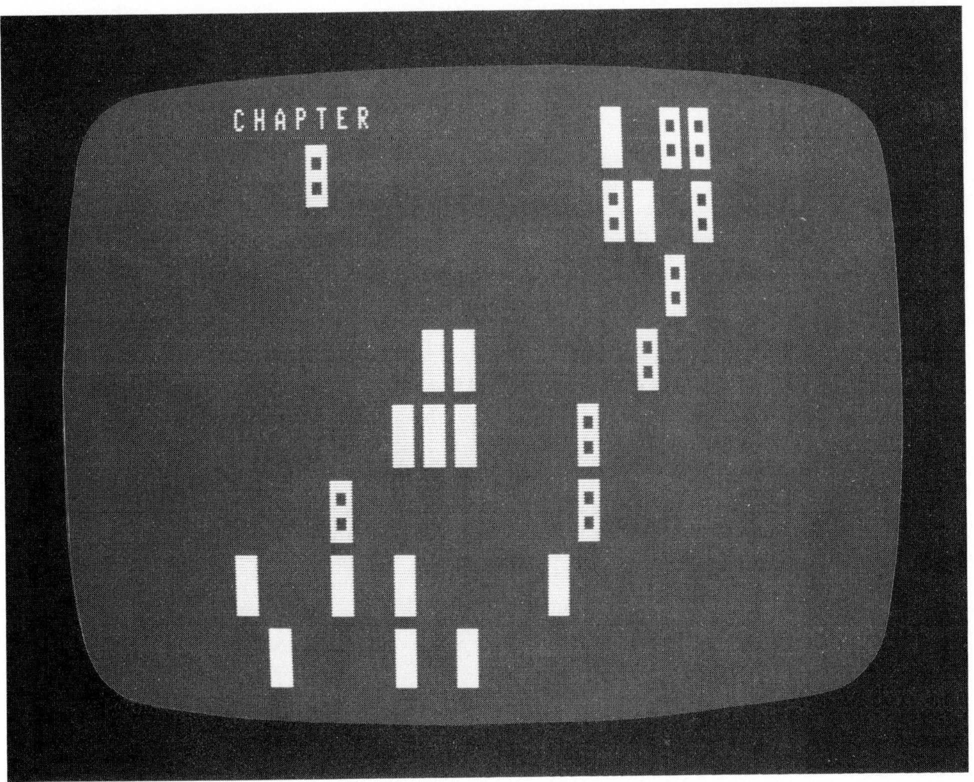

Motion Graphics

The previous chapters have shown you programs ranging widely in sophistication from a simple picture in the program Woodstock to a computerized map drawn using pixel graphics. There was little motion in the graphics examples because it is a difficult proposition to plan on paper and realize in code the effect of movement. Many factors contribute to this difficulty. The speed of the computer is one such factor because there is usually a lot of calculation when motion is involved. The translation of where each point "moves to" requires a calculation. The resolution of the video screen is another factor governing the way a picture looks. If the picture is rotated, then distortion can occur. Much planning must take place prior to writing a program. A third factor is that the BASIC programming language was not designed to facilitate the many primitive graphics operations that would be useful to have. Another, and probably the most important factor impeding a computer's ability to produce motion, is a lack of imagination and willingness to experiment on the part of the computer's programmer.

We will show you some programs that will illustrate the beginnings of how motion can be produced and the visual diversity and delight it can provide.

Bouncing Dots

In many games, as well as in serious graphing applications, you will want to have a dot move in a straight direction until it meets an obstacle and keeps moving in a new direction. Consider the possible bounces:

Vertical Wall Collision

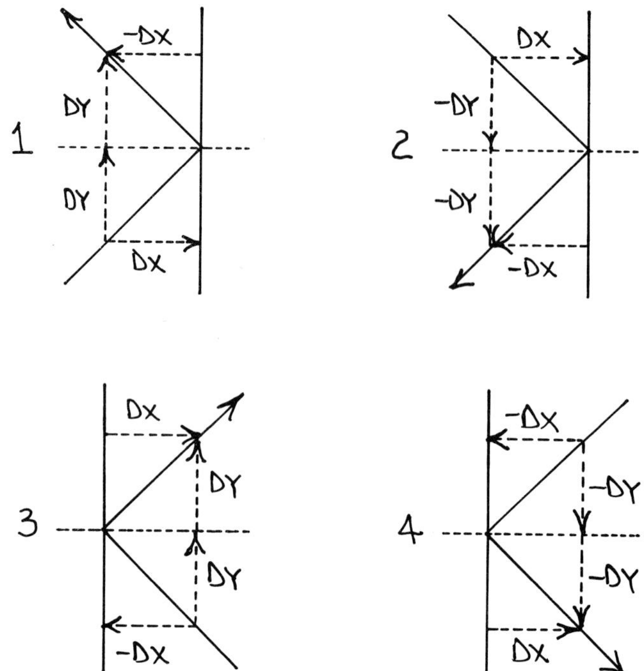

Each moving dot changes its X direction by an amount DX, and its Y direction by an amount DY. In all the conditions above, the Y direction increment DY never changes sign. In conditions 1 and 2, DX starts as positive, but changes sign to negative on the bounce.

If you investigate the four possible bounces from a horizontal wall, you will find that, as expected, the only change is the reversal of the sign of DY.

This understanding is all that is necessary to graph a moving and bouncing dot. The dot is a pixel drawn with a SET command. The coordinates of the SET are X and Y. The movement is provided by a SET at a new position X+DX, Y+DY followed by a RESET of the old dot at X,Y.

```
100 SET(X,Y)
110 X=X+DX: Y=Y+DY
120 SET(X,Y)
130 RESET(X-DX,Y-DY)
140 GOTO 110
```

To bounce the dot off the wall, you must "feel" ahead to see if any part of the surrounding territory is occupied. It is not enough to just sense the status of the next point. For example, suppose the dot is moving up and to the right, and it encounters a horizontal wall.

Next place to be set
is already occupied

If the "next place" is the only point that is considered on a bounce, the computer couldn't tell if the wall were horizontal or vertical.

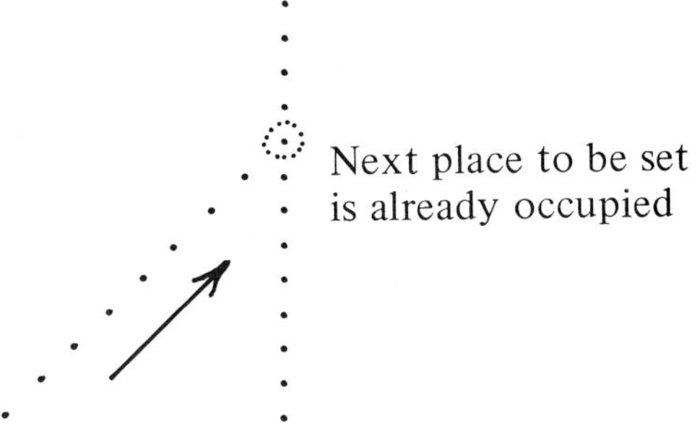

The only way to judge which direction increment, the DX or the DY, needs to change sign is to sense in all four directions.

Examples:

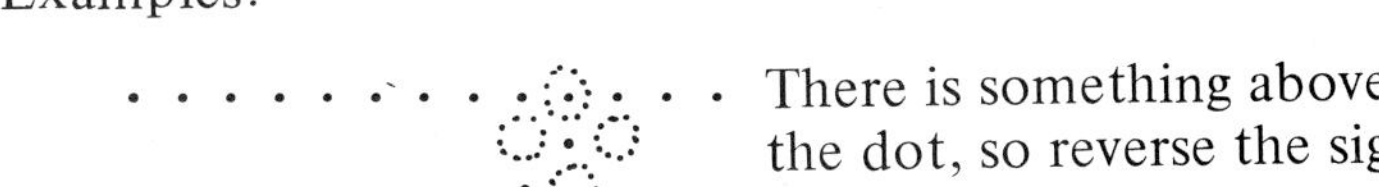

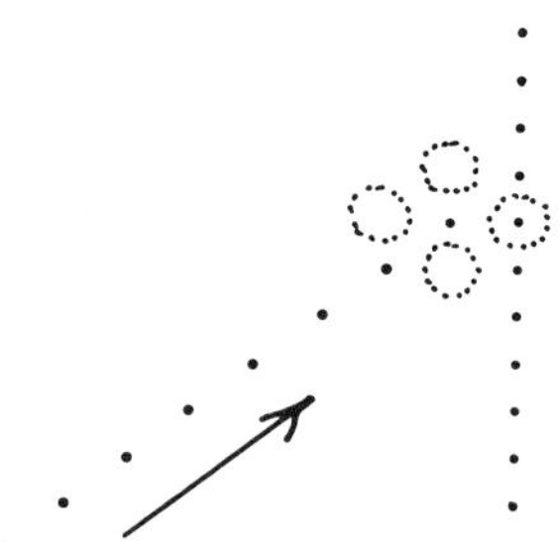

There is something to the right of the dot, so reverse the sign of DX

Problem 8.1

Write a program that bounces a dot off any wall set up in either a vertical or horizontal position.

Solution

```
10 'filename:"s8p1"
20 ' purpose: bouncing dot program
30 '   author: jps 2/80
40 INPUT "DX, DY BETWEEN 1 AND 2 INCLUSIVE";DX,DY
50 INPUT "STARTING COORDINATES";X,Y: CLS
60 FOR I=0 TO 127 ' this loop draws horizontal boundaries
70    SET(I,0): SET(I,1): SET(I,46): SET(I,47)
80 NEXT I
90 FOR I=0 TO 47 '   draw vertical boundaries
100    SET(0,I): SET(1,I): SET(126,I): SET(127,I)
110 NEXT I
120 SET(X,Y) '   put a point at location X,Y
130 '     change direction of dot if necessary
140 IF POINT(X+DX,Y) OR POINT(X-DX,Y) DX=-DX
150 IF POINT(X,Y+DY) OR POINT(X,Y-DY) DY=-DY
160 X=X+DX: Y=Y+DY: GOTO 120
9999 END
```

Discussion

- The program allows DX and DY to be defined for any value between 1 and 2.
- The walls are built on the four sides of the screen.

Suggestions

- Modify the program so that the rectangular area in which the dot bounces can be specified by the user.
- Turn the bouncing dot into a blob and write a program to bounce the blob off horizontal and vertical walls.

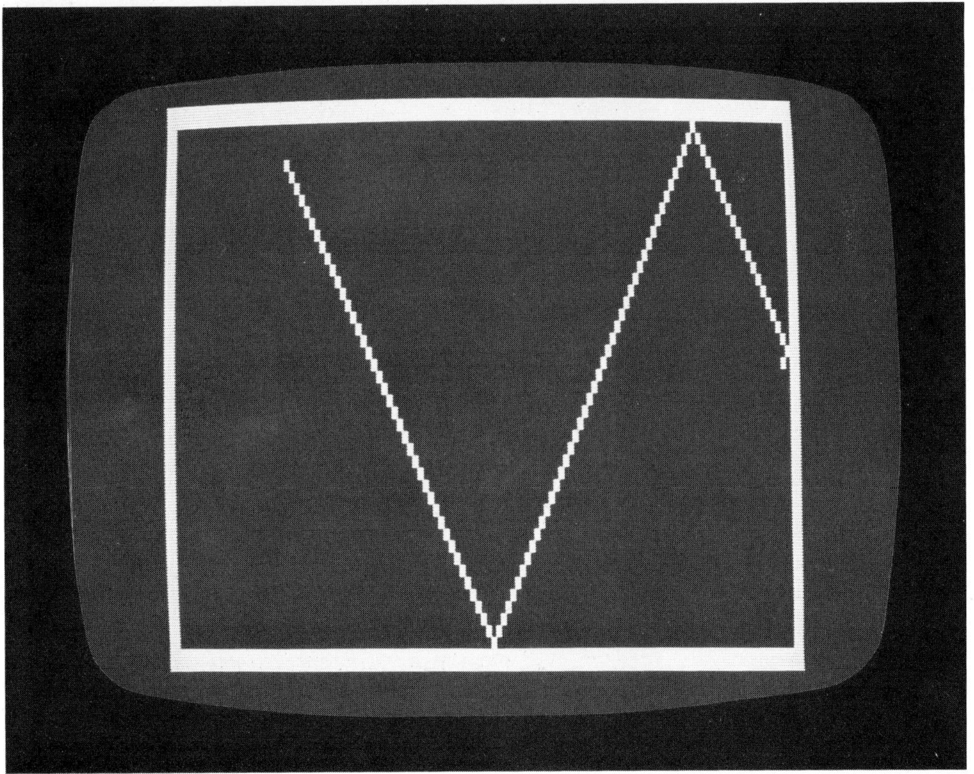

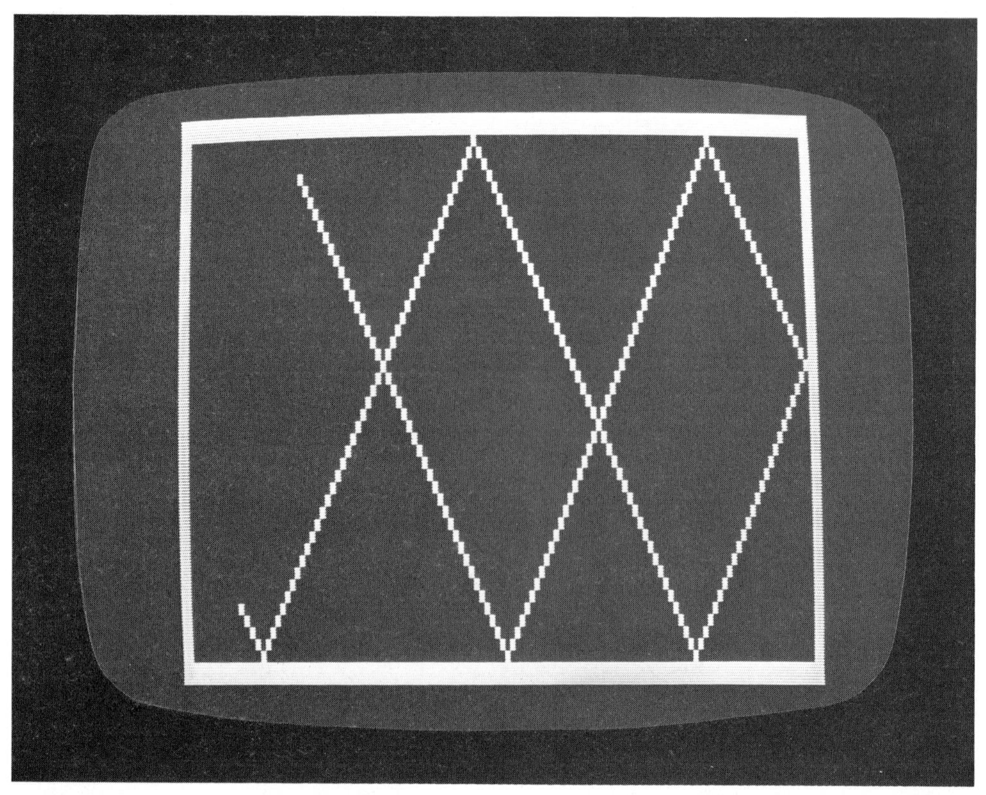

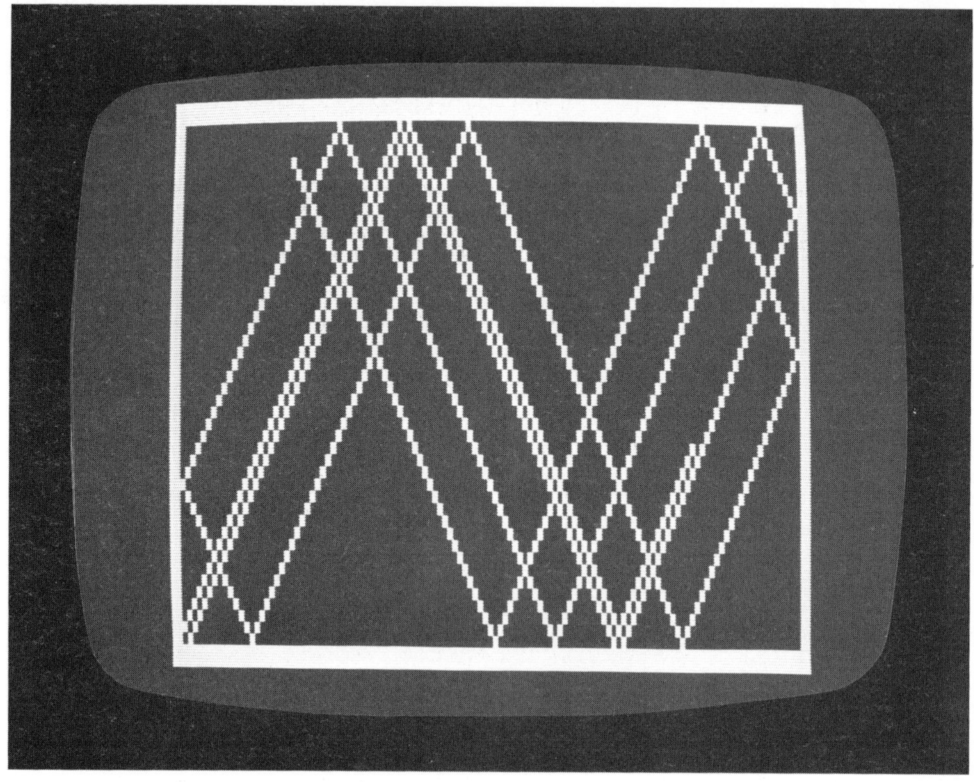

Problem 8.2

Write a program to produce a visual display by bouncing a dot off randomly placed lines on the video screen.

Solution

```
10 'filename:"s8p2"
20 ' purpose: creating computer art
30 '  author: sps 2/79
40 '  next line initializes variables; clears screen
50 RANDOM: CLEAR 1000: DEFSTR A: DEFINT B-Z: E=1: P=-1: CLS
60 CLOSE: PRINT "  PRESS:"
70 PRINT "      L-   TO LOOK AT OLD PICTURES"
80 PRINT "      M-   TO CREATE NEW PICTURES"
90 A=INKEY$: IF A="" THEN 90
100 IF A="L" THEN 790
110 '        user wants to create new art
120 CLS
130 '     the next loop draws 6 random lines on the screen
140 '              (3 vertical, 3 horizontal)
150 FOR T=1 TO 3
160 '       set up random variables
170    B0=RND(25)*2+4: B1=B+RND(50-.5*B)*2: B2=RND(21)*2+4
180    C=RND(11)*2+4: C1=C+RND(23-.5*C)*2: C2=RND(60)*2+4
190 '      draw the lines using the variables
200    FOR N=B0 TO B1: SET(N,B2): NEXT N
210    FOR N=C TO C1: SET(C2,N): NEXT N
220 NEXT T
230 '  the next two lines initialize the direction of the dot
240 S=INT(RND(100)/50): IF S=0 THEN S=-1
250 T=INT(RND(100)/50): IF T=0 THEN T=-1
260 '   the next two lines draw a boundary around the screen
270 FOR N=1 TO 125: SET(N,3): SET(N,47): NEXT N
280 FOR N=4 TO 46: SET(1,N): SET(125,N): NEXT N
290 '     next line gives the point a starting spot &
300 '         makes sure it isn't occupied
310 X=RND(61)*2+2: Y=RND(20)*2+5: IF POINT(X,Y) THEN 310
320 '      print the command statement on the screen
330 PRINT@ 10,"COMMAND(P,S, ,R,E):        ";
340 '
350 '
360 '       the rest is the main portion of the program
370 '   next 4 lines change the direction if necessary
380 IF POINT(X+1,Y) THEN S=-1
390 IF POINT(X-1,Y) THEN S=1
400 IF POINT(X,Y+1) THEN T=-1
410 IF POINT(X,Y-1) THEN T=1
420 '    previous point is blanked if P=1
430 IF P=1 THEN RESET(X,Y)
```

```
440 '   next 4 lines actually tell the dot where to move
450 IF S=1 THEN X=X+1
460 IF S=-1 THEN X=X-1
470 IF T=1 THEN Y=Y+1
480 IF T=-1 THEN Y=Y-1
490 ' next line erases point if it was white and E=1
500 IF POINT(X,Y) AND E=1 THEN RESET(X,Y) ELSE SET(X,Y)
510 '  the next line checks to see if a key was pressed-
520 '     if not, then go back to the main program
530 A=INKEY$: IF A="" THEN 380
540 '      print the letter that was pressed in the corner
550 PRINT@ 30,A;
560 '        execute the command
570 '     reverse the dot?
580 IF A="R" THEN T=-T: S=-S: GOTO 330
590 '     erase the dots trail?
600 IF A="P" THEN P=-P: GOTO 330
610 '     erase the dot when it runs over another?
620 IF A="E" THEN E=-E: GOTO 330
630 '     stop the motion of the dot?
640 IF A<>" " THEN 670
650 A=INKEY$: IF A="" THEN 650 ELSE 330
660 '      store the picture on disk?
670 IF A<>"S" THEN 330
680 '   store the file using random access
690 OPEN "R",1,"SCRNGRPH/DAT"'  open the file for access
700 FIELD 1, 255 AS B$: M=LOF(1): I=15359' initialize
710 A=""'     nullify A$
720 '   the next 5 lines copy the screen to disk
730 I=I+1
740 IF LEN(A)<255 THEN 770
750 M=M+1: LSET B$=A: PUT 1,M
760 IF M/4=INT(M/4) THEN 60 ELSE 710
770 A=A+CHR$(PEEK(I)): POKE I,46: GOTO 730
780 '      this portion copies the art on disk to the screen
790 OPEN "R",1,"SCRNGRPH/DAT": FIELD 1, 255 AS B$
800 IF LOF(1)<>0 GOTO 830
810 PRINT "SORRY, BUT THERE IS NO ART ON FILE...   <<CR>>";
820 A=INKEY$: IF A="" THEN 820 ELSE 60
830 CLS
840 FOR C=1 TO LOF(1) STEP 4
850    FOR D=0 TO 3: GET 1,C+D: PRINT B$: NEXT D
860    PRINT @970, "  <<CR>>";
870    A=INKEY$: IF A="" THEN 870 ELSE PRINT
880 NEXT C
9999 END
```

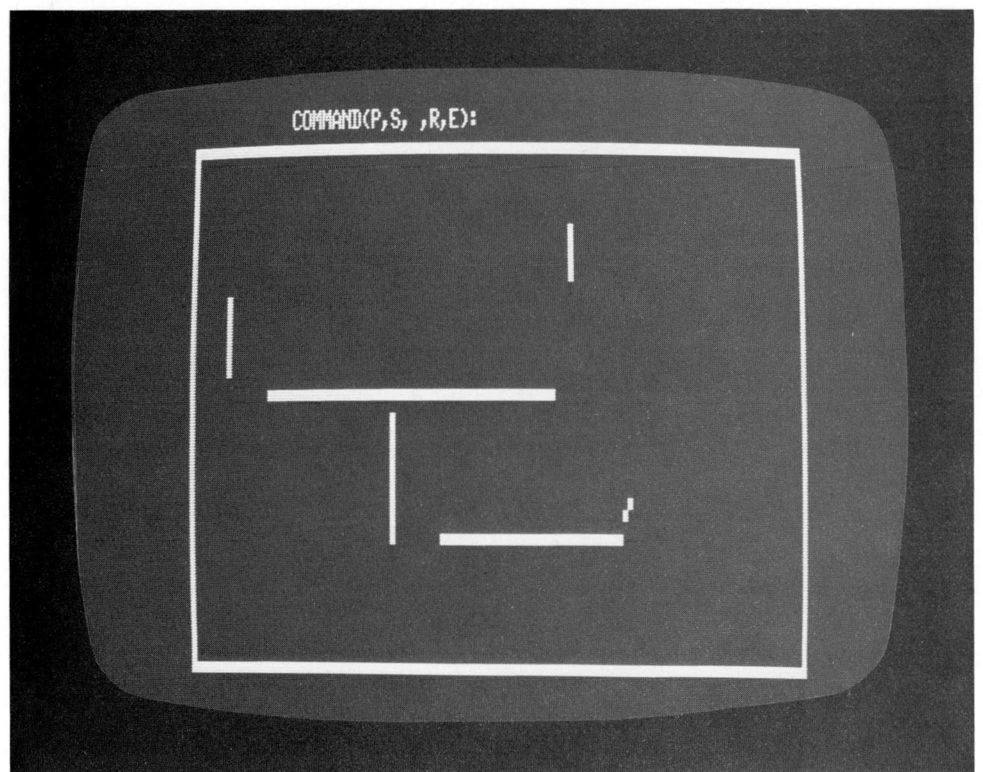
COMMAND(P,S, ,R,E):

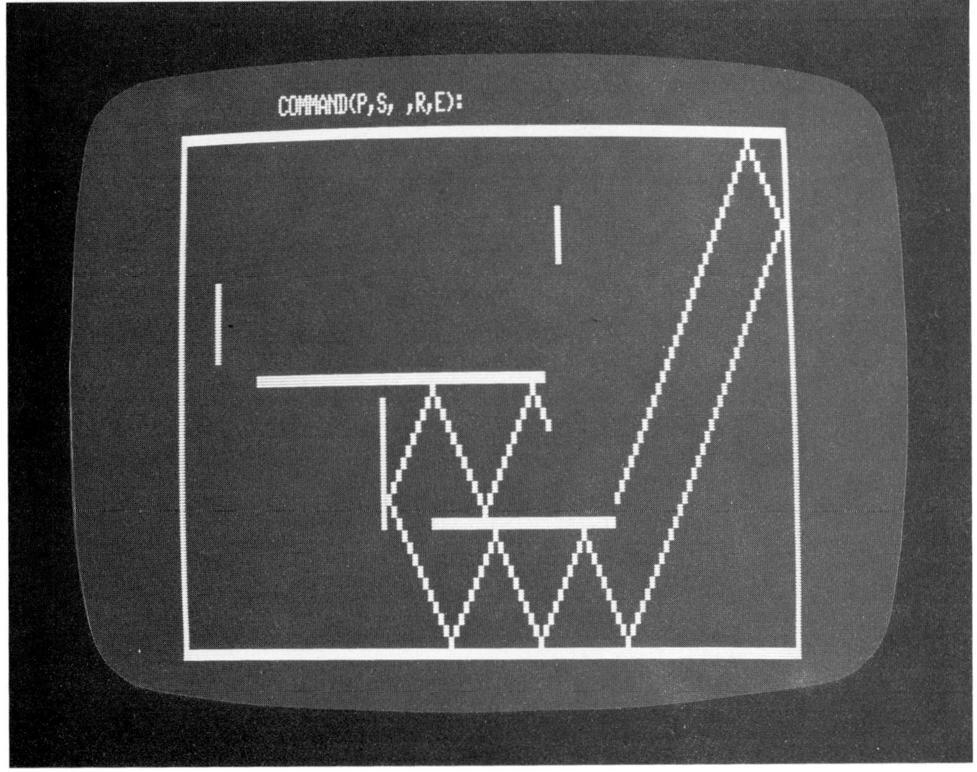
COMMAND(P,S, ,R,E):

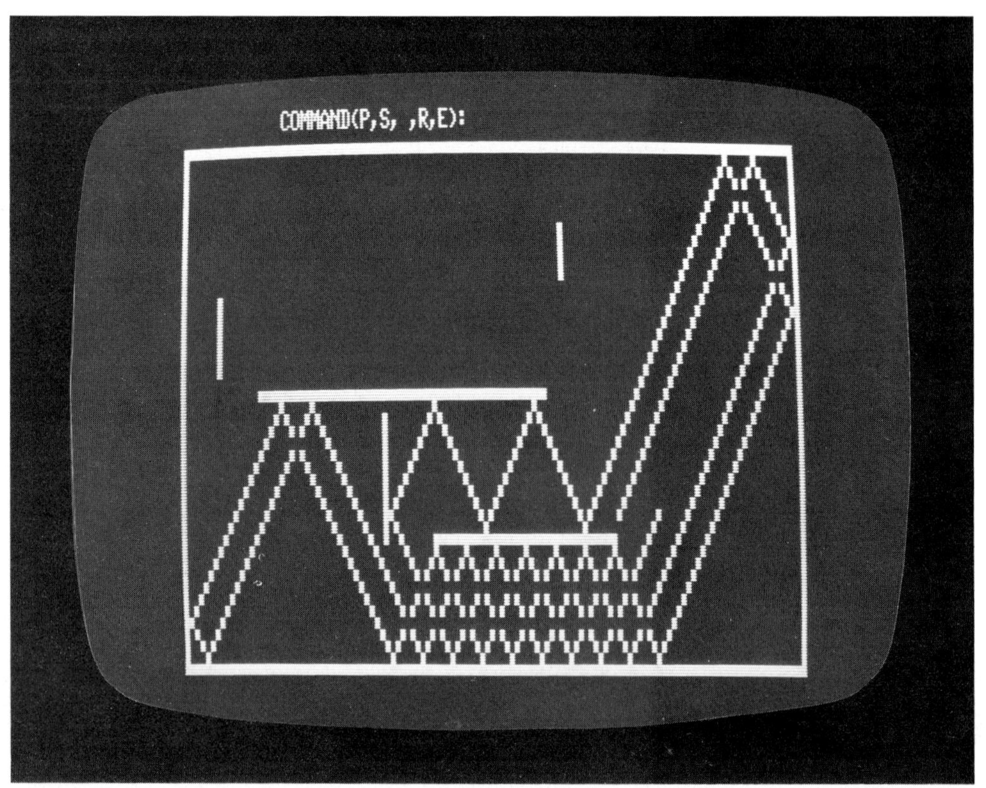
COMMAND(P,S, ,R,E):

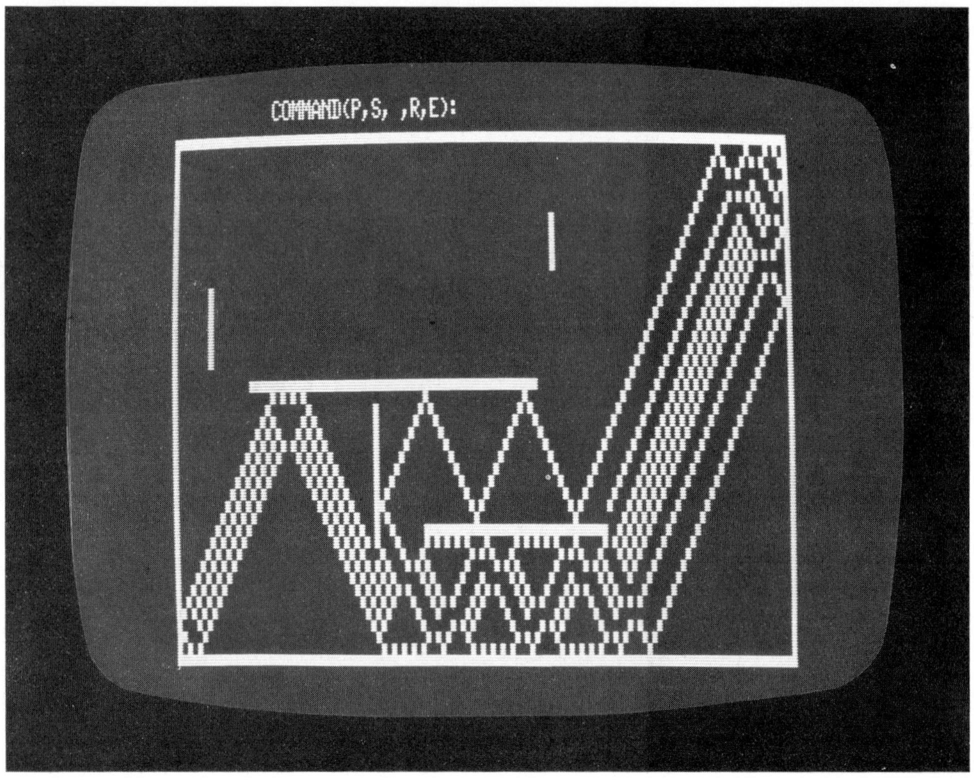
COMMAND(P,S, ,R,E):

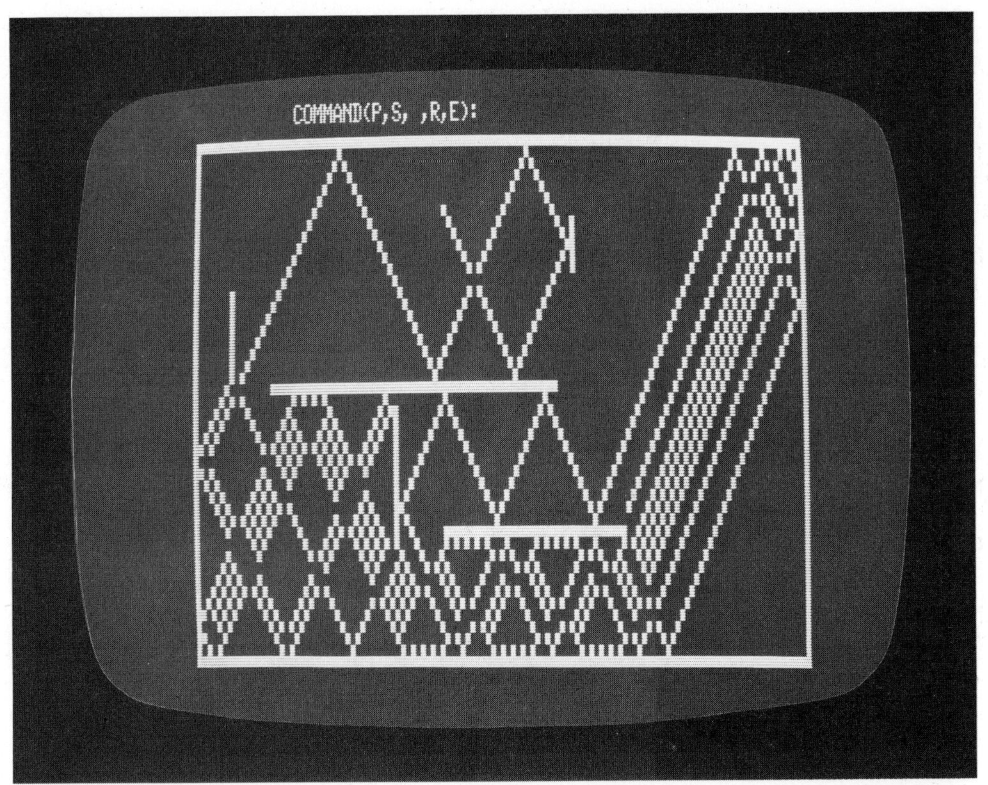
COMMAND(P,S, ,R,E):

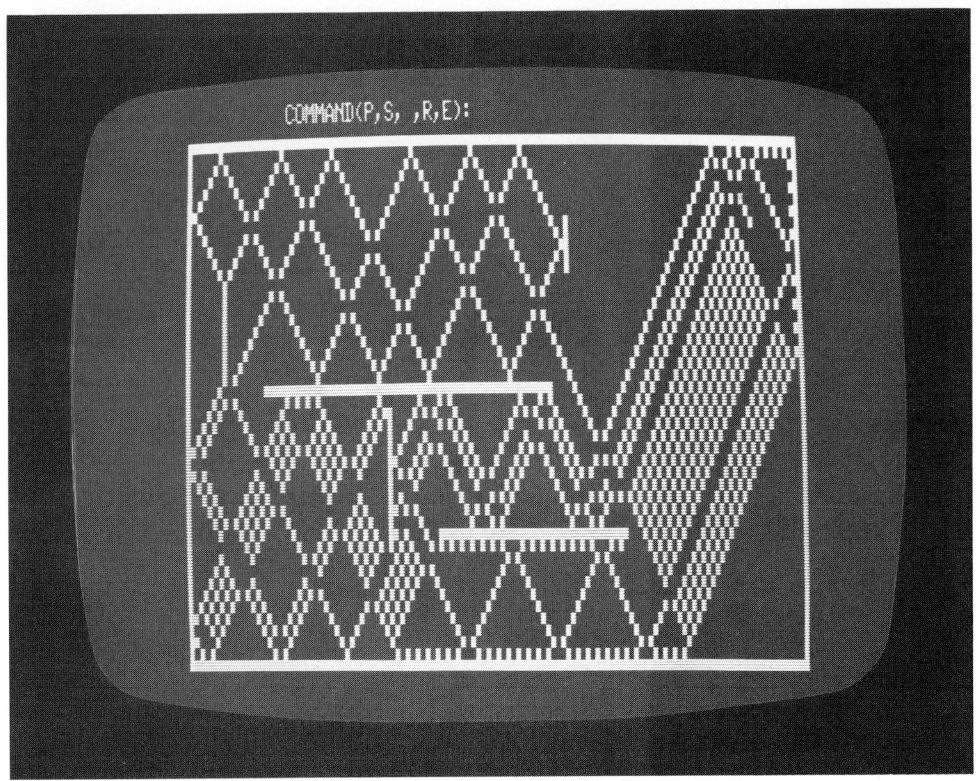
COMMAND(P,S, ,R,E):

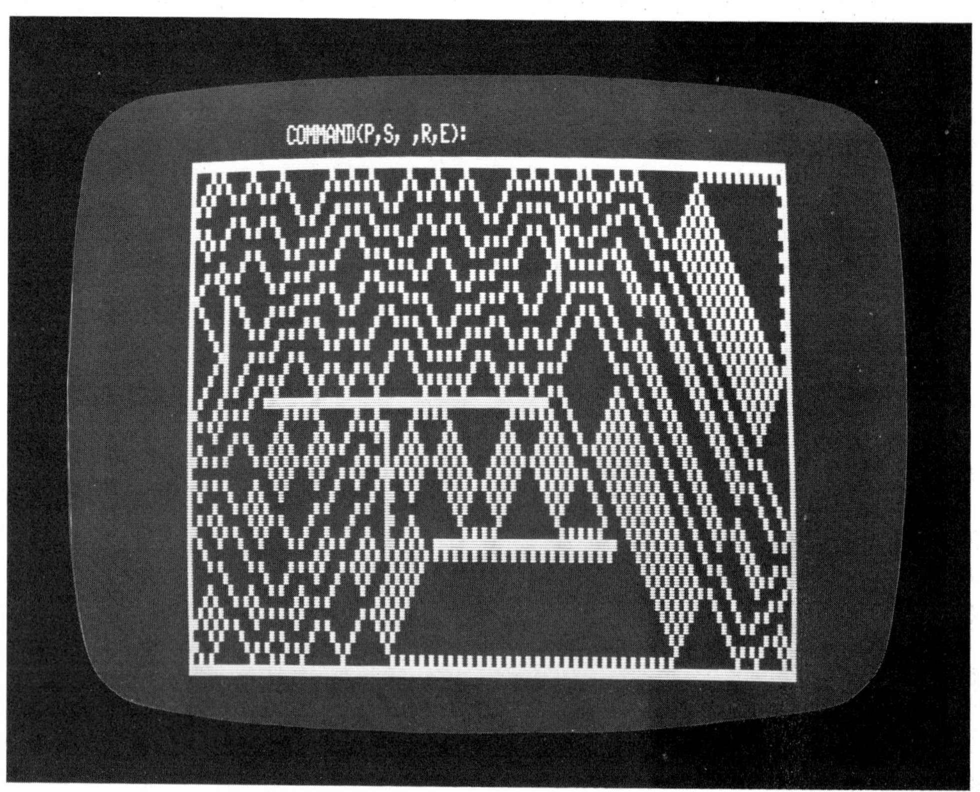

Discussion

- The program allows the user to participate in the way the graphic design proceeds.
  Typing an "R" reverses the dot's direction.
  Typing a "P" causes the dot's trail to be erased.
  Typing an "E" erases a dot that is run over by the moving dot.
  Typing a " " freezes the dot's motion.

- The program allows the user to save on disk the screen contents when a particularly interesting pattern is perceived.
  Typing an "S" stores the picture on a direct access disk file.

- All user input is through INKEY$. Depressing the ENTER key accidentally after typing any of the above keys can cause unpredictable and weird things to happen to the screen pictures.

Suggestions

- When a screen picture is saved, the status of the picture is lost and the picture can not be continued. Modify the program so that the dot picks up where it left off when interrupted by the typing of an "S".

Problem 8.3 Write a program that causes the screen of the TRS-80 to become a movie marquee hawking the latest flick.

Solution

```
10 'filename:"s8p3"
20 '  program: marquee display
30 '   author: jdr 8/80
40 '
41 CLS : CLEAR 300 : DEFINT A-Z
42 Z=600
43 READ E$,F$,G$
44 READ A$,B$,C$,R$
45 N=20 : M=5
46 'n=20, m=3  or n=20, m=5 or mod lines 60 & 120 step 2*p
47 'n=20, m=6, modify step in line 60 to be 2*p-1
50 FOR Q=1 TO 100
52 P=Q-INT(Q/M)*M+1
53 IF P<>2 THEN PRINT@Z-202,F$; : PRINT@Z-138,G$;
        ELSE PRINT@Z-202,R$+R$+R$; : PRINT@Z-138,R$+R$;
60 FOR I=P TO 63 STEP P
61    J1=64-I+INT(I/64)*64 : J3=127-J1 : J2=63-J1 : J4=64+J1
62    SET (J1,0) : SET (J3,0) : SET (J2,47) : SET (J4,47)
63    SET (J1,1) : SET (J3,1) : SET (J2,46) : SET (J4,46)
64  IF I-INT(I/5)*5<>0 THEN PRINT@Z-391,E$;
                       ELSE PRINT@Z-391,R$+R$;
100    IF J1<=59 THEN RESET (J1+4,0) : RESET (J1+4,1)
                  ELSE RESET (J1-60,0) : RESET (J1-60,1)
102    IF J2>=4 THEN RESET (J2-4,47) : RESET (J2-4,46)
                 ELSE RESET (J2+60,47) : RESET (J2+60,46)
105    IF J3>=68 THEN RESET (J3-4,0) : RESET (J3-4,1)
                  ELSE RESET (J3+60,0) : RESET (J3+60,1)
107    IF J4<=123 THEN RESET (J4+4,47) : RESET (J4+4,46)
                   ELSE RESET (J4-60,47) : RESET (J4-60,46)
110 NEXT I
115 IF P=1 THEN PRINT@Z,A$; : PRINT@Z+64,B$; : PRINT@Z+128,C$;
          ELSE PRINT@Z,R$; : PRINT@Z+64,R$; : PRINT@Z+128,R$;
120 FOR J=P TO 47 STEP P
121    SET (0,J) : SET (1,J) : SET (127,J) : SET (126,J)
122    FOR K=1 TO N : NEXT K
123    IF J>=4 THEN RESET (0,J-4) : RESET (1,J-4) :
                    RESET (127,J-4) : RESET (126,J-4)
130 NEXT J
993 DATA "           now playing"
994 DATA "T h e   H e d g e h o g   T h a t"
995 DATA "   A t e   C h e l m s f o r d"
996 DATA "   starring","Doug & Dinsdale","    Piranha"
997 DATA "                "
998 NEXT Q
999 END
```

now playing

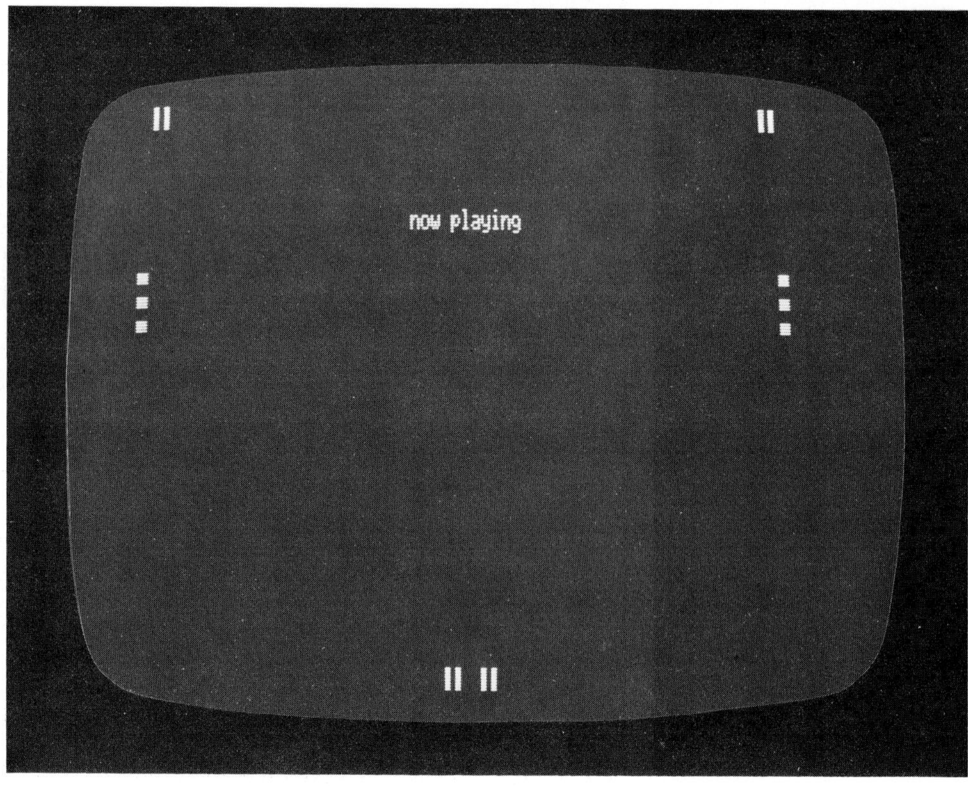
now playing

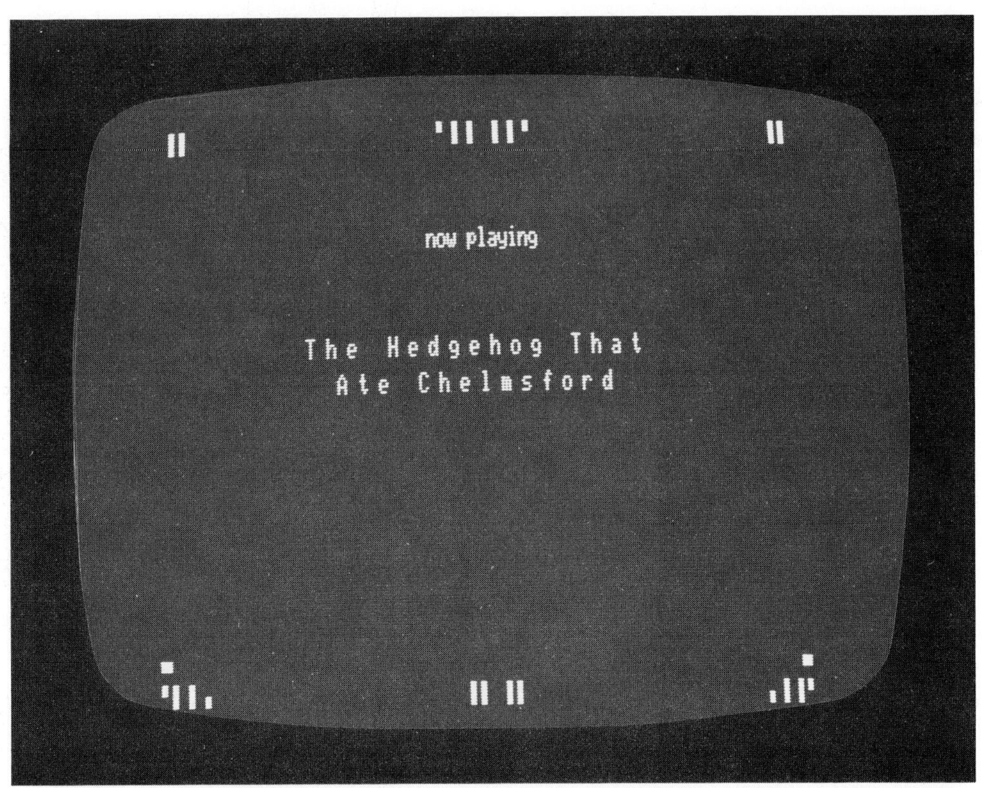
now playing
The Hedgehog That
Ate Chelmsford

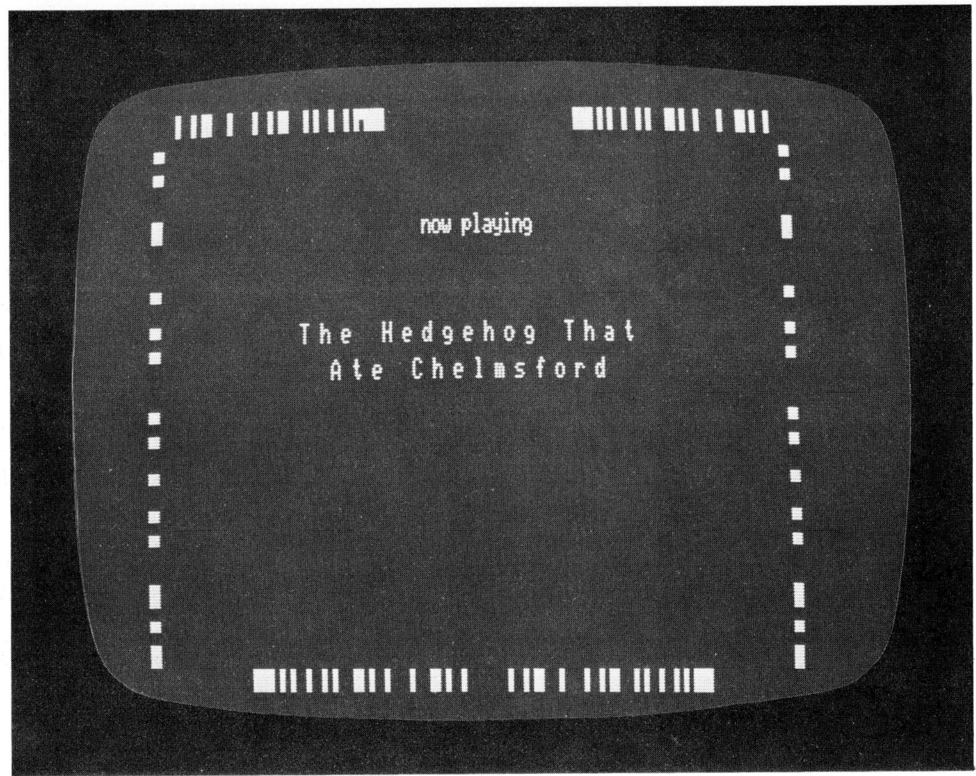
now playing
The Hedgehog That
Ate Chelmsford

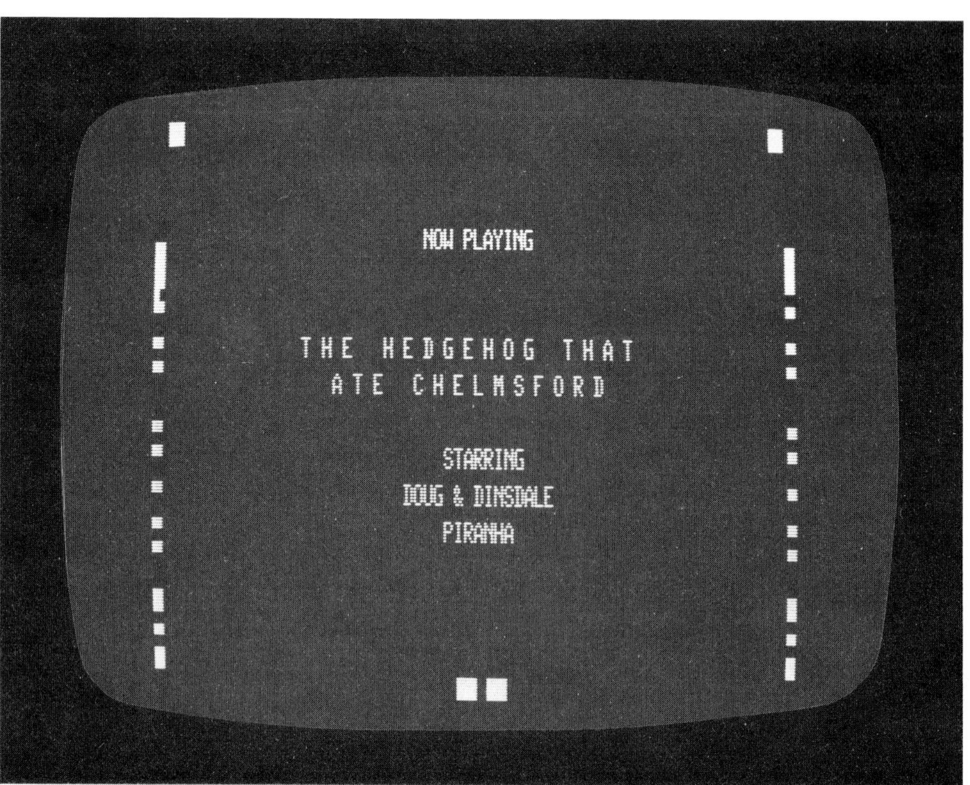

Discussion

- The marquee lights cycle from the center top toward the edges, then down the sides where they turn to converge at the center bottom of the screen.
- Some parameters have been built in to control speed, pattern, and cycle of the marquee lights.
- The movie's title and cast come and go giving added movement to the marquee.

Suggestions

- Run the program varying the parameters to get a feel for the type of visual displays that can be produced by the marquee.
- Experiment with the controlling loop structures to change the display. Some simple changes produce remarkable and unpredictable results.
- Change the size of the marquee.

Problem 8.4

Write a program that will cause a stick figure person to jump up and down on the video screen.

Solution

```
10 'filename:"s8p4"
20 '  purpose: bouncing Bentley
30 '   author: jdr 8/80
40 '
50 CLEAR 1000 : CLS : RANDOM
60 GOSUB 1000 : GOSUB 2000 : GOSUB 3000
65 PRINT@259,A$; : PRINT@585,C$;
66 PRINT@408,"Hello, I'm bouncing Bentley.";
67 FOR I=1 TO 700 : NEXT I
68 PRINT@408,"I feel a bouncing fit coming on!";
69 FOR I=1 TO 500 : NEXT I : CLS
70 FOR X=3 TO 47 STEP 2
72 Y=X+256 : Z=100
80    PRINT@X,A$; : PRINT@X+319,B$;
85 FOR I=1 TO Z : NEXT I : CLS
90    PRINT@Y,A$; : PRINT@Y+326,C$;
93 FOR I=1 TO Z : NEXT I : IF X<>47 THEN CLS
95 NEXT X
96 PRINT@408,"Geez, I'm pooped!";
98 FOR I=1 TO 500 : NEXT I
99 PRINT@408,"good bye .........";
100 FOR I=1 TO 10000
110     PRINT@RND(1023)-1," ";
120 NEXT I
160 STOP
1000 'bentley head
1010 A$=""
1020 FOR I=1 TO 74
1030     READ X
1040     IF X>=0
            THEN A$=A$+CHR$(128+X)
            ELSE A$=A$+CHR$(26)+STRING$(ABS(X),8)
1050 NEXT I
1060 DATA 63,3,3,3,3,3,3,3,51,51,19,3,43,21,-14
1070 DATA 63,0,32,60,60,16,0,62,3,3,43,20,42,21,-14
1080 DATA 63,0,63,0,0,63,0,63,0,0,42,21,42,21,-14
1090 DATA 63,0,63,48,48,63,0,63,48,48,58,21,42,21,-14
1100 DATA 15,12,12,12,12,12,44,12,12,12,12,12,14,5
1110 RETURN
2000 'body - up
2010 B$=""
2020 FOR I=1 TO 85
2030     READ X
2040     IF X>=0
            THEN B$=B$+CHR$(128+X)
            ELSE B$=B$+CHR$(26)+STRING$(ABS(X),8)
```

```
2050 NEXT I
2060 DATA 11,52,0,0,0,0,0,42,0,0,0,0,0,32,30,1,-15
2070 DATA 2,13,12,12,12,12,46,12,12,12,12,12,7,-7
2080 DATA 42,-5,40,23,3,3,3,3,3,3,61,-9
2090 DATA 42,21,0,0,0,0,0,0,63,-9
2100 DATA 42,21,0,0,0,0,0,0,63,-9
2110 DATA 42,21,0,0,0,0,0,0,63,-10
2120 DATA 56,7,0,0,0,0,0,0,0,2,45,16
2130 RETURN
3000 'body - down
3010 C$=""
3020 FOR I=1 TO 83
3030    READ X
3040    IF X>=0
           THEN C$=C$+CHR$(128+X)
           ELSE C$=C$+CHR$(26)+STRING$(ABS(X),8)
3050 NEXT I
3060 DATA 42,-10,8,12,12,12,12,12,12,12,12
3070 DATA 46,12,12,12,12,12,12,12,12,12,-10
3080 DATA 42,-6,63,3,3,3,3,3,3,3,3,3,43,21,-12
3090 DATA 63,0,0,0,0,0,0,0,0,0,42,21,-12
3100 DATA 63,0,0,0,0,0,0,0,0,0,42,21,-16
3110 DATA 3,3,3,3,3,0,0,0,0,0,0,0,0,0,2,3,3,3,3,1
3120 RETURN
```

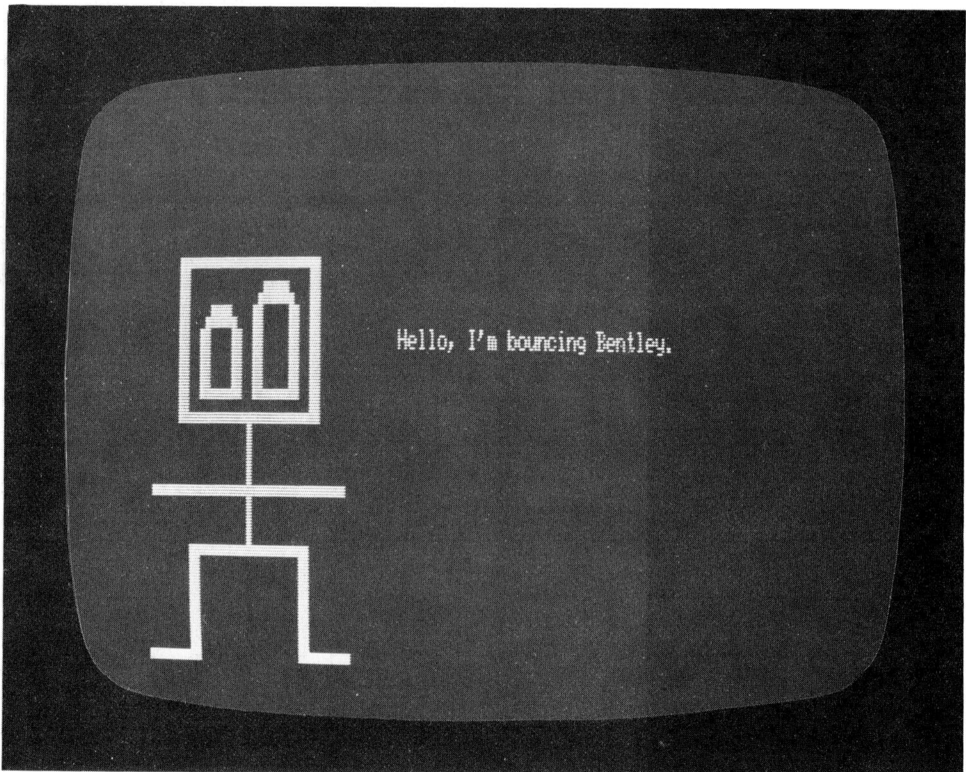

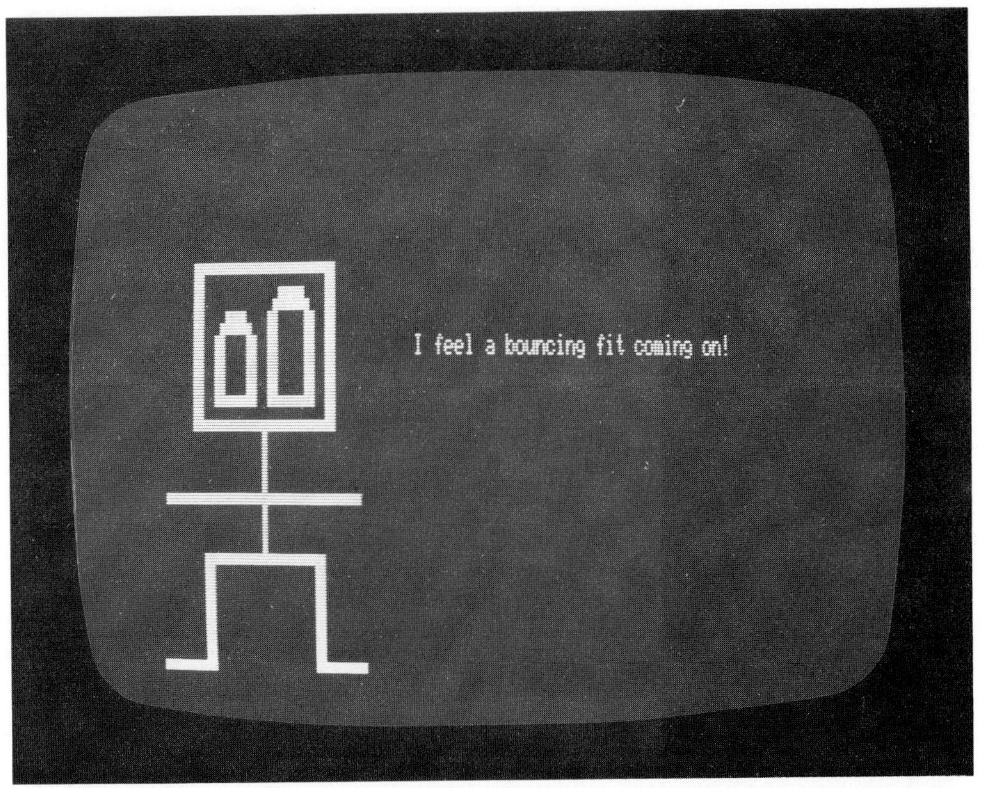
I feel a bouncing fit coming on!

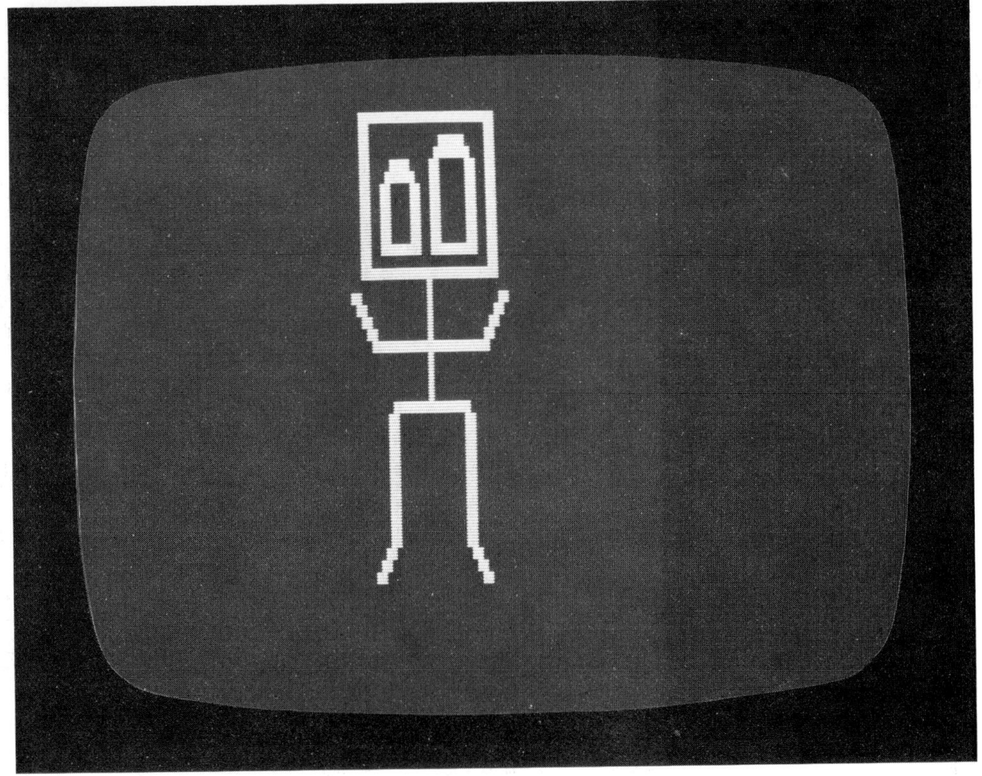

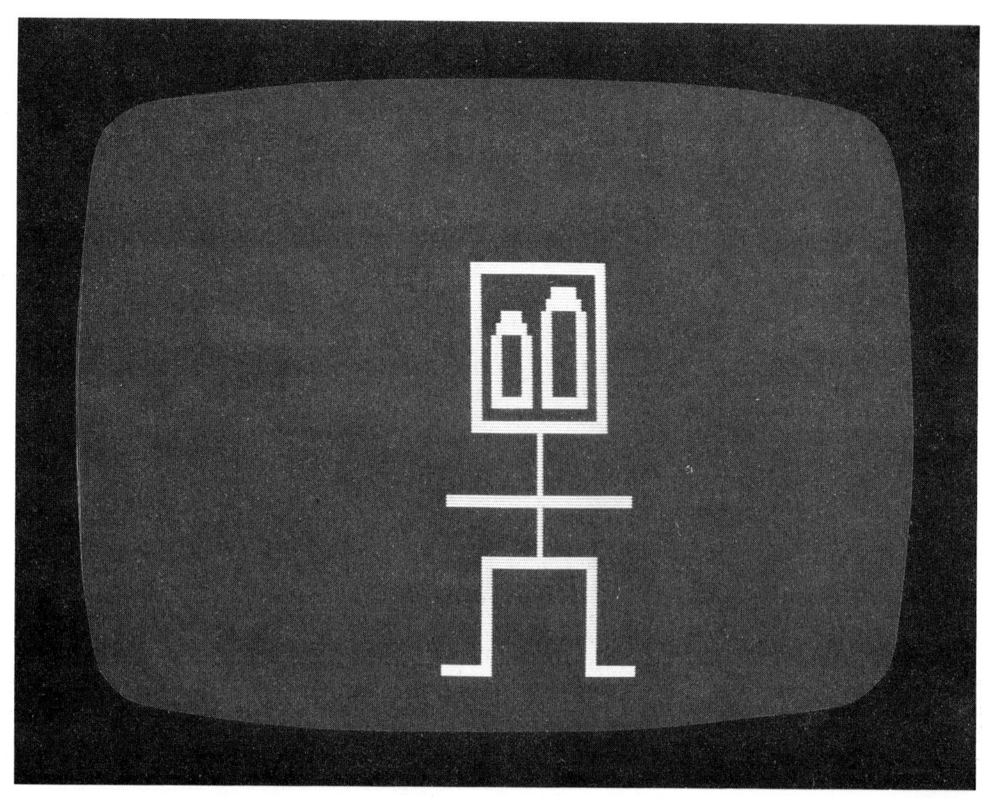

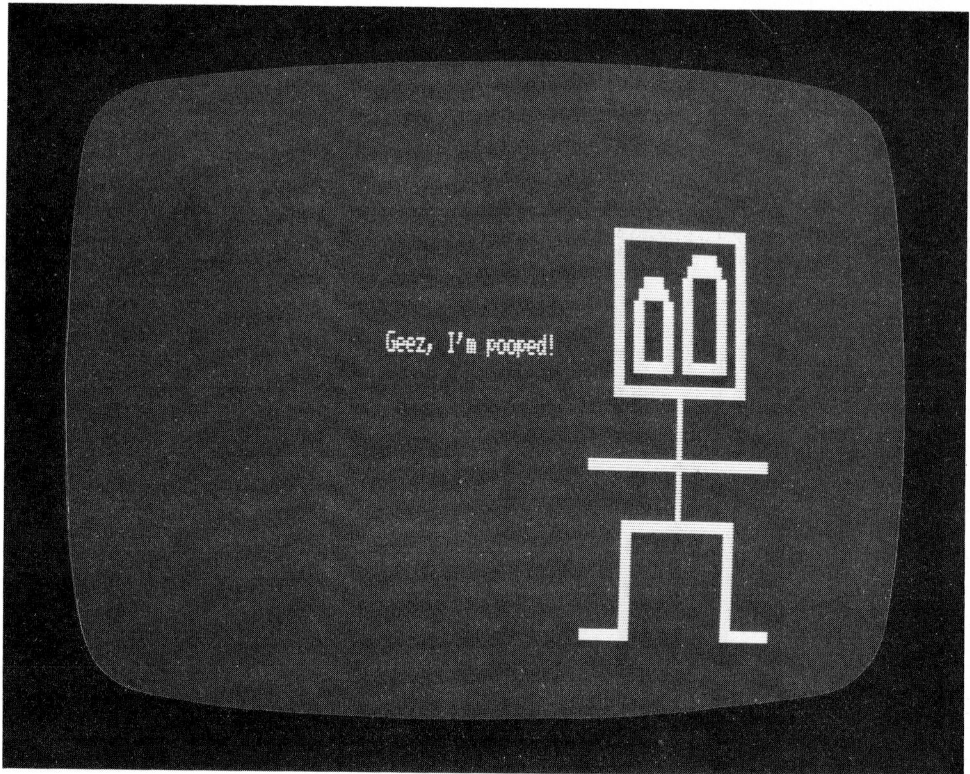
Geez, I'm pooped!

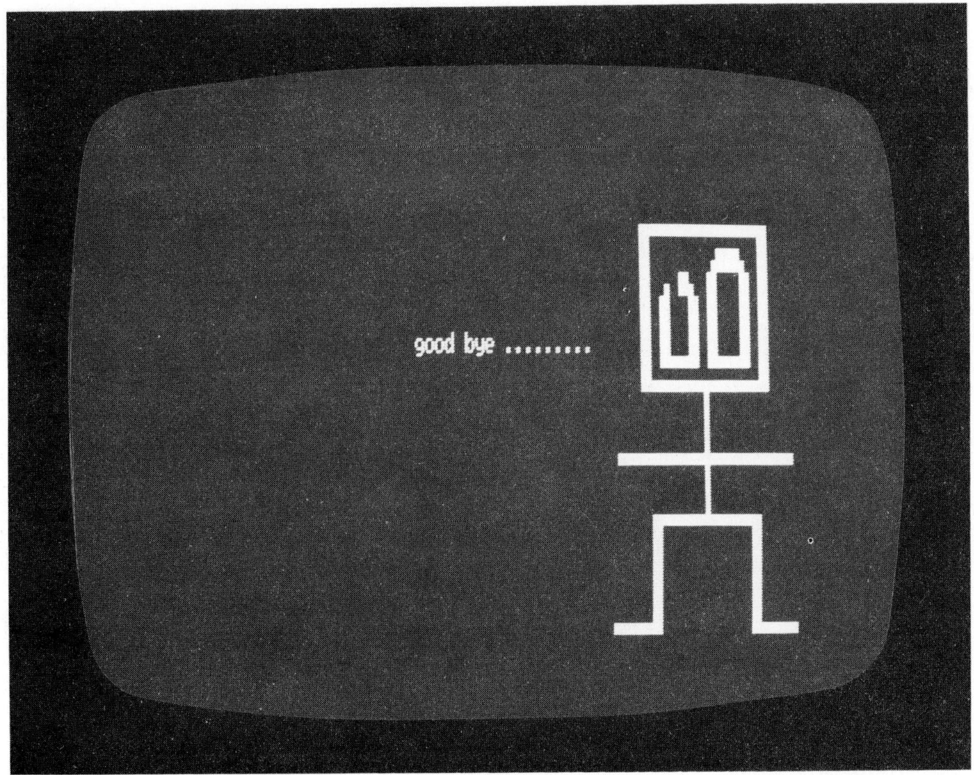

Discussion

- This program is an example of the kind of simple animation that can be programmed easily.
- Notice that the displaying of Bouncing Bentley is very rapid. Delay counting loops are incorporated at strategic positions to hold the picture for the viewer.
- The strings A$, B$, and C$ provide the body parts that are printed and cause the animation to unfold.

Suggestions

- Modify the program so that Bouncing Bentley doesn't progress from left to right during the bouncing fit, but starts at the center and bounces left or right at random.
- Add some intermediate stances to the bounce that Bentley performs.
- Using the basic ideas of this program, write a program that causes a stick figure to walk across the screen.
- Combining the stand up comedian with the stick figure, write a program that causes the stick figure to "shuffle off to Buffalo".

Appendix A ASCII Codes and Character Set

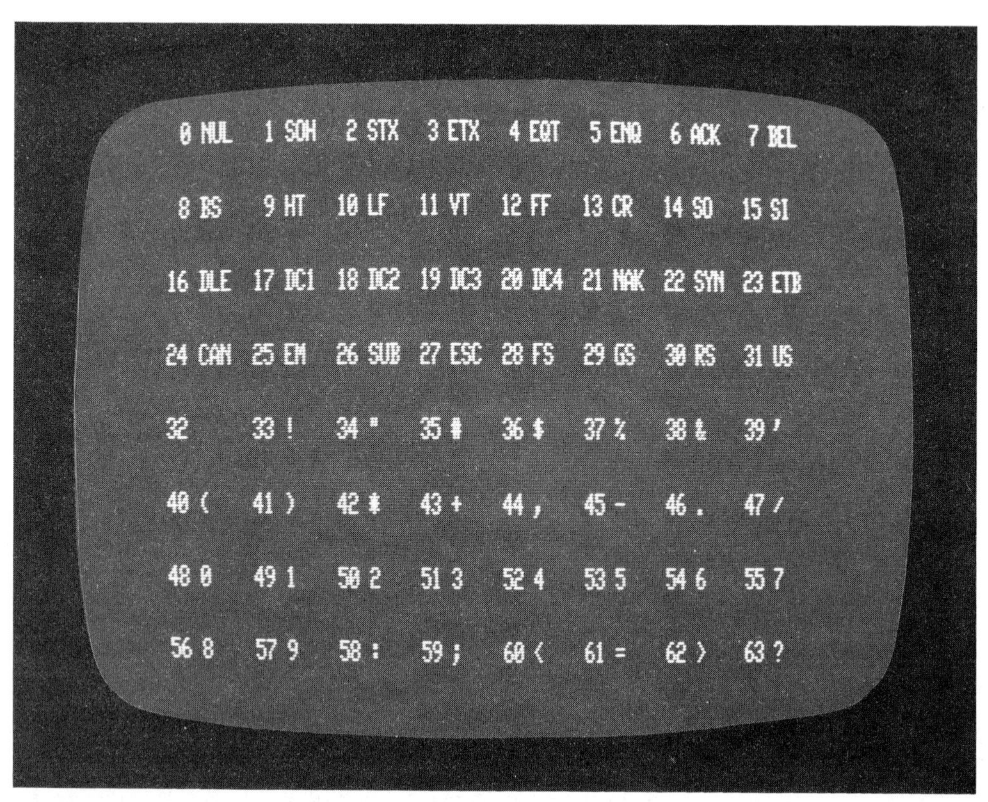

0 NUL 1 SOH 2 STX 3 ETX 4 EOT 5 ENQ 6 ACK 7 BEL
8 BS 9 HT 10 LF 11 VT 12 FF 13 CR 14 SO 15 SI
16 DLE 17 DC1 18 DC2 19 DC3 20 DC4 21 NAK 22 SYN 23 ETB
24 CAN 25 EM 26 SUB 27 ESC 28 FS 29 GS 30 RS 31 US
32 33 ! 34 " 35 # 36 $ 37 % 38 & 39 '
40 (41) 42 * 43 + 44 , 45 - 46 . 47 /
48 0 49 1 50 2 51 3 52 4 53 5 54 6 55 7
56 8 57 9 58 : 59 ; 60 < 61 = 62 > 63 ?

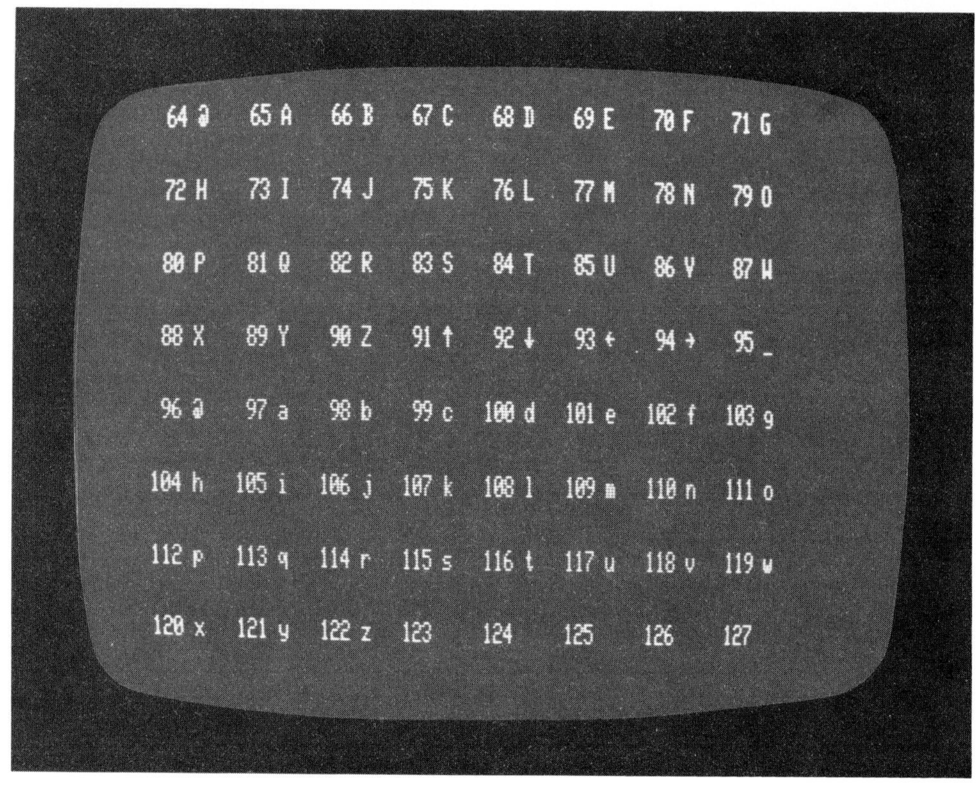

64 @ 65 A 66 B 67 C 68 D 69 E 70 F 71 G
72 H 73 I 74 J 75 K 76 L 77 M 78 N 79 O
80 P 81 Q 82 R 83 S 84 T 85 U 86 V 87 W
88 X 89 Y 90 Z 91 ↑ 92 ↓ 93 ← 94 → 95 _
96 @ 97 a 98 b 99 c 100 d 101 e 102 f 103 g
104 h 105 i 106 j 107 k 108 l 109 m 110 n 111 o
112 p 113 q 114 r 115 s 116 t 117 u 118 v 119 w
120 x 121 y 122 z 123 124 125 126 127

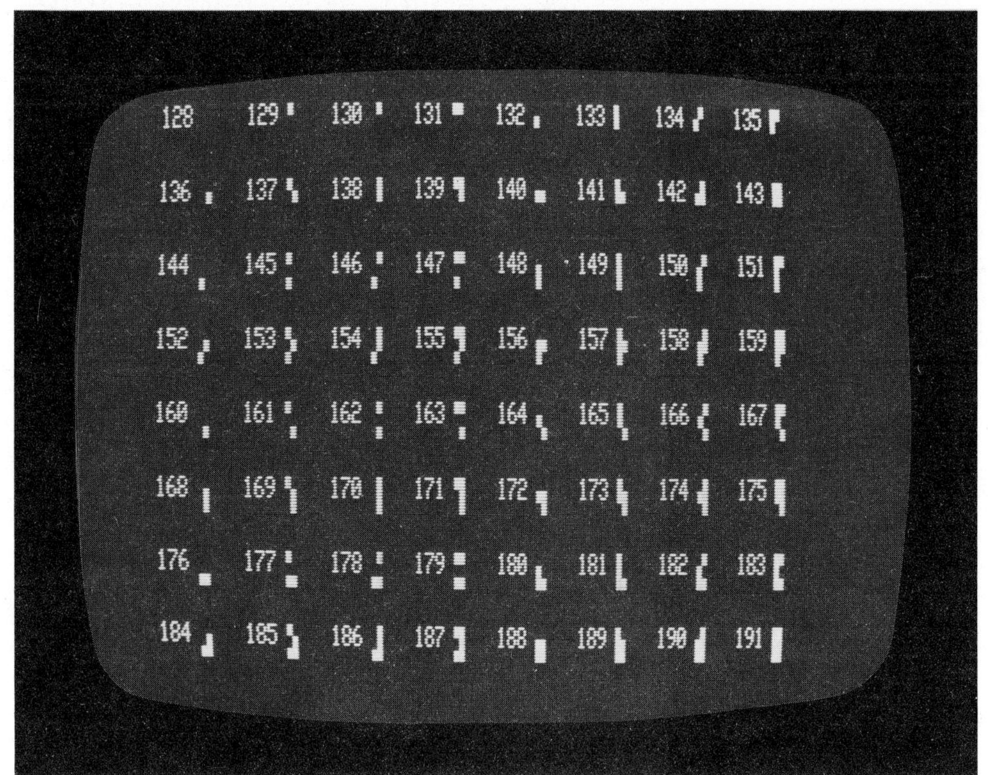

ASCII codes 192 through 255 are called space compression codes because printing one of these characters causes tabbing for 0 to 63 spaces.

And remember, you can preview any of our Wonderwares in your own home for a full 15 days—absolutely FREE!

Wm. C. Brown Company Publishers
2460 Kerper Blvd., Dubuque, Iowa 52001

ORDER TODAY!

Complete Order Form at right and mail to:

Wm. C. Brown Company Publishers
Direct Marketing, Inc.
2460 Kerper Blvd.
Dubuque, Iowa 52001

Gentlemen: Please send me the book(s) indicated. I understand that if I am not delighted with my selection(s), I may return them within fifteen days of receipt for a full and immediate refund—or that my credit card account will be credited for the full amount of any book(s) returned.

Total amount of order $ ________

California residents add sales tax $ ________

Postage and Handling ($1.00 per book) $ ________

TOTAL amount to be charged $ ________

Please check method of payment below:

Check or Money Order Enclosed

VISA Master Charge Interbank No. ________

Account No. ________

Exp. Date ________ Signature ________